KIDS ❤ LOVE Wisconsin

4th Edition

I0521995

An Organized Family Travel Guide to Exploring Kid-Friendly Wisconsin

500 Fun Stops & Unique Spots

Michele Darrall Zavatsky

Dedicated to the Families of Wisconsin

For the latest major updates corresponding to the pages in this book visit our website:

www.KidsLoveTravel.com

- **_REMEMBER_:** *Museum exhibits change frequently. Check the site's website before you visit to note any changes. Also, HOURS and ADMISSIONS are subject to change at the owner's discretion. Note: FAMILY ADMISSION RATES generally have restrictions. If you are tight on time or money, check the attraction's website or call before you visit.*

- **_EDUCATORS_:** *There are suggestions for finding FREE lessons plans embedded in many listings as helpful notes for educators.*

KIDS ♥ WISCONSIN ™ Kids Love Publications, LLC

TABLE OF CONTENTS

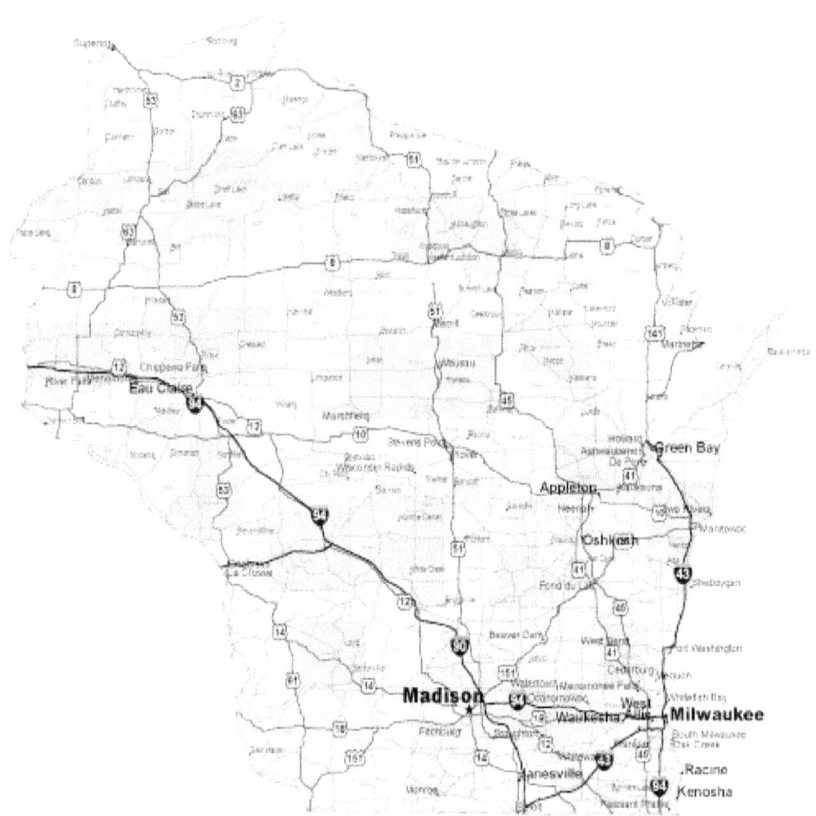

State Detail Map

(With Major Routes and Cities Marked)

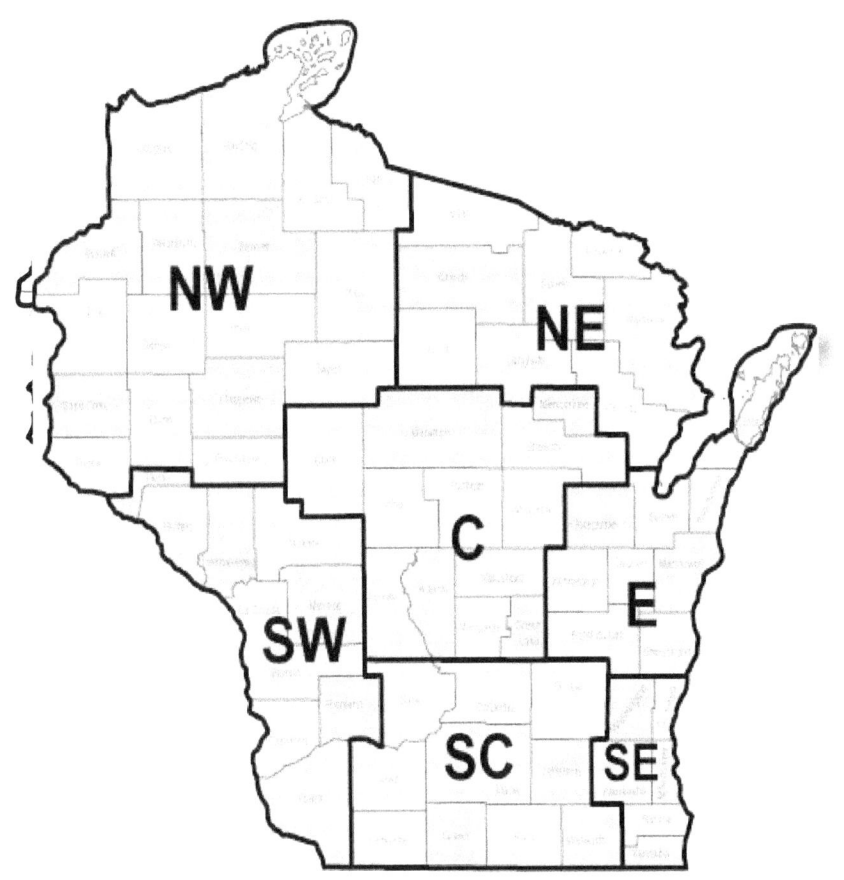

Chapter Area Map

(Chapters arranged alphabetically by chapter name)

HOW TO USE THIS BOOK

(a few hints to make your adventures run smoothly:)

BEFORE YOU LEAVE:

- Each chapter represents a two hour radius area of the state or a Day Trip. The listings are by City and then alphabetical by name, numeric by zip code. Each listing has tons of important details (pricing, hours, website, etc.) and a review noting the most engaging aspects of the place. Our popular Activity Index in back is helpful if you want to focus on a particular type of attraction (i.e. History, Tours, Outdoor Exploring, Animals & Farms, etc.).
- Begin by assigning each family member a different colored highlighter. At your leisure, begin to read each review and put a highlighter "check" mark next to the sites that most interest each family member or highlight the features you most want to see. Now, when you go to plan a quick trip - or a long van ride - you can easily choose different stops in one day to please everyone.
- Know directions and parking. Use a GPS system or print off directions from websites.
- Most attractions are closed major holidays unless noted.
- When children are in tow, it is better to make your lodging reservations ahead of time. Every time we've tried to "wing it", we've always ended up at a place that was overpriced, in a unsafe area, or not super clean. We've never been satisfied when we didn't make a reservation ahead of time.
- If you have a large family, or are traveling with extended family or friends, most places offer group discounts. Check out the company's website for details.
- For the latest critical updates corresponding to the pages in this book, visit our website: www.kidslovetravel.com. Click on *Updates*.

ON THE ROAD:

- Consider the child's age before you stop at an exit. Some attractions and restaurants, even hotels, are too formal for young ones or not enough adventure for teens.
- Estimate the duration of the trip and how many stops you can afford to make. From our experience, it is best to stop every two hours to stretch your legs or eat/snack or maybe visit an inexpensive attraction.
- Bring along travel books and games for "quiet time" in the van. (see tested travel products on www.kidslovetravel.com) As an added bonus, these "enriching" games also stimulate conversation - you may get to know your family better and create memorable life lessons.

ON THE ROAD: *(cont.)*

- In between meals, we offer the family snacks like: pretzels, whole grain chips, nuts, water bottles, bite-size (dark) chocolates, grapes and apples. None of these are messy and all are healthy.
- Plan picnics along the way. Many Historical sites and State Parks are scattered along the highway. Allow time for a rest stop or a scenic byway to take advantage of these free picnic facilities.

WHEN YOU GET HOME:

- Make a family "treasure chest". Decorate a big box or use an old popcorn tin. Store memorabilia from a fun outing, journals, pictures, brochures and souvenirs. Once a year, look through the "treasure chest" and reminisce.

WAYS TO SAVE MONEY:

- Memberships - many children's museums, science centers, zoos and aquariums are members of associations that provide FREE or Discounted reciprocity to other such museums across the country. AAA Auto Club cards offer discounts to many of the activities and hotels in this book. If grandparents are along for the ride, they can use their AARP card and get discounts. Be sure to carry your member cards with you as proof to receive the discounts.
- Supermarket Customer Cards - national and local supermarkets often offer good discounted tickets to major attractions in the area.
- Internet Hotel Reservations - if you're traveling with kids, don't take the risk of being spontaneous with lodging. Make reservations ahead of time. We don't use non-refundable, deep discount hotel "scouting" websites (ex. Hotwire) unless we're traveling on business - just adults. You can't cancel your reservation, or change them, and you can't be guaranteed the type of room you want (ex. non-smoking, two beds). Instead, stick with a national hotel chain you trust and join their rewards program (ex. Choice Privileges) to accumulate points towards FREE night stays.
- State Travel Centers - as you enter a new state, their welcome centers offer many current promotions.
- Hotel Lobbies - often have a display of discount coupons to area shops and restaurants. When you check in, ask the clerk for discount pizza coupons they may have at the front desk.
- Attraction Online Coupons - check the websites listed with each review for possible printable coupons or discounted online tickets good towards the attraction.
-
-

AIRPORTS - All children love to visit the airport! Why not take a tour and understand all the jobs it takes to run an airport? Tour the terminal, baggage claim, gates and security / currency exchange. Maybe you'll even get to board a plane.

ANIMAL SHELTERS - Great for the would-be pet owner. Not only will you see many cats and dogs available for adoption, but a guide will show you the clinic and explain the needs of a pet. Be prepared to have the children "fall in love" with one of the animals while they are there!

BANKS - Take a "behind the scenes" look at automated teller machines, bank vaults and drive-thru window chutes. You may want to take this tour and then open a savings account for your child.

CITY HALLS - Halls of Fame, City Council Chambers & Meeting Room, Mayor's Office and famous statues.

ELECTRIC COMPANY / POWER PLANTS - Modern science has created many ways to generate electricity today, but what really goes on with the "flip of a switch". Because coal can be dirty, wear old, comfortable clothes. Coal furnaces heat water, which produces steam, that propels turbines, that drives generators, that make electricity.

FIRE STATIONS - Many Open Houses in October, Fire Prevention Month. Take a look into the life of the firefighters servicing your area and try on their gear. See where they hang out, sleep and eat. Hop aboard a real-life fire engine truck and learn fire safety too.

HOSPITALS - Some Children's Hospitals offer pre-surgery and general tours.

NEWSPAPERS - You'll be amazed at all the new technology. See monster printers and robotics. See samples in the layout department and maybe try to put together your own page. After seeing a newspaper made, most companies give you a free copy (dated that day) as your souvenir. National Newspaper Week is in October.

PETCO - Various stores. Contact each store manager to see if they participate. The Fur, Feathers & Fins™ program allows children to learn about the characteristics and habitats of fish, reptiles, birds, and small animals. At your local Petco, lessons in science, math and geography come to life through this hands-on field trip. As students develop a respect for animals, they will also develop a greater sense of responsibility.

PIZZA HUT & PAPA JOHN'S - Participating locations. Telephone the store manager. Best days are Monday, Tuesday and Wednesday mid-afternoon. Minimum of 10 people. Small charge per person. All children love pizza – especially when they can create their own! As the children tour the kitchen, they learn how to make a pizza, bake it, and then eat it. The admission charge generally includes lots of creatively made pizzas, beverage and coloring book.

KRISPY KREME DONUTS - Participating locations. Get an "inside look" and learn the techniques that make these donuts some of our favorites! Watch the dough being made in "giant" mixers, being formed into donuts and taking a "trip" through the fryer. Seeing them being iced and topped with colorful sprinkles is always a favorite with the kids. Contact your local store manager. They prefer Monday or Tuesday. Free.

SUPERMARKETS - Kids are fascinated to go behind the scenes of the same store where Mom and Dad shop. Usually you will see them grind meat, walk into large freezer rooms, watch cakes and bread bake and receive free samples along the way. Maybe you'll even get to pet a live lobster!

TV / RADIO STATIONS - Studios, newsrooms, Fox kids clubs. Why do weathermen never wear blue/green clothes on TV? What makes a "DJ's" voice sound so deep and smooth?

WATER TREATMENT PLANTS - A giant science experiment! You can watch seven stages of water treatment. The favorite is usually the wall of bright buttons flashing as workers monitor the different processes.

U.S. MAIN POST OFFICES - Did you know Ben Franklin was the first Postmaster General (over 200 years ago)? Most interesting is the high-speed automated mail processing equipment. Learn how to address envelopes so they will be sent quicker (there are secrets). To make your tour more interesting, have your children write a letter to themselves and address it with colorful markers. Mail it earlier that day and they will stay interested trying to locate their letter in all the high-speed machinery.

General State Agency & Recreational Information

Call *(or visit websites)* for the services of interest. Request to be added to their mailing lists.

WISCONSIN TOURISM - www.travelwisconsin.com

WISCONSIN STATE PARKS - www.dnr.wi.gov/org/land/parks/ - Become a Wisconsin Explorer and discover the natural world. Pick up a booklet at the nature center. The booklets are full of hands-on, exciting and educational activities for days on the beach, rainy days at home, or starry nights. Complete at least half of activities and return it to any state park, forest or recreation area. Receive a patch and certificate for completing the activities.

WISCONSIN CAMPGROUND DIRECTORY - www.travelwisconsin.com/PDF/waco.pdf or www.wisconsin-campgrounds.com

WISCONSIN HISTORICAL SOCIETY - www.wisconsinhistory.org

CYCLE SOUTHWEST WISCONSIN - www.cyclesouthwestwisconsin.com. Let Cycle Southwest Wisconsin be your guide to biking through southwest Wisconsin's challenging rolling hills and picturesque farm land. A newly developed bike trail map details 28 loops that combine the area's history and quaint small towns with excellent shopping, art and eateries.

ASSOCIATION OF WISCONSIN SNOWMOBILE CLUBS - www.awsc.org

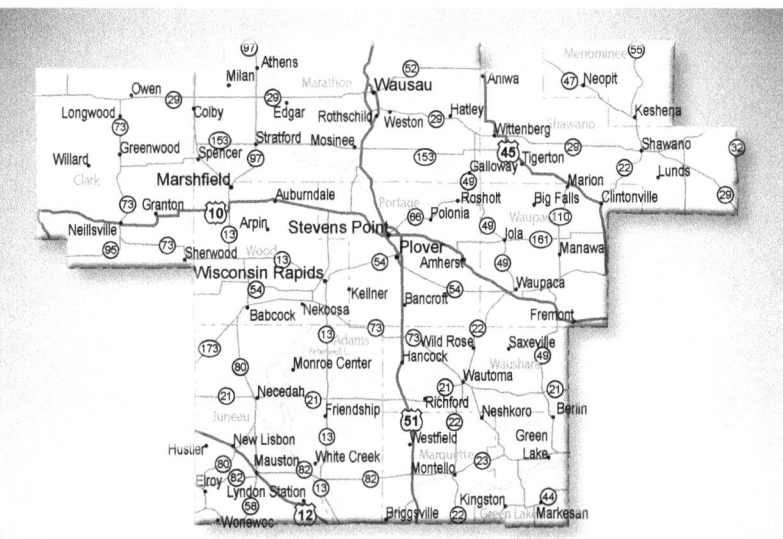

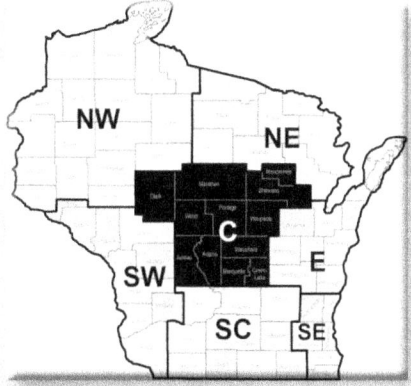

Chapter 1
Central (C)

QUICK LOOK...

Cheese Factory Tours

State Parks & Wildlife Areas

Nature Centers

Jurustic Park

Cranberry Festival & Tour

Fremont (Zittau)
- Union Star Cheese Factory

Friendship
- Roche-A-Cri State Park

Marion
- Dupont Cheese Factory

Marshfield
- Jurustic Park
- Wildwood Zoo

Necedah
- Buckhorn State Park
- Necedah National Wildlife Refuge

Nekoosa
- Nekoosa Giant Pumpkin Fest

Prairie Du Sac
- Wisconsin State Cow Chip Throw

Shiocton
- Navarino Wildlife Area & Nature Center

Stevens Point
- Central Wisconsin Children's Museum

- Museum Of Natural History / Planetarium, UWSP
- Schmeeckle Reserve Nature Center
- Stevens Point Sculpture Park

Thorp
- Holland's Family Cheese Factory

Waupaca
- Chief Waupaca / Lady Of The Lakes Boat Tours
- Hartman Creek State Park
- Wheelhouse Restaurant

Wausau
- Dells Of The Eau Claire Park
- Granite Peak Ski Area
- Rib Mountain State Park

Wisconsin Rapids
- Cranberry Blossom Festival

Wisconsin Rapids (Rudolph)
Wisconsin Dairy State Cheese Co.

Sites and attractions are listed in order by City, Zip Code, and Name. Symbols indicated represent:

 Restaurants   Lodging

UNION STAR CHEESE FACTORY

7742 County Road II (five miles southeast of town) **Fremont (Zittau)** 54940

- Phone: (920) 836-2804 **www.unionstarcheese.com**
- Tours: Monday, Thursday, Friday & Saturday 8:00am-8:30pm.

As one of the few privately owned and operated small cheese factories in Wisconsin, they use fresh milk from local farms to produce small batches of handcrafted cheeses. The factory is open seven days a week to sample cheeses for purchase but also take a cheese factory tour and learn about cheesemaking. They start the process at 4:00am with the pasteurizing milk process. After adding good bacteria and rennet, by 6:00am the milk in the vat has changed into a yogurt-like consistency. Then comes the stirring and the cooking. Why do they then add salt? It's not just for flavor but also chemistry. Come in, watch them make cheese, then taste it. Fresh curds are ready to eat between 9:00am-10:00am. Kids like string cheese? They make that, too.

ROCHE-A-CRI STATE PARK

1767 Hwy 13 (1 & 1/2 miles S of SR 21, 3 miles N of Friendship)
Friendship 53934

- Phone: (608) 565-2789
  http://dnr.wi.gov/topic/parks/name/rocheacri/
- Admission: Daily $8.00-$11.00 per vehicle.

The park's French name refers to the 300-foot-high rock outcropping that is the central feature of this quiet park. Climb the stairway to the top for a panoramic view (open sunrise to sunset). Native American petroglyphs can also be seen on the rocks. Features 41 campsites, a dumping station, handicap-accessible picnic area and campsites, seasonal naturalist programs, lookout tower, vistas, fishing, 6.1 miles of hiking trails, 4.2 miles of cross-country ski trails. The Spring Peeper Trail is a quarter-mile trail named for the small frogs that abound in this area of the park. The trail goes through mature oak and maple woods adjacent to Carter Creek. In season, you'll see dragonflies, swallowtail butterflies, and nesting birds. Overnight camping.

DUPONT CHEESE FACTORY

N10140 Hwy 110 (5 miles south of town) **Marion** 54950

- ☐ Phone: (800) 895-2873 **www.dupontcheeseinc.com**
- ☐ Hours: Monday-Friday 8:00am-4:00pm, Saturday 8:00am-3:00pm.

Dupont Cheese has been making the highest quality, best tasting cheese for the past 38 years. They have a newly remodeled cheese store, where you can sample from a wide variety of freshly made cheese, or choose from hundreds of other wonderful Wisconsin products. You can even watch skilled cheesemakers practicing their craft through the viewing window. Fresh cheese curds are available on Thursday and Friday.

JURUSTIC PARK

222 Sugar Bush Lane **Marshfield** 54449

- ☐ Phone: Best to contact by email: Clyde@Jurustic.com **www.jurustic.com**
- ☐ Hours: Most days 10:00am-4:30pm. Contact them to be sure.

Clyde Wynia works with iron and irony. His Jurustic Park is filled with metal sculptures. Clyde will tell you, with a straight face and a little twinkle in his eye, that he discovered these creatures buried in nearby McMillan Marsh north of Marshfield. Clyde's collection of extinct animals from the "iron" age include the monstrous Marsh Dragons - the Attack Dragon and the Statue of Liberty Dragon plus the smaller variety of junkyard dogs and cats. Try to find the scary fish, the gator and the spider. Amongst the whimsical array of junkyard creatures, you'll find the fanciful Hobbit House where Clyde's wife plies her glass and fiber crafts and a unique jewelry shop.

WILDWOOD ZOO

608 W. 17th Street **Marshfield** 54449

- ☐ Phone: (715) 384-4642 **https://www.ci.marshfield.wi.us/visitors/ wildwood_park_and_zoo/index.php**
- ☐ Hours: Daily 7:30am-6:00pm. Extended summer hours. Reduced winter hours.
- ☐ Admission: FREE. Donations accepted.

Wildwood Zoo is a municipal zoo established in 1937. The park and zoo cover over 60 acres and boast a variety of birds and mammals from North America. Key exhibits are the grizzly bear, mountain lions, lynx, sandhill cranes and timber wolves. A special feature is the drive-by viewing option of the large animals, which include buffalo, elk and the timber wolf exhibit. Be sure to look for the foxes, bison and the prairie dogs.

BUCKHORN STATE PARK

W8450 Buckhorn Park Avenue (8 miles NE of I-90/94 on County Highway G)
Necedah 54646

☐ Phone: (608) 565-2789
http://dnr.wi.gov/topic/parks/name/buckhorn/
☐ Admission: Daily $8.00-$11.00 per vehicle. Annual passes available.

Buckhorn is a 2,500-acre peninsula jutting into the Castle Rock Flowage of the Wisconsin River. Unique cart-in campsites offer a rustic flavor. Features wildlife blind, 24 campsites, winter camping, backpack camping, handicap-accessible picnic area and campsites, seasonal naturalist programs, shoreline with marked beach area, canoeing, boating, fishing, 3 miles of nature trails, 3.5 miles of hiking trails, 4.5 miles of snowmobile trails, 3.5 miles of cross-country ski trails. Open 6:00am-11:00pm with overnight camping.

The Sandblow Walk leads you out onto a typical central Wisconsin sandblow. This desert-like area recalls the park's Ice Age history when the region was covered by glacial Lake Wisconsin. There are interpretive signs at this site.

NECEDAH NATIONAL WILDLIFE REFUGE

W7996 20th Street West **Necedah** 54646

☐ Phone: (608) 565-2551 **www.fws.gov/midwest/necedah/**
☐ Hours: Open daylight hours. Visitors Center Monday-Saturday 9am-4pm.

This Refuge is located in the Great Central Wisconsin Swamp, the largest wetland bog in the state (7,800 square miles). Whooping cranes, wolves, Karner blue butterflies, and white-tailed deer call Necedah National Wildlife Refuge "home." Ringed bog hunter dragonflies live in sedge meadows, flying squirrels in upland hardwood timber. Trumpeter swans inhabit the marshes, and badgers the savanna.

NEKOOSA GIANT PUMPKIN FEST

Nekoosa - The Annual Nekoosa Giant Pumpkin Fest is home to some of the largest pumpkins you'll ever see. Stop by to see the giant pumpkin weigh-off or cheer on your favorite participant in the annual Pumpkin Boat Regatta. Other activities include a craft show, farm and flea market, children's games and activities (some are free), pumpkin and scarecrow decorating contests, bake-off, classic car show, antique tractor show, and lots of great food. **www.nekoosagiantpumpkinfest.com** *Admission. (first weekend in October)*

WISCONSIN STATE COW CHIP THROW

Prairie du Sac - Marion Park. Life doesn't get any more authentic than tossing farm animal byproducts "for fun." More than 1,000 competitors and 50,000 spectators gather each year for one of the most unique and hilarious state competitions in the country. Competitors from around the world take their shot at breaking the men's and women's records. Anyone can get in on the fun, including kids-- with their parent's permission of course. Also food, entertainment, clowns, cloggers, and a big parade. Can you imagine being on the Cow Chip Picking Committee? **www.wiscowchip.com** *FREE (early September weekend)*

NAVARINO WILDLIFE AREA & NATURE CENTER
W5646 Lindsten Road **Shiocton** 54170

- ☐ Phone: (715) 758-6999 **www.navarino.org**
- ☐ Hours: Navarino Nature Center: open different times daily except Sunday, generally 8:00am-3:00pm. Weekend lobby hours: 8:00am-5:00pm. The Wildlife area is open daily from dawn to dusk.
- ☐ Admission: FREE

The Navarino Wildlife Area is a 15,000 acre WDNR property located in Southeast Shawano County and Northeast Waupaca County. There are 56 miles of hiking trails on the wildlife area, 12 of which are groomed for cross-country skiing during the winter months. Recently 2 new snowshoeing trails have been established, following this the nature center rents out snowshoes for use on the wildlife area. Habitats on the wildlife area include: upland forests, lowland forests, sedge marshes, bogs, flowages, and restored prairie habitats. New to the Center - bees! New to the trails - boardwalks over bogs.

CENTRAL WISCONSIN CHILDREN'S MUSEUM

1100 Main Street (suite 200 upstairs) **Stevens Point** 54481

- Phone: (715) 344-2003 **www.cwchildrensmuseum.org**
- Hours: Wednesday-Saturday 9:00am-4:00pm, Sunday Noon-4:00pm.
- Admission: $5.00 general (age 1+).

The Central Wisconsin Children's Museum hosts daily activities and boasts several play areas, including a pretend grocery store, pretend farm, stage with costumes and musical instruments, building area with giant Legos, and quiet room for listening to music and stories. Camp indoors in a Pine Log. Kids might also like to wear a lab coat, check x-rays and pretend dentist or make it with paper with a room overflowing with art supplies and themed projects. Babies and toddlers have their own area In the Robin's Nest. The place is for children 6 months to 10 years and their families.

MUSEUM OF NATURAL HISTORY / PLANETARIUM, UWSP

900 Reserve Street and Room 106 Albertson Learning Resources Center (University of Wisconsin) **Stevens Point** 54481

- Phone: (715) 346 2858
- **www.uwsp.edu/physastr/plan_obs/Pages/default.aspx** or **uwsp.edu/ cols-ap/museum**
- Hours: MUSEUM - School Year - Monday-Thursday 7:45am-12:00am. Friday 7:45am-9:00pm, Saturday 9:00am-9:00pm, Sunday 11:00am-1:00am. PLANETARIUM - Programs designed for all ages. Planetarium - Various programs available such as Sunday program @ 2:00pm & Night Sky program Monday @ 8:00pm (mid-September - mid-May). Visit website for most current schedule.
- Admission: Most programs are FREE.
- Tours: MUSEUM - Open when school is in session at which time the public is welcome to walk through to visit the exhibits.

Interact with the natural world. Explore the origins of Earth, discover dinosaurs, and witness natural habitats and rare collections of species. Most everything is set in artistic dioramas to give me "real" appeal to the eye and willingness to read the placards at each station.

SCHMEECKLE RESERVE NATURE CENTER

2419 North Point Drive (near Interstate 39 / US 51) **Stevens Point** 54481

- ☐ Phone: (715) 346-4992
- ☐ **www.uwsp.edu/cnr-ap/schmeeckle/Pages/home.aspx**
- ☐ Hours: Monday-Friday 9am-4pm, Saturday 10am-4pm, Sunday Noon-3pm.

275 acres of wetlands, forests, prairies and a lake attract an array of songbirds, raptors and waterfowl. 5 miles of nature trails. The Center is home of the WISCONSIN CONSERVATION HALL OF FAME. The WCHF houses a hands-on forum for learning about the history of conservation in Wisconsin. Learn how animals have had to adapt to human homesteading and trapping for furs. Lumberjacks cut and left behind scarred trees. The pines were gone in less than 60 years. Wisconsin settlers came over to own farm and three-fourths of northern Wisconsin was farmland. Most of these farms failed within a few years doomed by short growing seasons and sterile soils. Since the last glacier moved through, which waterfowl and fish have survived in the waters of Wisconsin?

STEVENS POINT SCULPTURE PARK

901 North Second Street (I-39 exit 161, alongside Zenoff Park) **Stevens Point** 54481

- ☐ **www.stevenspointsculpturepark.org**
- ☐ Hours: Daily sunrise to sunset.
- ☐ Admission: FREE.

The 20-acre Stevens Point Sculpture Park features artwork from local, regional and national artists. The park connects to the Green Circle Trail, a 30.5-mile hiking and biking trail that loops around the Stevens Point area through natural forests and wetlands. A nice wayside off the trail.

HOLLAND'S FAMILY CHEESE FACTORY

200 W Liberty Drive **Thorp** 54771

- ☐ Phone: (715) 669-5230 **www.hollandsfamilycheese.com**
- ☐ Tours: Don't forget to take a self-guided tour anytime of the year, or guided tour during our tour season of June-August. Tours by appointment are greatly encouraged.
- ☐ Note: Cafe open daily 8am-4pm.

Rolf and Marieke Penterman emigrated from the Netherlands in 2002 to pursue their passion for dairy farming. The cheeses are smooth, creamy Gouda cheeses with a slightly sweet, nutty flavor that becomes more complex as it ages on wooden shelves. The 2007 U.S. Championship Cheese Contest gave them Best of Class with their Feonegreek Gouda. The store in the front of the factory is filled with wooden shoes, chocolates, coffees from Holland and key chains with little wooden shoes attached. Samples of flavored goudas are plentiful.

Tours are offered June through September, and teach you about dairy cattle and cheese making (tours $2). Cheese making days are Monday, Tuesday, Thursday and Friday. The cheese factory has viewing windows into the separate rooms so you can watch each individual process. The Pentermans have used some very innovative ideas to conserve time and energy. A special pipeline brings the milk from the dairy directly to the factory. This means the already warm milk demands less energy to heat up to the required temperature of 145 degrees Fahrenheit.

CHAIN O' LAKES CRUISES

N2757 Cty Road QQ (Clear Water Harbor) **Waupaca** 54981

- Phone: (715) 258-2866 **https://clearwaterharbor.com/boat-cruises/**
- Hours: Public cruises Daily (mid-May - October). Call or see website for departure times, generally 11:30am, 1:00pm, 2:30pm, 5:00pm (summers).
- Admission: $17.49 adult, $11.99 child (3-12).
- Note: After your cruise drop by the harborside restaurant for burgers, fish and other North Woods foods. While eating, the kids can watch the boat traffic along the adjacent waters of the Chain O' Lakes.

Lake cruises aboard a sternwheeler or motor launch "Lady of the Lakes". Tour: 90-minute narrated ride that lets you enjoy the scenery and learn the history of the lakes. Learn about the glacial impact, the wildlife, the islands and the folklore of the lakes while appreciating their natural beauty.

HARTMAN CREEK STATE PARK

N2480 Hartman Creek Road (2 miles E of Cty D, 6 miles west of town) **Waupaca** 54981

- Phone: (715) 258-2372
  http://dnr.wi.gov/topic/parks/name/hartman/
- Admission: A vehicle admission sticker is required. Daily $8.00-$11.00.

Located on the beautiful Chain O'Lakes, Hartman Creek is a quiet and friendly natural gem. Features 101 campsites, winter camping, handicap- accessible picnic area and campsites, seasonal naturalist programs, vistas, shoreline with marked beach area on Hartman Lake, canoeing, fishing, 13.7 miles of hiking trails, 3.5 miles of horseback trails (State Trail Pass required), 1 mile of surface bicycle trails, 5.8 miles of off- road bicycle trails (State Trail Pass required), 4 miles of snowmobile trails, 8.6 miles of cross- country ski trails. Open 6:00am-11:00pm with overnight camping.

WHEELHOUSE RESTAURANT

E 1209 Cty Tk Q **Waupaca** 54981

- ☐ Phone: (715) 258-8289 **www.wheelhouserestaurant.com**
- ☐ Hours: Daily Lunch/Dinner on weekends. Summers - weekday lunches/ dinners. Winters - weekday dinners only.

Their famous wheel House pizza features homemade crust, sauce and the freshest ingredients. All pizzas come dressed in real Wisconsin mozzarella cheese and are built to your order - fresh. Not in the mood for pizza? Try a Bomber sandwich (Jeff's homemade Italian sausage). Some items are only $5.00 with most sandwiches averaging $8.00 and most entrees $10.00. Live Music, Indoor and Outdoor Dining, Child Friendly Atmosphere and Video Game Room at Scoopers Ice Cream Parlor next door. Fun for the Whole Family located in the heart of the Chain O' Lakes. _____ |◉|

RIB MOUNTAIN STATE PARK

4200 Park Road (1-1/2 miles W of US 51, 2 miles S of Wausau) **Wausau** 54401

- ☐ Phone: (715) 842-2522
  http://dnr.wi.gov/topic/parks/name/ribmt/
- ☐ Admission: A vehicle admission sticker is required. Daily $8.00-$11.00. Annual passes available.

Rib Mountain has the highest skiable downhill run in the state, 73 kilometers of groomed cross-country ski trails, 750 miles of groomed snowmobile trails, sheets of indoor ice for hockey, curling and figure skating, plus snowshoeing or sledding. 1,172-acre park with camping, hiking, and spectacular scenic overlooks. The top of the 60-foot observation tower offers spectacular views of the Wausau area and Wisconsin River. Granite Peak Ski Area is on the north face of the mountain and offers downhill skiing and snowboarding during winter. Open 6:00am-11:00pm .

CANDLELIGHT SNOWSHOE WALKS - Nighttime walks in the snow. (February)

GRANITE PEAK SKI AREA

3605 N Mountain Road **Wausau** 54402

☐ Phone: (715) 845-2846 **www.skigranitepeak.com**

One of the Midwest's top downhill and snowboarding areas; 700-ft vertical drop, 74 runs, hi-speed chairlifts and a new chalet. Open Thanksgiving thru early April, daily 9:00am-9:00pm.

DELLS OF THE EAU CLAIRE PARK

P2150 County Road Y (On Hwy Y about 15 miles east of Wausau) **Wausau (Aniwa)** 54408

☐ Phone: (715) 261-1550 **https://www.marathoncounty.gov/Home/ Components/FacilityDirectory/FacilityDirectory/38/60**

This 190 acre park along the Eau Claire River features a spectacular rock gorge with waterfalls and rapids, carved by the continual flow of water since glacial times. Wisconsin Trails Magazine voted this park "The Best Place to Picnic" in 1992. In addition to picnic facilities that include a playground and both an open-sided and a reservable log and stone enclosed shelter, there are miles of hiking trails, a rustic campground with 26 sites (16 have electricity), a group campground, and a swimming area on a quiet stretch of river away from the falls and rapids. The park is located on the Ice Age National Recreation Trail and also includes a state scientific area that features the unusual rock formations and associated riverine plant and animal communities.

DID YOU KNOW? Dells are actually from the French word "dalles" which means "gorge" formed from ancient volcanic rock eroded by the river.

CRANBERRY BLOSSOM FESTIVAL

Wisconsin Rapids - *About Blossom Time: "Crane Berries" - Early settlers thought the cranberry blossom resembled the head a crane, hence, the name "crane berry," which was shortened to cranberry. Cranberry blossoms, pretty, delicate pink flowers, come out in late June and early July. Small, green fruit develops behind the flower, growing and changing from green to white to dark red through the months of August and September.*

The Wisconsin Rapids Area is the largest inland-producing cranberry region in the world. They produce nearly 30% of the world's cranberries and are home to several processing, juicing and value-added manufacturing facilities.

Events including live music, parade, arts and crafts, cranberry blossom tours, and of course, culinary treats featuring Wisconsin's tart and tangy fruit, the cranberry!

Cranberry Blossom Tours: GLACIAL LAKE CRANBERRIES (2480 County Road D, Wisconsin Rapids). Tour one of the oldest cranberry marshes in Central Wisconsin with an actual grower. History, videos, cranberry gifts, and tours are offered. Call ahead (715-887-4161) to verify tour times.

Want to tour during harvest season in the fall? History, videos, cranberry gifts, and tours are offered Monday-Friday at 9:00, 11:00am, 1:00 and 3:00pm during harvest and other times by appointment. Call ahead to verify harvest and tour times. **www. blossomfest.com** *(long weekend in June)*

WISCONSIN DAIRY STATE CHEESE CO.

6860 State Road 34 (7 miles north of W Rapids at corner of Main Street and Hwy 34) **Wisconsin Rapids (Rudolph)** 54475

- ☐ Phone: (715) 435-3144 **http://dairystatecheese.com**
- ☐ Hours: Retail outlet open Monday-Friday 8am-5pm, Saturday 8am-4pm.

Most cheese factories are great quick stops. Why? They offer an observation window and play a video on cheesemaking (in case you've arrived late morning and the workers are done making curds and whey). Either way, you'll get the idea. The movie focuses on Wisconsin's rich dairy heritage, too. The store offers many varieties plus fresh cheese curds and ice cream. A trip to the cheese shop is guaranteed to make you hungry. Cheese curds are the best car-friendly snack.

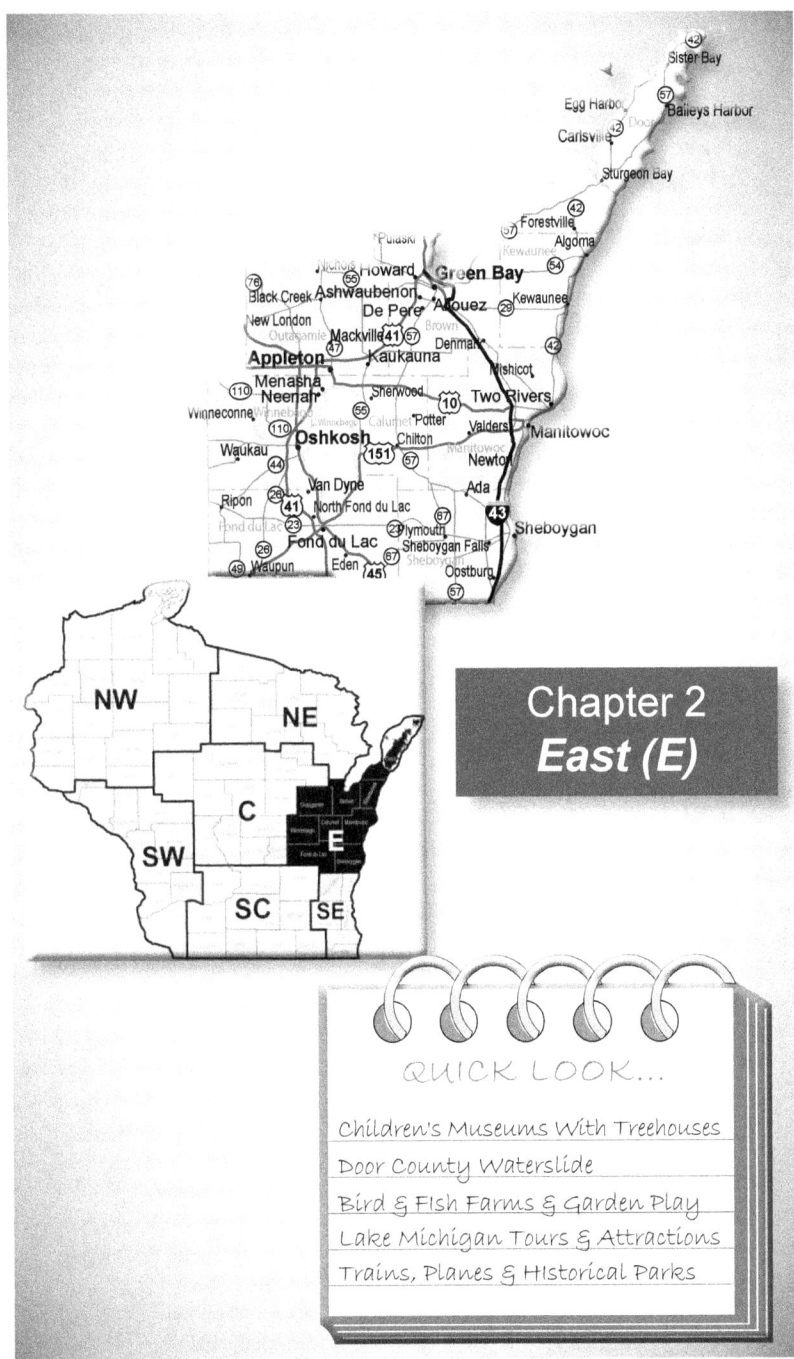

Chapter 2
East (E)

QUICK LOOK...

Children's Museums With Treehouses

Door County Waterslide

Bird & Fish Farms & Garden Play

Lake Michigan Tours & Attractions

Trains, Planes & Historical Parks

Appleton
- Building For Kids
- Funset Boulevard
- Gordon Bubolz Nature Preserve
- History Museum At The Castle
- Simon's Specialty Cheese Factory

Campbellsport
- Reuss Ice Age Visitor Center

Cana Island
- Cana Island Lighthouse

Chilton
- Ledge View Nature Center

De Pere
- Oneida Nation Cultural Museum Festivals

Egg Harbor
- Plum Loco Animal Farm

Egg Harbor (Carlsville)
- Renaissance Fantasy Faire, Door County

Ellison Bay
- Newport State Park

Ellison Bay (Rowleys Bay)
- Gravity Trails

Ephraim
- Fyr Bal Festival

Fish Creek
- American Folklore Theatre
- Door County Trolley
- Fish Creek Winter Festival
- Peninsula State Park

Fond Du Lac
- Children's Museum Of Fond Du Lac
- Galloway House & Village

Fond Du Lac (cont.)
- Kristmas Kringle Shoppe
- Lakeside Park & Lighthouse
- Walleye Weekend

Green Bay
- Bay Beach Amusement Park
- Bay Beach Wildlife Sanctuary
- Green Bay Botanical Garden
- Green Bay Packers Hall Of Fame
- Green Bay Packers Training Camps
- Heritage Hill State Historical Park
- Lambeau Field Tours
- National Railroad Museum
- Neville Public Museum
- New Zoo
- Winterfest On Broadway

Greenbush
- Wade House Historic House

Kaukauna
- 1000 Island Environmental Center
- Wisconsin International Raceway

Kewaunee
- Agricultural Heritage Farm
- C.D. Besadny Anadromous Fish Facility
- Tug Ludington

Kiel
- Hennings Cheese Store & Museum

Kohler
- Harvest Days, Kohler

Little Chute
- Great Wisconsin Cheese Festival
- Little Chute Windmill

Manitowoc
- Beerntsen's Confectionary
- Cedar Crest Ice Cream Parlor

- Lincoln Park Zoo
- Pine River Dairy
- Pinecrest Historical Village
- S.S. Badger Lake Michigan Carferry
- Wisconsin Maritime Museum

Menasha

- Heckrodt Wetland Reserve
- Weis Earth Science Museum & Barlow Planetarium

Mt. Calvary

- Villa Loretto Tours

Omro

- Knigge Farms

Oshkosh

- EAA Air Adventure Museum
- Menominee Park And Zoo
- Oshkosh Public Museum

Ripon

- Larson's Famous Clydesdales
- Little White Schoolhouse

Seymour

- Hamburger Festival

Sheboygan

- Above & Beyond Children's Museum
- Blue Harbor Resort & Indoor Waterpark
- Kohler-Andrae State Park

Sherwood

- High Cliff State Park

Sister Bay

- Al Johnson's Swedish Restaurant
- Corner Of The Past / Old Anderson House Museum

Sturgeon Bay

- Door County Maritime Museum
- Potawatomi State Park
- The Farm
- Whitefish Dunes State Park

Two Rivers

- Historic Washington House
- Londondairy Alpacas & Fiber Studio
- Point Beach State Forest
- Rogers Street Fishing Village

Washington Island

- Washington Island Ferry Line

Sites and attractions are listed in order by City, Zip Code, and Name. Symbols indicated represent:

 Restaurants Lodging

BUILDING FOR KIDS CHILDREN'S MUSEUM

100 West College Avenue (intersection of College Ave & Appleton Street)
Appleton 54911

☐ Phone: (920) 734-3226 **www.buildingforkids.org**
☐ Hours: Tuesday-Sunday 9:00am-4:00pm.
☐ Admission: General $11.00 (age 1+).

The Building for Kids is one of the largest children's museums in the Midwest. The brightly colored museum hosts hands-on exhibits that arouse children's curiosity and invite them to learn by doing. A 2-story tree house is the centerpiece of the building accompanied by a water play area, a mini Kwik Trip, "The Happy Baby Garden" designed especially for children aged 0-3, the Amazing Heart, Castle Adventure, and other educational exhibits. Girls love dressing in scrubs to help in the doll hospital. The Move-It exhibit is a giant wall of levers and pulleys that the kids have to reach for to make the simple machine work. Or, maybe your kids want to combine art and science in a craft, fly a plane, drive a fire truck or don a hardhat in the construction zone. Again, the nicest part is the vividly-colored playspaces.

GORDON BUBOLZ NATURE PRESERVE

4815 N Lynndale Dr (Cty A) **Appleton 54913**

☐ Phone: (920) 731-6041 **www.bubolzpreserve.org**
☐ Hours: Building Hours: Tuesday-Friday 8:00am-4:30pm. Saturday 11:00am-4:00pm. Sunday Noon-4:00pm. Trails open during daylight hours.

This 775-acre white cedar swamp features a nature center, hiking trails and wildlife watching. Woodland bird species include great horned owls, pileated woodpeckers, yellow-bellied sapsuckers, herons, cranes, Cooper's hawks, harriers migrating ducks and shorebirds. Ski and snoeshoe trails and rentals.

HISTORY MUSEUM AT THE CASTLE
330 East College Avenue **Appleton** 54911

- Phone: (920) 735-9370 **www.myhistorymuseum.org**
- Hours: Daily 10:00am to 4:00pm.
- Admission: $10.00 adult, $7.50 child (3-17). $22.00 family.
- Note: A Houdini walking tour map with articles and magic tricks is available at the History Museum for 25 cents.
- Educators: wonderful curriculum links: Teachers' Resources. We especially liked the Time Capsules Curriculum and the School Days lessons. http://www.myhistorymuseum.org/curriculumlanding.html

Appleton's Harry Houdini pushed the limits in his quest for the ultimate illusion as a magician, escapologist and stunt performer. An unusual dreamer, Houdini flew airplanes and held a 1921 patent for an underwater diving suit he designed. His life and illusions are immortalized at this museum where a large exhibit space lets you experience some of Houdini's tricks through hands-on activities.

Other exhibit spaces highlight Native Americans, WWII and the Fur Trade history in Fox Valley. Did you know Appleton is also the location of the world's first home lighted by a central hydroelectric station, Hearthstone Historic House Museum. What we like best about this place is that they took the time to engage kids at every station with One-of-a-kind artifacts, multi-sensory activities, and audio-visual technology. History is alive and here.

SIMON'S SPECIALTY CHEESE FACTORY
2735 Freedom Road (just off Hwy 41) **Appleton** 54913

- Phone: (920) 788-6311 **www.simonscheese.com**
- Hours: Monday-Friday 8:00am-6:00pm, Saturday 8:00am-5:00pm.

Get a close up look at Wisconsin's dairy industry heritage at this large manufacturer of specialty cheeses. Watch a video of cheese production, look through a mini-museum, sample a variety of freshly made cheeses, enjoy a quick lunch and shop for Wisconsin-themed gifts in the gift shop. Plus fresh cheese curds, FREE cheese & fudge samples with 16 varieties of fudge including their special recipe of Homemade Chocolate Cheese Fudge, hand-dipped ice cream, fresh pizzas and many Wisconsin specialty gifts & gourmet items.

FUNSET BOULEVARD

3916 West College Avenue **Appleton** 54914

- ☐ Phone: (920) 993-0909 **www.funset.com**
- ☐ Hours: Monday-Thursday 4:00pm-10:00pm, Friday 4:00pm-11:00pm, Saturday Noon-9:00pm, Sunday Noon-9:00pm. (additional hours in summer).
- ☐ No admission but each activity costs $3.00 to $8.00. Packages/ wristbands for certain activities available for $12.95+.

This one-of-a-kind facility is filled with more than 100 video games, a laser tag arena, virtual reality games, a mini-bowling alley, a miniature golf course, bumper cars, a train ride, and full-size carousel. Funset is attached to a state-of-the-art movie theater complex. Funset Grill features pizza and snacks.

REUSS ICE AGE VISITOR CENTER

N2875 Hwy 67 (off Hwy 67 NE of Hwy 45) **Campbellsport** 53010

- ☐ Phone: (920) 533-8322
  https://dnr.wisconsin.gov/topic/parks/kmn/naturecenter
- ☐ Hours: Open year round Wednesday-Sunday 9:30am-4:30pm, Weekends 9:30am-5:00pm. Winter hours vary.

Learn how the glaciers of the last Ice Age shaped the landscape of the Kettle Moraine area. The history of glacial activity is depicted in a 20-minute Ice Age film, exhibits, panoramas, and staff-led programs. A back deck overlooks an outwash plain and provides a perfect photo spot with Dundee Mountain in the background.

CANA ISLAND LIGHTHOUSE

(north of Baileys Harbor off County Highway Q) **Cana Island** 54202

- ☐ Phone: (920) 743-5958 www.dcmm.org/cana-island-lighthouse/
- ☐ Hours: Daily 10:00am-5:00pm (May-October).
- ☐ Admission: $12.00 adult, $10.00 child (5-17). $4.00 additional per person to climb the tower (must be 42" or taller - other rules apply).

Cana Island is an island you can walk to! Walk across the rock causeway from the Door County mainland to the island (be aware occasional wind and weather cause water to flow over the causeway). Come prepared with boots or other footwear that can withstand the water and protect your feet). Or, ride a hay-wagon over the causeway to explore the island, including the 89-foot-tall

For updates & travel games visit: **www.KidsLoveTravel.com**

light tower, oil storage house and lighthouse keeper's home. The highlight of any Cana Island visit is climbing the 97 steps of the tower's spiral staircase to reach the gallery deck, which delivers a sweeping panoramic view of Lake Michigan and the Door County peninsula.

The Lighthouse was built in 1869 and is 89 feet tall and still operational. Begin your tour of the buildings at the base of the light. Step inside the Keepers' House where the first of a number of lighthouse keepers tended to the light which guided sailors and protected them from the dangerous shoals extending out from the island into Lake Michigan. Note that the climb is confined and somewhat aerobic so be sure you qualify as a climber before you pay the fee.

LEDGE VIEW NATURE CENTER
W2348 Short Rd (one mile south of Chilton between Hwys G and 57)
Chilton 53014

- ☐ Phone: (920) 849-7094 **http://ledgeviewnaturecenter.org/**
- ☐ Hours: Park open dawn to dusk. Nature Center: Monday-Saturday 8:00am-4:00pm.
- ☐ Admission: FREE to enter park.
- ☐ Tours: Public cave tours weekends May-October, some summer weekdays. Call to confirm. Recommended minimum age is 5 years old.
- ☐ Note: Maple Syrup Sunday open house (end of March) and Halloween Candlelight Cave Tours.

Cliffs, caves and plenty of color are what make Calumet County a nature lover's paradise. This 105-acre preserve has indoor exhibits on Lake Sturgeon, Wisconsin Bats, Birds, Niagara Escarpment; live animals; honeybee observation hive; hiking/xc ski trails; fun trail; 60-foot observation tower; labeled arboretum, butterfly garden, rain garden; three caves and a quarry.

- CAVE TOURS - There is no access to the caves except on a scheduled tour. The caves are accessed via stairs and ladders. All cave tours are guided by a naturalist and include information about the biology, geology, and human history of the caves. Tours last about two hours. There is no electrical lighting in the caves, nor any concrete walkways. Visitors will have opportunities to crawl through passageways and explore. Visitors should bring a flashlight and plan on getting dirty! (You are welcome to bring a change of clothes.)

For the general public, walk-in tours are offered most weekends and some weekdays, May through October. Tours visit Carolyn's Caverns, or Carolyn's and Mothers Cave. Only one or two tours will run on any scheduled date, and participants need to have "registered" at the front desk by the tour start time. The charge is a flat per-person rate of $5.00. The Mothers Cave tour is $6.00 per person (all crawling).

ONEIDA NATION CULTURAL MUSEUM

W892 County Road EE (7 miles west of Green Bay city limits at County Roads E and EE) **De Pere** 54115

- ☐ Phone: (920) 869-2768 **www.facebook.com/oneidamuseum**
- ☐ Hours: Tuesday-Friday 9:00am-5:00pm (June-August), Saturday 10am-3pm. Tuesday-Friday 9:00am-5:00pm (September-May). The museum is closed Sunday & Monday, and holidays.
- ☐ Tours: $5.00 per person
- ☐ Admission: $4.00 adult, $2.00 senior (55+) and child (under 18).

Largest exhibit of Oneida Nation history, culture and artifacts in the world. The historic village and longhouse and the crafts exhibits and demos are worth a look. Best to plan family visits around events. They have many new exhibits that are most festive during a celebration.

ONEIDA NATION CULTURAL FESTIVAL

De Pere - *Oneida Nation Cultural Museum - Enjoy traditional Oneida music, dancing, food, children's activities, craft vendors, arts and craft demonstrations, raffles and more. The museum offers monthly events throughout the year. See the Calendar section on their website. FREE. (first Saturday in June)*

PLUM LOCO ANIMAL FARM

4431 Plum Bottom Road **Egg Harbor** 54209

- ☐ Phone: (920) 743-1617 **www.plumlocoanimalfarm.com**
- ☐ Hours: Daily 9:30am-4:30pm (closed Wednesday). (Memorial Weekend - Labor Day) Weekends Only 9:30am-4:00pm (Labor Day - November 1).
- ☐ Admission: $9 adult, $8 seniors, $7 child (2-17).
- ☐ Note: Snacks, drinks, souvenirs available.

Escape the crowds and unwind in wide-open spaces. Enjoy the antics of farm animals- each with their own "house" - the goats have a Swiss chalet.

Picnic or relax in rustic cedar gazebos. Or let the kids pretend in the mini play farm village complete with a scaled-down farm house equipped with a fully-stocked kitchen, garden and laundry wash line. The barn contains landscaping equipment, tool bench, pedal-tractors, gas pump, wheel-barrows and corral with plush horses the children can ride and brush. The 1880's style General Store is complete with a farmer's market stand, cash register, shopping carts and items to buy and sell. Share some family time with a lawn or board game. There are all kinds of things to do on the farm, including petting the animals, feeding carrots to ponies, horses and donkeys or grains for the sheep, pigs and goats. The couple that runs this place is so accommodating and pleasant - we think it makes the animals behave likewise.

RENAISSANCE FANTASY FAIRE, DOOR COUNTY

Egg Harbor (**Carlsville**) - *(off Highway 42, head east on Monument Road. Go 1/2 mile). The Door County Renaissance Fantasy Faire brings visitors back in time to experience the middle ages in a family friendly, festival setting. Featuring make-believe knights, faire ladies, wenches, wizards, dragons and royalty, the fair recreates a 12th-16th Century European Country Market Faire with mythical creatures and characters as its guests. In addition to entertainment, Renaissance Fantasy Faire aims to educate through interactive history and showcase the talent of Door County actors. Admission. FREE parking.* **www.DoorCoWIRenaissance.com** *(two weekends leading up to July 4th)*

NEWPORT STATE PARK

475 County Highway NP (2-1/2 miles SE of SR 42, 5 miles E of Ellison Bay)
Ellison Bay 54210

- ☐ Phone: (920) 854-2500
  http://dnr.wi.gov/topic/parks/name/newport/
- ☐ Admission: A vehicle admission sticker is required. Daily $8.00-$10.00. Annual passes available.

Newport's wilderness philosophy offers quiet forests and miles of Lake Michigan shoreline as quiet alternatives to bustling Door County. Features 16 campsites, winter camping, backpack camping, handicap-accessible picnic area, nature center, seasonal naturalist programs, shoreline, canoeing, fishing, 2 miles of nature trails, 30 miles of hiking trails, 13 miles of off- road bicycle trails, 23 miles of cross- country ski trails.

GRAVITY TRAILS

1041 County Rd. ZZ **Ellison Bay (Rowleys Bay)** 54210

- ☐ Phone: (414) 704-3982 **www.gravitytrails.com**
- ☐ Admission: Zip ~$45.00/ Kayak ~$60.00-$65.
- ☐ Tour Times: 8:00am to dusk on the hour every hour. By reservation.
- ☐ Note: Minimum age is 8. Gem Mining flume - starts at $15/bucket.

Gravity Trails is a multi-recreational activity center located at the Wagon Trail Resort. Activities offered include guided kayak tours, cruiser style biking, and nearly 2000 feet of zip lining. Gravity Trails has access to Newport State Park, The Mink River Estuary, Sand Bay Beach, and over 50+ acres of hiking trails behind the Wagon Trail Resort.

ZIP LINE - Zip Line next to ponds, sand dunes and fly through the air up to a version of an ewok village in the trees. A beginner to Intermediate Climbing Wall ascends to a 20 ft platform, from there you zip to a 14 ft platform that zips to a 10 ft platform and from there you zip down to the ground.

FYR BAL FESTIVAL

Ephraim - *Downtown, waterfront. Visitors can celebrate the summer solstice at this colorful Scandinavian festival in Door County. The event includes ethnic food and music, traditional Scandinavian dancers and singers, a community fish boil, crafts, Ephraim Historical Walking Tours, village chieftain ceremony, sailboat regatta, Viking ship, bonfires along the shores of Eagle Harbor on Green Bay and fireworks on Saturday evening. There's a pet parade and trolley tours, too.* **www.ephraim-doorcounty.com** *(third weekend in June, Fathers Day weekend)*

NORTHERN SKY THEATER

AFT Amphitheatre - Peninsula State Park (shows performed at 3 locations)
Fish Creek 54212

- ☐ Phone: Business office - (920) 854-6117 **www.northernskytheater.com**
- ☐ Hours: Summer season (mid-June - August). Fall season at Town Halls (September-October). Most performances late afternoon or early evening.
- ☐ Admission: Early shows $10-$25. Evening shows $18-$37.

Humble yet polished, hopeful, yet not sentimental, historical yet hysterical... That's the oddball wonder called AFT. This production team write original musical comedies for the whole family. They build their shows on the rock of

American folk culture: great tales, turns of events and aching melodies. Want an example of their regional twists? How about Cheeseheads, the Musical, Lumberjacks in Love, Guys and Does, Northern Lights or Guys on Ice - an ice fishing musical comedy. Clever and cute.

DOOR COUNTY TROLLEY

Pickup locations are at various hotels and major attractions
Fish Creek 54212

- Phone: (920) 868-1100 **www.doorcountytrolley.com**
- Hours: generally daily May - October, several times per day.
- Tours: start at the basic 30 minute Family Tour ($9.95-$12.95) or the 1.5 hr Scenic Trolley Tour at $22.95-$27.95 per person.

Year-round tours of Door County including scenic, lighthouse & winter tours. Folks love these tours, mostly because the guides love what they do and tell stories of legend and lore unique to this area. Often, you'll hear trolleys go by with passengers laughing. In the end, everyone learns something new about historic Door County. We'd suggest taking this tour in the early part of your visit to Door County and find out what "must see" sights you plan to visit next. Lunch is often included in many of the 2 hour tours. Winters they offer a sleigh ride, too. Call or visit Web site for schedule.

PENINSULA STATE PARK

9462 Shore Road (off SR 42) **Fish Creek** 54212

- Phone: (920) 868-3258
  http://dnr.wi.gov/topic/parks/name/peninsula/
- Admission: A vehicle admission sticker is required. Daily $8.00-$10.00. Annual passes available.

High bluffs and sandy beaches, an 1860s lighthouse, a challenging 18-hole golf course and professional summer theater performances make this park extremely popular. Features 469 campsites, 100 electric sites, winter camping, handicap- accessible picnic area and campsites, concessions, nature center, seasonal naturalist programs, lookout tower, vistas, shoreline with 8 miles of marked beach area, canoeing, boating, fishing, 2.5 miles of nature trails, 20 miles of hiking trails, 7 miles of surfaced bicycle trails, 8 miles of off- road bicycle trails (State Trail Pass required), 18 miles of snowmobile trails, 18 miles of cross- country ski trails.

EAGLE BLUFF LIGHTHOUSE - www.eagleblufflighthouse.org. (920) 839-2377. Keeper's dwelling is completely restored. Guided tours daily from Memorial Day through the third weekend of October, 10:00am-4:30pm. Admission fee.

The WHITE CEDAR NATURE CENTER is located in Peninsula State Park, a 776-acre area that includes seven miles of accessible shoreline and nearly 500 campsites. The nature center, located on Bluff Road near the Woodyard, is a year-round facility featuring bird and fish displays, children's area, and more. A large stuffed black bear greats you. Half-mile interpretive nature trail adjacent to building. Open daily Memorial Day - Labor Day, 10:00am-2:00pm. Open limited days September - May. Family nature programs offered daily during the summer, limited times through out the year.

FISH CREEK WINTER FESTIVAL

Fish Creek - Downtown. Nestled in the heart of picturesque Door County, the town of Fish Creek, sets its sight on the "weird and hysterical" in the annual event. Perhaps the main attraction is the Costumed Bed Racing Competition in which teams race down the street in their luxury sleepers. Or, watch as toilet seats and bikes take to the air for the toilet seat throw and bike toss. And few things bring more laughs than the hijinks during the snowshoe dance contest. Kid's obstacle course, treasure hunt, tube toss and more. Other events for the whole family include crazy golf, sleigh rides, the arctic basketball toss, raffles and the Sock Hop at the Parkway Supper Club. (twelve days starting early February) **https://www.facebook.com/fishcreekwinterfest/**

CHILDREN'S MUSEUM OF FOND DU LAC

75 W Scott Street **Fond du Lac** 54935

- ☐ Phone: (920) 929-0707 **www.cmfdl.org**
- ☐ Hours: Tuesday -Thursday 9:00am-5:00pm, Friday-Saturday 9:00am-4:00pm.
- ☐ Admission: $8.00 (age 1+), $7.00 senior (65+).
- ☐ Educators: click on Educators/Schools icon, then Educator Packets for a pdf of extension activities to conduct for each museum station.

Adventure and excitement await you. Take your family on a journey around the world as you experience all the hands-on, educational fun that the museum has to offer. Throughout the museum passport stations give information as they show pictures and items from different countries. Match the correct flags or animals or answer the questions to collect stamps in your passport. Build a house in Beijing, cast your shadow in our African safari, make a pizza in Italy, and much more. Go to the Great Toddler Reef (Australia) and see how healthy habits help in HealthWorks! (North America). Designed for children ages 0-11.

GALLOWAY HOUSE & VILLAGE

336 Old Pioneer Road (midway between SR 175 and US 45)
Fond du Lac 54935

☐ Phone: (920) 922-1166 **www.fdlhistory.com**
☐ Hours: Wednesday-Sunday 11:00am-4:00pm (Memorial day to Labor day).
☐ Admission: $10.00 (ages 7+). Family $30.00 (2 adults and dependent children).

See what life was like in the late 1800s. Tour this authentic village and 30-room mid-Victorian mansion boasting 4 fireplaces, Italianate details, and many pieces of original furniture. The 30-room mansion was the "farmhouse" of the Galloway family for three generations. Purchased as a simple but decorative house, the Galloways built ornate additions to turn the house into a showplace of gracious living and entertaining.

Surrounded by 25 historic buildings such as a church, photographers' shop, townhall, newspaper print shop, and one-room school. The Blakely Museum contains historical collections from Native American to present day. In the CCC Barracks Museum learn about the CCC (Civilian Conservation Corps) workers in the 1930s. CCC was President Roosevelt's most successful "New Deal" program, designed to put young men to work during the Great Depression.

KRISTMAS KRINGLE SHOPPE

1330 South Main Street (Hwys 41 & Main St Exit) **Fond du Lac** 54935

☐ Phone: (920) 922-3900 or (800) 721-2525 **www.kristmaskringle.com**
☐ Hours: Daily 10:00am-5:00pm. Special holiday & extended hours on Friday night.

This Midwest favorite has long been a destination for shoppers of all ages. The two-story Bavarian style shop boasts an interior that resembles streets of quaint European shops, lined with more than 70 themed Christmas trees, collectibles, animated figures, and imported ornaments.

LAKESIDE PARK & LIGHTHOUSE

555 N Park Ave end of N Main St & end of N Park Ave) **Fond du Lac** 54935

- ☐ Phone: (800) 937-9123 **www.fdl.com/to-do/lakeside-park/**
- ☐ Hours: Daily 10:00am-4:00pm (summers).
- ☐ Admission: FREE for park. Rides are small fee.
- ☐ Note: Park glows with thousands of holiday lights and animated displays including holiday music each December. Decorated and spotlighted for the holidays every December.

Bring the family for fun in Fond du Lac's 400-acre Lakeside Park, on Lake Winnebago, Wisconsin's largest inland lake. Walk-up lighthouse. Picnic areas, shelters, playground, deer park, ball diamonds, marina, and boat launch ramps. Train ride, old fashioned carousel, bumper boats, aqua bikes, and canoes.

Lighthouse & Observation Deck - Climb this 40-ft tall working lighthouse for a spectacular view of Lake Winnebago and Lakeside Park. Built in 1933 during the Great Depression, wooden Cape Cod style painted white with a flagstone base, free telescope views. Self-guided tours April 15 - October 15, weather permitting. 8:00am to dusk.

WALLEYE WEEKEND

*Fond du Lac - Lakeside Park. A national walleye fishing tournament includes a Familyland area, entertainment and the "world's largest fish fry." Walleye Weekend, Fond du Lac's signature event, has been luring more than 100,000 people for the past 32 years. Filled with three days of free family fun, Walleye Weekend offers something for everyone. The familyland area features a children's entertainment stage, balloon artists, inflatables and such. The festival also features five music stages with live performances from regional and national acts, and more than eight sporting events including the featured Mercury Marine National Fishing Tournament. Admission, parking, shuttles, attractions and entertainment at Walleye Weekend are free to the public. Through its efforts, Walleye Weekend benefits more than 100 non-profit organizations. **www.fdlfest.com** (second weekend in June)*

HERITAGE HILL STATE HISTORICAL PARK

2640 South Webster Avenue (On SR 172, 2-1/2 miles E of US 41)
Green Bay 54301

- Phone: (920) 448-5150 **www.heritagehillgb.org**
- Hours: Tuesday-Saturday 10:00am-4:00pm, Sunday Noon-4:00pm (May-October). Monday-Friday 10:00am-4:30pm for Stroll Though the Park (rest of year).
- Admission: $12.00 adult, $10.00 senior (62+), $8.00 child (6-17). Stroll Through the Park is a reduced rate.
- Educators: Heritage Kits can be rented from the park.

Experience living history at this 49-acre outdoor museum. Twenty-five historic buildings dating from 1672 through 1905, with costumed interpreters share the history of Northeast Wisconsin and its people. Historic guides challenge guests to think of what it would have been like to live as a fur trader (very rough), a farmer, an officer's wife, a soldier, or a trades person. If you're a fan of Laura Ingalls, you will feel like you're on the set of the later shows when you visit the farm & community areas. Is your favorite chore washing, churning or baking?

The Fort Howard guard house adds to the feeling of a military outpost era in early 1800s Wisconsin. Learn about soldier's regimented days, chores and military marching (even practice some maneuvers).

BAY BEACH AMUSEMENT PARK

1313 Bay Beach Road **Green Bay** 54302

- Phone: (920) 448-3365 **http://baybeach.org/**
- Hours: Daily 10:00am-9:00pm (summers). Weekends until 6:00pm May & September. Daily 10:00am-6:00pm (last 2 weeks of August).
- Admission: There is no admission charge and parking is free. Ride tickets are $0.25 cents each, with the rides requiring one or two tickets per rider.

Inexpensive and affordable are the claims you'll hear most from folks that visit this park. Because it's pay as you go, you only go on the rides kids really like best. Choose from classic fair rides like carousel, ferris wheel, giant slide, bumper cars, Scrambler, etc. Best for younger families as they don't really have thrill rides. For about $5.00, you can let your child ride a bunch of rides, wear out, and home you go. And you can bring in a cooler with your picnic lunch and drinks so you can eat and drink much more affordably!

BAY BEACH WILDLIFE SANCTUARY

1660 East Shore Drive (I-43 Webster Ave. exit) **Green Bay** 54302

- ☐ Phone: (920) 391-3671 **www.baybeachwildlife.com**
- ☐ Hours: Nature Center: Daily 8:00am-7:30pm (May-Labor Day). Closes 4:30pm (rest of year). Observation Building generally closes before Nature Center. Hiking trails close at 4:30pm year round.
- ☐ Admission: FREE.

This sanctuary is a 700-acre urban wildlife refuge with live animal exhibits, interactive nature center, trails & serves as a wildlife rehabilitation site. It includes both a Raptor center and a live Nature Center. Meet their Eagle Matriarch, the bats, Bob the bobcat and Sammy and Sadie otters. Naming their creatures creates a connection with your kids - some of the names have meaning, some are just silly - but memorable. Their naturalists on staff lead regular live animal talks, hikes, Wisconsin's wildlife tours and pond studies. Along the trail, there's a lookout tower that oversees the deer habitat. They also have a wolf area and the kids have trouble seeing many differences from domestic dogs - but there are. Can you tell who's the alpha?

GREEN BAY BOTANICAL GARDEN

2600 Larsen Road **Green Bay** 54303

- ☐ Phone: (920) 490-9457 **www.gbbg.org**
- ☐ Hours: Monday-Saturday 9:00am-4:00pm (January-March), Daily 9:00am-5:00pm (April, May, September, October), Daily 9:00am-8:00pm (June-August), Monday-Friday 9:00am-5:00pm (November, December).
- ☐ Admission: $13.00 adult, $11.00 senior (62+), $5.00 child (3-17).
- ☐ Note: Story Hours and family gardening in the Peas in a Pod program. Educators: For pre-and post visit materials: click on the online Education icon, then Teachers and Students, then Curriculum. FREEBIES: S.E.E.D. Packs can be checked out for no additional charge after paid admission.

This place has tons of formal gardens but the kids will naturally gravitate to the only Children's Garden in the state of Wisconsin. The Children's Garden captures the imagination of children with a tree house, slide, vine maze, re-circulating pond, and giant sundial. Children can learn about the wonders of plants and nature through their exploration of the Einstein Garden, Butterfly Garden, Peter Rabbit Garden, Sensory Garden, Dragon Fly Bridge, and Frog Bridge. Children can be educated in the Children's Gardening Patch, Compost Demonstration Area, Wetting Zoo and Wild Ones Prairie Planting.

As you pay admission, ask for a FREE S.E.E.D. activity filled backpacks created in four main themes: Discovery, Gardening, Birds and Butterflies, and Forestry. Within the Packs are short lessons about a topic relating to the theme of the Pack, accompanied by a hands-on activity. These activities include games, scavenger hunts, journaling activities, and observation activities that encourage users to explore the Garden more closely.

GARDEN OF LIGHTS

Green Bay - Green Bay Botanical Garden. Recently added, a 60' long walk-through caterpillar that stands 7' tall and 7' wide and boasts 20,000 energy-saving LED lights. Also see the area's largest tree, a five-story, 45' metal frame tree trimmed with 20,000 LED lights. Along with nightly entertainment, there are visits from Santa and Mrs. Claus. Visitors center with refreshments and gifts. Wagon rides. Admission. (Friday, Saturdays, Sundays from Thanksgiving weekend thru Christmas weekend)

NEVILLE PUBLIC MUSEUM

210 Museum Place (I-43 exit 189, off US 141) **Green Bay** 54303

- Phone: (920) 448-4460 **www.nevillepublicmuseum.org**
- Hours: Hours: Wednesday-Saturday 9:00am-5:00pm. Tuesday Noon-8:00pm 1st Wednesday FREE admission from 5:00-8:00pm. Sunday Noon-5:00pm.
- Admission: $11.00 adult (16+), $9.00 senior (62+), $6.00 child (3-15).
- Educators: Education packets for every major permanent or traveling exhibit is found under the Education icon, then School Year Programs.

Learn about science, art, and local history at Green Bay's largest museum. Its signature exhibit, "On the Edge of the Inland Sea" teaches patrons the history of the Great Lakes Region, from the last Ice Age to the present. The Discovery Room is where hands-on happens. Discovery Baskets (each with a separate theme such as insects, dinos, art) with props, books, and toys plus added instructional activity sheets.

Kid-sized tables and chairs invite children to sit down and use their hands to write, color or create. "Please Touch" signs abound. In another space labeled: Hometown Advantage, a video theater shows eight short films about the relationship of the Green Bay Packers to the local community. After all, the city owns the team. Learn what happens OFF the field in Green Bay. Although the building has been there for a while and many permanent exhibits are the same, temporary exhibits and the Discovery Room keep proud locals coming back.

DID YOU KNOW? Green Bay is the Toilet Paper Capital of the World - toilet paper production, wood-processing plants, mills, and paper-company offices form the core of the city's business world.

GREEN BAY PACKERS HALL OF FAME

1265 Lombardi Avenue **Green Bay** 54304

☐ Phone: (920) 569-7512 or (888) 442-7225
   www.packers.com/lambeau-field/hall-of-fame/visit.html
☐ Hours: (Non-Game days) Monday-Saturday 9:00am-6:00pm, Sunday 10:00am-5:00pm. (Training Camp Hours - August 1 - September 3), Monday-Saturday 8:00am-6:00pm, Sunday 10:00am-6:00pm. The day before a game the Hall of Fame is open from 8:00am-7:00pm.
☐ Admission: $18.00 adult (18-61), $15.00 senior (62+), Military, & college, $12.00 youth (6-17).
☐ Note: Located in the Lambeau Field Atrium, the HOF is complimented by a number of dining, entertainment and retail options. Curly's Pub is a popular family restaurant, especially during away games. Curly's Game Zone, on the Atrium's second level, features more than 50 exciting and interactive games.

Pure Packers adrenaline fills the 25,000-square-foot HOF where you can see, touch and feel more than eighty years of NFL football history. There are nearly eighty exhibits including three Super Bowl trophies and a re-creation of Vince Lombardi's office. Extensive videos – many of them updated – allow the Packers' legendary memories to carry on. There is a special exhibit on Brett Favre's memorable career here. Discover the origin of the "Lambeau leap," and then try to kick a winning field goal or throw a touchdown.

• CHEESEHEADS - Fans of Chicago sports called Wisconsin fans "cheeseheads" as an insult. Milwaukeean Ralph Bruno turned that cheesy comment into big business, fashioning the now infamous cheesehead hat out of polyurethane foam. By the end of the 1987 season, the wedge-shaped hats had become a Wisconsin fan's slice of heaven. The cheesehead hat are the color of cheddar with Swiss cheese holes - pure Wisconsin. www.cheesehead.com.

• VINCE LOMBARDI - Arguably the most legendary football coach of all time, Vince Lombardi honed his coaching skills by improving the skills of underdogs in the emerging sport of football. Backed with military training and a hard-work ethic the Packers needed to shape their potential, Lombardi arrived in Green Bay in 1959. By the time he left in 1967, the green and gold dominated professional football, collecting six division titles, five NFL championships, two Super Bowls (I and II) and acquiring a record of 98-30-4.

LAMBEAU FIELD TOURS

1265 Lombardi Avenue **Green Bay** 54304

☐   Phone: (920) 569-7513
     www.packers.com/lambeau-field/stadium-tours.html
☐   Hours: Daily 10:00am-4:00pm. Hours may vary daily. Please see website for
     schedule. Generally most days there are four tours.
☐   Admission: $34.00 adult (18-61), $28.00 senior (62+), military, college,
     $22.00 youth (6-17). Includes visit to HOF.
☐   Tours: Tickets are sold on a first-come, first-served basis for each day's
     available tours. Stadium Tours do sell out on a regular basis, so please arrive
     early. Tickets go on sale at 9:00am Monday-Saturday, 10:00am on Sundays.
     During Training Camp tickets will go on sale at 8:00am.

Who would ever guess that a kid kicking around a salt sack filled with sand, leaves and pebbles because he couldn't afford a football would become the man behind the mighty Green Bay Packers? Earl "Curly" Lambeau eventually got a ball, grew up and convinced his employer, the Indian Packing Company, to donate money to start up a football team. Lambeau revolutionized professional football by legitimizing passing in a game that had focused on running while placing building blocks for the Packers and their forever home at Lambeau Field.

Lambeau Field stadium tours allow fans to experience the Packers' history-rich facility first-hand and see several behind-the-scenes areas. Each one-hour tour begins in Harlan Plaza at the statues of Curly Lambeau and Vince Lombardi. Tour guides will lead fans through the all-new Atrium, up to the Club Level for an exclusive look at the private boxes, club seats and the Legends Club, and then visit the upgraded concourse and check out the turf of football's most famous gridiron. You'll learn the history of Lambeau Field. And you'll even walk through the team tunnel on the same concrete that every Packers player has walked on since Lombardi's teams took the field.

PACKERS HERITAGE TROLLEY TOUR: 100 years of history with stops at famous landmarks. 90 minutes. $40.00 per person.

NATIONAL RAILROAD MUSEUM

2285 South Broadway **Green Bay** 54304

- ☐ Phone: (920) 437-7623 http://.**nationalrrmuseum.org/**
- ☐ Hours: Monday-Saturday 9:00am-5:00pm (April-December). Closed Mondays (January - March). Sunday 11:00am-5:00pm (year-round).
- ☐ Admission: $12.00 adult, $10.00 senior (62+), $8.00 child (2-12).
- ☐ Tours: Train Rides - (additional $4.00 charge, April-September & weekends in October). Train Ride tickets must be purchased with a Museum admission.
- ☐ Educators: A thorough Scavenger Hunt, worksheets, games and puzzles are located under EDUCATION icon.

Explore America's railroad heritage. Marvel at the Union Pacific Big Boy, the world's largest steam locomotive (you can actually climb aboard!), and Eisenhower's World War II command train. They show a movie about the "Big Boy" engine and train safety. Over 70 pieces of railroad equipment on display - explore their interiors-some still look elegant, others used and worn. Next, hands-on models allow kids to role play and touch railroad equipment. Outside, you can climb the yard observation tower for a nice view of Green Bay. Ride a full-size train around the yard before you leave. Any kid who likes trains will be in awe…especially at the size of the engines. Many dads seem to take to this place, too.

DAY OUT WITH THOMAS

Green Bay - *National Railroad Museum. Ride along with Thomas the Tank Engine. Have your picture taken with Sir Topham Hatt. Stop by the Imagination Station for temporary tattoos! There will be arts & crafts and story telling, too! Advance tickets. (5 days in early to mid-June)*

WW II REENACTMENT

Green Bay - *National Railroad Museum. Experience the Eisenhower command train and the Museum's World War II era locomotives through the eyes of those who fought the war. This WWII reenactment allows visitors to explore Axis and Allied camps, observe a daily battle, and receive exclusive tours of the Eisenhower train. Reenactment included in Museum admission. (second weekend in July)*

THE GREAT PUMPKIN TRAIN

Green Bay - *National Railroad Museum. Hey kids! Ride the train to the pumpkin patch and select your pumpkin! Enjoy family entertainment and children's activities. General admission. (third weekend in October)*

POLAR EXPRESS

Green Bay - *National Railroad Museum. The classic Christmas tale comes alive in a dramatic reading and a simulated train ride to the North Pole! Gather the entire family for this holiday adventure. Don't forget to wear your pajamas & winter jackets. Advance reservations are highly recommended. (last long weekend in November and first long weekend in December)*

NEW ZOO

4378 Reforestation Road (Hwy 41/141 exit 176 west. 10 miles from downtown) **Green Bay** 54313

- ☐ Phone: (920) 434-7841 **www.newzoo.org**
- ☐ Hours: Daily 9am-6pm. Reduced winter hours and pricing.
- ☐ Admission: $11.00 adult (16+), $8.00 senior (62+) & child (3-15). Adventure Park (zipline, climbing wall, ropes course) extra $10.95-$23.95.
- ☐ Note: Carousel & Train Rides. Mining sluice. Restaurant. Seasonal holiday events like Easter EggStravaganZoo. FREEBIES: Zoo Scavenger Hunt is downloadable from the Visit page.

The NEW Zoo (Northeast Wisconsin Zoo) is a great zoo because it is just the right size. It isn't too big but still has plenty of animals to see. Favorite areas where the interaction with the animals is more noticeable are the wolves (play and run alongside the fence like dogs) and the new giraffes where you can watch them and then feed them (specified times, $1.00 for 2 giraffe crackers). The Australia section has really cute wallabies hopping around. Other cute animals to watch for a while are the Prairie Dogs and the river otters - very active bunch.

The Children's Zoo petting area has you typical goats and sheep but also reindeer. Kids who like to touch things will notice the various Discovery Carts along the paths. Feed giraffes. It's fun to see the goats navigate the swinging bridge above. It is smaller then the Milwaukee zoo, but it has a lot of personality.

GREEN BAY PACKERS TRAINING CAMPS

Green Bay - *Clarke Hinkle Field. Green Bay's legendary Packers strap on the pads and hit the pre-season practice fields for the opening of training camp. Packer fans from across the country line the fences of Ray Nitschke Field, located just east of Lambeau Field, for the opportunity to get an upclose and personal vantage point of some of their favorite players as they sweat through practices full of drills, conditioning and scrimmages. In addition, fans can take a tour of historic Lambeau Field and the Green Bay Packers Hall of Fame.* **https://www.packers.com/training-camp/** *(mid-July thru August)*

WADE HOUSE HISTORIC HOUSE

W7824 Center Street (7 miles west of Plymouth, just off WI-23)
Greenbush 53026

- ☐ Phone: (920) 526-3271 **http://wadehouse.wisconsinhistory.org/**
- ☐ Hours: Wednesday-Sunday,(late-May - early November). Saturday only (winters).
- ☐ Admission: $15.00 adults, $13.00 senior (65+) $8.00 child (5-12). Prices slightly higher for special events. Reduced winter admission.
- ☐ Note: Gift shop and lunch served at the Greenbush Cupboard Café. Fall and Christmas events.

Authentically costumed guides lead tours of the 27-room Stagecoach Inn, forge iron at the Dockstader Blacksmith Shop and demonstrate the sawyer's craft at the Herrling Sawmill – the nation's only working reproduction of a muley-type up-and-down sawmill. Visitors enjoy a relaxing horse-drawn carriage ride to the WESLEY JUNG CARRIAGE MUSEUM, featuring the state's largest collection of horse-drawn wagons and carriages (ride included with admission). Inside the Carriage Museum, an interactive scavenger hunt tour engages children with more than 120 horse- and hand-drawn vehicles from 1870 to 1915, all restored to their former glory. At times they have stations where kids can practice candle dipping.

1000 ISLAND ENVIRONMENTAL CENTER

1000 Beaulieu Court (Hwy 41 to Hwy 55 south through town to Dodge St, east to Beaulieu Ct) **Kaukauna 54130**

- ☐ Phone: (920) 766-4733 **www.1000islandsenvironmentalcenter.org**
- ☐ Hours: Tuesday-Friday 8:00am-4:00pm, Saturday 10:00am-3:30pm.

- Admission: FREE
- Note: Cross county skiing, snowshoeing, canoeing, fishing available.

The 1000 Island Environmental Center is a 300-acre preserve whose miles of boardwalk trails provide access for all. The facility harbors a herd of Whitetail deer, with a large indoor display of North American, Asian and African mounted animals. You might also hear the song birds or ducks coo and catch the wink of an owl or the flight of an eagle. Seasonally, they have Nature Studies and maintain a butterfly garden. Boardwalk trails are great for those families who don't quite "rough" hike yet.

WISCONSIN INTERNATIONAL RACEWAY

W1460 County Road KK **Kaukauna** 54130

- Phone: (920) 766-5577 **www.wirmotorsports.com**
- Hours: Schedule - See web site for racing dates and times. (April-October).
- Admission: Spectator viewing $12.00.

Speedsters of all ages will thrill to stock car and drag racing at one of the Midwest's premier racing sites. In addition to stock car and drag racing WIR also features figure 8's and the infamous Eve of Destruction.

AGRICULTURAL HERITAGE FARM

N2251 State Road 42 (5 miles south of Kewaunee on Hwy 42)
Kewaunee 54216

- Phone: (920) 388-0604 **https://www.facebook.com/ heritagefarmkewaunee/**

Events like Heritage Days, Spring Shearing Days, Barn Dances, Oktoberfest, "Country Crossroad" Motor Coach and "Land to Learning" school tours all create awareness and pride in the unique rural heritage in northeastern Wisconsin. The Wayside School is the newest edition to the farm village. See Facebook page for calendar of events (spring thru fall)

CHRISTMAS ON THE FARM

Kewaunee - Agricultural Heritage Farm. Santa visits. Free activities, treats and activity books available all day. Winter wonderland of Trees. Kringles and Hoska plus homemade candies for sale. (weekend before Thanksgiving)

C.D. BESADNY ANADROMOUS FISH FACILITY

3884 Ransom Moore Lane (off of County Highway F, west of Kewaunee, on the west bank of the Kewaunee River) **Kewaunee** 54216

- ☐ Phone: (920) 388-1025 **http://dnr.wi.gov/topic/fishing/hatcheries/ cdbesadny.html**
- ☐ Hours: Site is open daily, dawn to dusk. Building - Monday-Friday 8:00am-4:00pm (March-December). Closed winters.

Kewaunee, Wisconsin is the place to be each September and October to watch the salmon run. Steelhead and salmon egg-gathering station with fish ladder and observation window. The Besadny fishery has a partially underwater tank with Plexiglas where you can see the salmon "Up Close and Personal" both under water and during their last jump. Fish going against the stream is a wondrous thing. Spring and summer view steelhead. In addition, visitors can hike nature trails (River Trail & Ice Age Trail), stroll by large prairie gardens, and view wildlife.

TUG LUDINGTON

Harbor Park, Downtown **Kewaunee** 54216

- ☐ Phone: (920) 388-5000 **https://cityofkewauneewi.gov/tug-ludington/**
- ☐ Tours: Daily 10:00am-4:00pm (May-mid October). Self guided.
- ☐ Admission: $3.00-$5.00 per person.

Tug Ludington was fourth in a series of eight seagoing tugboats constructed specifically for World War II in 1943. Tugs were often strafed by enemy planes and submarines, but were considered too small a target to waste a torpedo on. Still, a tug's armament consisted of 2 mighty mounted machine guns. This tug participated in the D-Day invasion of Normandy, towing ammunition barges across the English Channel. Since its arrival in Kewaunee, Tug Ludington assisted in the construction and maintenance of many harbors on the Great Lakes.

HENNINGS CHEESE STORE & MUSEUM

20201 Point Creek Road (3 miles north of town on Hwy 67 to Cty X, east 3.5 miles) **Kiel** 53042

- ☐ Phone: (920) 894-3032 **www.henningscheese.com**
- ☐ Hours: Monday-Friday 7:00am to 3:00 or 4:00pm, Saturday 8:00am-Noon.

This factory specializes in Cheddar, Colby, fresh curds, Monterey jack, string cheese and mozza whips, reduced-fat and salt farmers cheese and flavors. Fresh warm cheese curds are made weekdays (and they sell breaded cheese curds for deep frying). A dream of Everett Henning's, the son of founder Otto Henning, had always been to build a cheese museum showcasing the cheese equipment used during the early 1900's. The museum features an old cheese vat, press, separator, and old butter making equipment. Other items include cheese forms and cheese making equipment (wooden rake and shovel). While visiting the store and museum, you can watch cheese being made through two large viewing windows that overlook the factory, watch a video on how to make cheese, and enjoy lots of samples of cheese and ice cream.

LITTLE CHUTE WINDMILL

130 West Main Street (Island Park on the Fox River) **Little Chute** 54140

- ☐ Phone: (920) 788-2629 **www.littlechutewindmill.org**
- ☐ Hours: Tuesday-Friday 10:00am-4:30pm, Saturday Noon-4:30pm (April-Oct).
- ☐ Admission: $6.00 adult, $4.00 child (5-17).

The Little Chute Windmill is an authentic 1850s design from the province of North Brabant in the Netherlands. Visitors have the opportunity to tour the different levels of the Windmill and see it in action as it harnesses wind power to grind grain into flour. The windmill is 100 feet tall.

The Van Asten Visitor Center features exhibits on the history and legacy of Dutch settlement in the Fox River Valley and northeast Wisconsin. Watch a video on the building of the windmill and history of Little Chute. The gift shop here sells bags of flour ground in the windmill.

GREAT WISCONSIN CHEESE FESTIVAL

*Little Chute - Doyle Park. Cheese lovers will have a "dairy" good time at this festival. The festival started in 1989, as a response to Rome, N.Y.'s claim of having the best cheese in the nation. Little Chute invited the mayor of Rome to the Cheese Festival for a cheese-tasting competition to settle the dispute. Today, the festival trumpets this victory with three days of "cheesy" fun, including a cheese breakfast, parade, cheese-carving demonstrations, a cheesecake contest and, of course, plenty of cheese tasting. Cheese carving and tasting, parade, children's games. See an authentic Dutch windmill open to visitors. Admission. **https://www.littlechutewi.org/226/Great-Wisconsin-Cheese-Festival** (first full weekend in June)*

BEERNTSEN'S CONFECTIONARY

Manitowoc - *108 North 8th Street 54220. Phone: (920) 684-9616* **http://beerntsens. com/**. *Hours: Daily 10:00am-9:00pm. Located in an old stagecoach inn, this candy store has been a town landmark since 1932. They still use the same family methods - copper kettles and wooden paddles to make their hard candies and they still dip chocolates by hand. You may catch a glimpse of the ladies "dipping". No matter, the smell of warm chocolate and the showcases of decorative varieties for sale will have you putting together your own treat bag for a walk around town or a cruise on the Badger. Oh, and they have ice-cream, too.* 🍽️ _____

CEDAR CREST ICE CREAM PARLOR

Manitowoc - *2000 S. 10th Street 54220.* **www.cedarcresticecream.com**. *Phone: (920) 682-5577 Hours: Open daily at 11:30am. Closed December through March. Featuring 32 flavors of Cedar Crest hand dipped ice cream, sherbet and frozen yogurt. The ice cream parlour is their ice cream manufacturing plant, cleverly hidden behind the "The Big Cow." In a crazy mood? Try a scoop of Blue Moon or Unicorn. Did you know? The average number of licks to finish a single-scoop cone is 50. It's not hard to find this place. Just look for the biggest cow in Wisconsin! She's only 35 feet tall and weighs 4 tons!* 🍽️ _____

LINCOLN PARK ZOO

1215 North 8th Street **Manitowoc** 54220

- ☐ Phone: (920) 683-4685 **www.manitowoc.org/parkandrec/Zoo/zoo.htm**
- ☐ Hours: Daily 9am-7pm (Memorial DAy-Labor Day), Monday-Saturday 9:00am-5:00pm, Sunday, 1:00pm-5:00pm (Labor Day-October & April to Memorial Day). Monday-Saturday 7:00am-3:00pm (rest of year).
- ☐ Admission: FREE, donations of $1.00-$2.00 suggested.

Featuring animals and birds native to the North woods...everything from a timber wolf to a bald eagle. Located in beautiful wooded park setting with private and public picnic areas. Children's playground.

PINE RIVER DAIRY

10115 English Lake Road (off SR 42, west of town) **Manitowoc** 54220

- ☐ Phone: (920) 758-2233 **www.pineriverdairy.com**
- ☐ Hours: Monday-Friday 8:00am-5:00pm, Saturday 8:00am-1:00pm.
- ☐ Note: Want some bread to go with that butter? Swing on over to NATURAL

OVENS BAKERY OF MANITOWOC on 4300 County Road CR. Open daily except Sundays: **www.naturalovens.com**.

Over 250 varieties of cheese available in the retail store. Enjoy a 25 cent hand dipped ice cream cone while browsing through many gifts and souvenirs. Today, the Olm family, now in it's sixth generation of dairy food producers, continues to operate the business manufacturing and selling butter and butter blends at the wholesale level. Come view the butter manufacturing process through their observation window. Pine River Dairy utilizes the fresh cream from Eastern Wisconsin cheese factories to manufacture high quality butter products. It's cool to see butter made vs. cheese, for a change. Do you know how much a "slab" of factory butter weighs? Ask them.

PINECREST HISTORICAL VILLAGE

924 Pine Crest Lane (3 miles west of I-43 exit 152) **Manitowoc** 54220

- Phone: (920) 684-5110 **www.manitowoccountyhistory.org/**
- Hours: $14.00 adult, $13.00 senior (65+), $10.00 child (4-17).
- Admission: Wednesday-Sunday 10:00am-4:00pm (June - September). Friday-Saturday only (May). Thursday-Friday only 10am-2pm (winter).
- Tours: Using the new digital tour players, you can experience "Voices from the Past" audio tour on your next visit to Pinecrest Village. A different historical character will bring each building to life.

In the scenic Ice Age Kettle Moraine countryside, Pinecrest Historical Village, a 60 acre open air museum, features more than 25 historical buildings complete with furnishings from Manitowoc County. Authentic Norwegian and German log houses show how immigrant settlers lived at the turn of the century. The self-guided tour around the outdoor museum explores how they lived during the 1850-early 1900s. Buildings such as Blacksmith, General Store (Gift Shop), Church, dance hall, railroad passenger car, the Cheese shop (sample cheese curds and watch them making butter), seamstress shop (crafts), schoolhouse, and also furnished homesteads. There's also a new carpentry shop. Even more interaction is had on their weekend programs and festivals when costumed interpreters abound.

A self-guided Nature Trail winds past native trees and shrubs. Interpretive signs provide information on the area's glacial origins, vegetation and early settlement. Special programs and festivals are held throughout the year.

GERMAN FEST

Manitowoc - *Pinecrest Historical Village. Celebrate Manitowoc County's German Heritage with authentic music, German food and beer, craft demonstrations, family activities and an evening dance. Admission. (second Saturday in July)*

VILLAGE FAIR

Manitowoc - *Pinecrest Village. Re-live an 1870s county fair with livestock judging, music, displays, games, contests, and more! (second weekend in August)*

FALL HARVEST FESTIVAL

Manitowoc - *Pinecrest Historical Village. Take a break from the fall harvest and enjoy a day of discovery and an evening barn dance. Enjoy food, family activities, historic craft demonstrations, and live music. Admission. (first Saturday in September)*

A HOLIDAY IN HISTORY

Manitowoc - *Pinecrest Historical Village. Celebrate holiday traditions of the past with sleigh rides, live holiday music, beautiful decorations, and family activities in the stove heated buildings. Admission. (second weekend in December)*

S.S. BADGER LAKE MICHIGAN CARFERRY

Lake Michigan docks, 900 S. Lakeview Drive **Manitowoc** 54220

- ☐ Phone: (231) 843-1509 or (800) 841-4243 **www.ssbadger.com**
- ☐ Admission: One way ~$59.00 adult or RT ~$111.00. Child one way $24.00, round trip $39.00 (ages 5-15).Vehicle fares extra ~$80.00.
- ☐ Tours: 4 hour cruises depart Manitowoc at 1:55pm (CT) daily during season (Mday thru early October). Arrive Manitowoc Noon the next day. Extra crossing in summer. Closed Winter season.
- ☐ Round Trip Mini-Cruises: Travel round trip without a vehicle returning within 48 hours and pay just $70 per person (age 5+). Children under 5 are free. This offer cannot be combined with any other discount or promotion. (Must call to receive this discount.)

Ready for a giant cruise on a giant lake? You have to experience the S.S. Badger. With the excitement and romance of a sea voyage, plus uninterrupted time with family and friends…the journey is as much fun as the destination. The Badger has expanded their focus on family amenities designed to appeal to passengers, children and even pets. Parents have more time to enjoy the cruise while their children have entertaining things to do. The children's program includes a KidsPort playroom, face-painting, a free activity book (coloring prizes), and trivia for prizes. Adults head for the spacious deck areas ("steel beach") for walking or relaxing in the fresh air (also a great place to avoid motion sickness, if you're prone - they also offer Sea Bands), two food service areas (serving really good food, beverage and snacks), private staterooms (extra fee), and satellite TV or quiet rooms (place for reading or comfortable cat napping). The Main Lounge and Midship is where kids gravitate. They watch movies in the theatre; browse in the ship's store; but mostly participate in the games - like their famous Badger Bingo. By the end of the trip, most every player wins. Kids can also navigate and track the steamship's progress over open water. What an adventure on the sea!

WISCONSIN MARITIME MUSEUM

75 Maritime Drive **Manitowoc** 54220

- Phone: (920) 684-0218 or (866) 724-2356 **www.wisconsinmaritime.org**
- Hours: Daily 9:00am-5:00pm (June =August), Daily, except closed Tuesday & Wednesday, 10am-4pm (Sept-May).
- Admission: $20.00 adult, $17.00 senior (65+) & veterans, $13.00 child (4-12).
- Tours: Allow 3-4 hours to fully explore the Museum and tour USS COBIA. Tours of the submarine are offered daily but vary with season and are subject to change. Daily 9:30am-4:30pm (summer). See website for other schedules.

Enjoy a museum where kids and adults can tour a fully restored World War II submarine, operate a real steam engine, scan the harbor through a periscope; time-travel back to a 19th century shipbuilding town and sail their own boat in the Children's Waterways room; land a record setting salmon at the Sportfishing Simulator; and think like a scientist in their Aquatic Species Investigation Lab -- all at the region's only Smithsonian affiliate and the largest maritime museum on the Great Lakes. Outdoors, the Cobia is the most functional WWII sub in existence; 85% of her machinery and controls still work. The Cobia was manufactured nearby at the Manitowoc Shipping Company, which was one of three shipyards awarded contracts to build subs for the U.S. war effort. The Cobia ran six successful war patrols from 1944-45, sinking twelve enemy vessels and rescuing seven downed Allied pilots. This sub is a hero ship. You can tour the galley and crew's mess hall, sleeping quarters, officers quarters, and torpedo room. Everything is cramped but it's effective. If you like, stay overnight during one of their Family Overnights.

HECKRODT WETLAND RESERVE

1305 Plank Road (Highway 114) **Menasha** 54952

- ☐ Phone: (920) 720-9349 **https://heckrodtnaturecenter.org/**
- ☐ Hours: Nature Center - Tuesday-Friday 8:00am-4:30pm, Saturday 11:00am-4:00pm. Trails open everyday 6:00am-9:00pm.

76 acres of forested wetland, wetland meadow, open water and upland field communities on the northern shore of Lake Winnebaro. Wheelchair and stroller friendly 3+ mile trail system accesses the wetland. 5,000 sq ft Nature Center includes live and mounted animals, indoor play area, and bird watching solarium.

WEIS EARTH SCIENCE MUSEUM & BARLOW PLANETARIUM

1478 Midway Road (UW - Fox Valley campus) **Menasha** 54952

- ☐ Phone: (920) 832-2925
  https://uwosh.edu/weis/ or www.barlowplanetarium.org
- ☐ Hours: Wednesday-Friday Noon-4:30pm, Saturday 10:00am-4:30pm.
- ☐ Admission: $3.00 adult, $2.00 senior (65+) & junior (13-17), $1.00 child (3-12).

WEIS EARTH SCIENCE MUSEUM

Wisconsin is a scenic wonder — the Kettle Moraine, the Baraboo Hills, the Wisconsin Dells, the Driftless Area, Door County, the Apostle Islands. But Wisconsin didn't always look this way. At various times in the distant past Wisconsin was home to mountains as high as the Himalayas, volcanoes like those in the Pacific Northwest, tropical reefs resembling those in the Caribbean, and glaciers rivaling those of Antarctica.

The official state museum of geology features interactive learning tools and self-guided tours offering information about fossils, geology, paleontology and agriculture as well as the state's mineral and mining heritage. Interactive and hands-on exhibits, video displays, colorful graphics, and specimens of real fossils, minerals and rocks await you at the Weis Earth Science Museum. Kids like to make an earthquake, blast a quarry, touch a dino bone, walk through a mine tunnel, and make it rain. In fact, you'll learn that every rock tells a story, and you can read them yourself.

BARLOW PLANETARIUM

One of only 29 in the world with similar capabilities, the world-class 98-seat facility boasts state-of-the-art technology and equipment. The planetarium features awesome and exciting shows about stars, galaxies and planets in a three-dimensional setting. The Curler Science Gallery, designed to inform visitors about the latest space happenings, is located in the planetarium's lobby.

KNIGGE FARMS

4577 Poygan Avenue (20 miles west of Oshkosh off Highway 21)
Omro 54963

☐ Phone: (920) 685-5531
   www.facebook.com/pages/Omro-WI/Knigge-Farms/58810262752
☐ Hours: Daily 8:00 am-7:00pm.
☐ Admission: $2.00-$5.00 per person (age 4+)
☐ Tours: Daily, but call to make an appointment.

Half hour guided tour of a working family dairy farm using robotic milking technology. You will tour a free stall dairy barn where cows milk themselves 24 hours a day. Visit calves and feed them if your visit is during their feeding time. Cats, chickens and Jack the farm dog are other animals for you to see.

MENOMINEE PARK AND ZOO

5205 Siewert Trail (Hazel Street And Merritt Avenue) **Oshkosh** 54901

☐ Phone: (920) 236-5082 **https://www.ci.oshkosh.wi.us/Parks/
   MenomineeParkZoo/**
☐ Hours: Zoo - 9:00am-6:00pm. (May-September).
☐ Admission: Nominal admission.

This 110-acre park, located on the shores of scenic Lake Winnebago, invites folks to play baseball, tennis and soccer or to skate, bike or hike on the two-mile recreation trail. A swimming beach, boat launch, and several picnic shelters are available, and a miniature train, paddle boats, bumper boats, wooden castle playground, and merry-go-round delight little ones. From May through September, Menominee Park also boasts a seasonal zoo. Animals are leased from facilities in other parts of the country for a summer up north and returned when colder weather starts. The lease program allows the zoo to present a changing variety of animals – 30 to 50 each season.

OSHKOSH PUBLIC MUSEUM

1331 Algoma Boulevard Oshkosh 54901

- ☐ Phone: (920) 236-5761 or (920) 236-5799 **www.oshkoshmuseum.org**
- ☐ Hours: Tuesday-Saturday 10:00am-4:30pm, Sunday 1:00pm-4:30pm.
- ☐ Admission: $8.00 adult, $6.00 senior (62+) and students, $4.00 child (4-17).
- ☐ Educators: Discovery Boxes are loaned for home or classroom use.

Step back onto the streets of old Oshkosh and explore the development of this historic city on the water. The museum exhibits include the fun interactive 'Grandma's Attic' and new pioneer log cabin. Step inside the interactive People of the Waters and explore Wisconsin's prehistoric past and Native American culture that spans at least 13,000 years. Tour the grand 1908 Edgar Sawyer home-the famous Tiffany Studios of New York designed the interiors of this magnificent home. Visitors love the eight-foot-tall 1895 Apostles Clock, considered one of Wisconsin's top ten attractions. For being a smaller town, these museum exhibits have quality dioramas, display cases and lighting.

EAA AIR ADVENTURE MUSEUM

3000 Poberezny Rd (right next to Highways 41 and 44, adjacent to Wittman Regional Airport) Oshkosh 54902

- ☐ Phone: (920) 426-4818 **www.airventuremuseum.org**
- ☐ Hours: Daily 10:00am-5:00pm. Pioneer Airport is open on Fridays, Saturdays, and Sundays from the first weekend in May until the second weekend in October.
- ☐ Admission: $15.00 adult, $13.00 senior (62+), $12.00 student (6-18), $37.00 family. Allows admission to all of the museum's exhibits, theaters and Pioneer Airport. Simulators and airplane rides cost extra.
- ☐ Note: MaxFlight Simulator gives the pilot sitting inside the cockpit the opportunity to soar thru combat flight in a vintage fighter jet. $6.00 extra.

Celebrate the history of aviation from early barnstormers to modern jet fighters. The Experimental Aircraft Association museum was founded in 1962 after the donation of an "air racer" was made. Through the years, the collection has grown to include more than 250 historic aircraft and 20,000 other aeronautical artifacts. Five different theaters show films about aviation including the new HD Skyscape Theater.

The world's largest collection of aerobatic, air racing and homebuilt aircraft, and record breaking airplanes - including the smallest that has ever flown!

Bring the family for "hands on" fun in KidVenture Gallery, a children's museum of aviation with over 25 interactive exhibits and flight simulators will keep all kids entertained. If you time your visit right, you may get to watch an authentic war plane take off outside. Interested? Take a ride in a vintage airplane at Pioneer Airport—a real working aerodrome right out of the "golden age" of aviation.

EAA AIRVENTURE

Oshkosh - EAA Air Adventure Museum. The Wittman Regional Airport in Oshkosh offers a unique service – valet parking for airplanes – during the annual EAA AirVenture show each summer. It's the world's largest and most significant annual aviation event drawing more than 10,000 planes of every size, shape and description of aircraft from home-built and antique to military and space shuttles to Wisconsin. On the ground, aviation enthusiasts savor the opportunity to inspect planes close-up and watch daily flying exhibitions by expert pilots. Admission. (last week in July)

CHRISTMAS IN THE AIR

Oshkosh - EAA Air Adventure Museum. Musical, Madrigal and choral groups from the Oshkosh area will be performing throughout the day. Cookies and refreshments will be available. See Santa arrive by helicopter to meet all of his fans. (early weekday in December)

LARSON'S FAMOUS CLYDESDALES
W12654 Reeds Corner Rd (17 miles west of FDL, Hwy 23W to KK)
Ripon 54971

- Phone: (920) 748-5466 **https://www.facebook.com/people/larsons-clydesdales/100081351425097/**
- Tours: Monday-Saturday at 10:00am only (mid-May thru mid-October). Reservation only. $25.00 per person.

One of the only places in the United States where one can see many Famous Clydesdales, close-up and personal. Begin with a fun 90 minute guided Tour with a short grandstand Show. Included in the show is the newest mascot, Mac Gregor, a great Scottie dog. Don't forget to visit the Clydesdale museum, Clydesdale gift-shop, and to pet and take pictures of the Rare Baby Clydesdale.

LITTLE WHITE SCHOOLHOUSE

1074 W Fond Du Lac Street **Ripon** 54971

- ☐ Phone: (920) 748-6764 **https://lwsh.org/**
- ☐ Hours: Daily 10:00am-4:00pm. (June-Labor Day). Weekends in May, September and October.
- ☐ Admission: Free

In this schoolhouse, on March 20, 1854, the first mass meeting in the country was held that definitely and positively cut loose from old parties and advocated a new party. Ripon citizens voted to form and become members of a new political party called "Republican." The birth of the Republican Party brought a dedicated following of individuals who pledged to organize together and fight against the spread of slavery. The Little White Schoolhouse tells an intriguing story of how the Republican Party came to be.

HAMBURGER FESTIVAL

Seymour - Main Street, Lake Park & the Seymour High School. Hungry hamburger fans will want to visit Seymour, the "Home of the Hamburger" as it pays tribute to hamburger inventor Charles Nagreen. According to local legend, meatball salesman Nagreen served the first burger in 1885 at the Outagamie County Fair. Basically, the first burger was a squished meatball on a bun. The accomplishment is honored by a 14-foot statue of "Hamburger Charlie." Kids of all ages will enjoy numerous games, music all day, hot air balloons ascending over the city, the ketchup slide, burger press and hamburger-eating contest, as well as the, "World's largest hamburger parade." Not only do they have a giant frying pan, but the chef at this event swings by harness, suspended by overhead crane, across hundreds of sizzling patties. He sweeps over the pan, sprinkling salt and pepper. This routine is part of the entertainment at the festival. Admission. www.homeofthehamburger.org (first or second Saturday in August)

ABOVE & BEYOND CHILDREN'S MUSEUM

902 N. 8th Street **Sheboygan** 53081

- ☐ Phone: (920) 458-4263 **www.abkids.org**
- ☐ Hours: Tuesday-Saturday 9:00am-4:00pm.
- ☐ Admission: $6.00 per person. Children under the age of two are free.

Twelve hands-on interactive exhibits for children are available at this museum with highlights including the marketplace, a shipyard and schoolhouse. Rachel's Favorite exhibit shows what you can accomplish with everyday household items if you put your mind to it, and even illustrates some simple machine concepts to boot.

Of all, the Skycrawl may be the kids favorite way to burn energy. If there is a longer skycrawl in the United States, we haven't found it (at least not a blue one anyway). This (like all the museum activities) is 'grown up safe' so parents can enjoy it too! Best for children from 2 to 12 years of age.

BLUE HARBOR RESORT & INDOOR WATERPARK

725 Blue Harbor Drive (I-43 exit 123, Hwy 28 east. Lake Michigan shoreline)
Sheboygan 53081

- Phone: (920) 452-2900 **www.blueharborresort.com**
- Hours: Waterpark generally open 12 hours on weekends. Limited hours on Monday and Thursday. Closed (except for holidays and school breaks) on Tuesday and Wednesdays. Occassional Sunday day passes are $40.

The creators of Great Wolf Lodges have begun a new themed indoor adventure resort in a nautical atmosphere. In addition to luxurious accommodations and in-room amenities, Blue Harbor Resort offers over 43,000 spectacular square feet of indoor waterpark. Not full of thrill slides but catered more to young families or families who want to base from here but spend time exploring the area, too. Not a guest at the resort? Not a problem. They offer day passes to the general public, too. The resort option experience offers 182 family-sized suites and 64 villas; a 54,000 square-foot indoor entertainment area; Elements Spa featuring Aveda products; Kids Spa; Arcade; fitness center; Crew Club craft and activity room; two casual themed restaurants - On The Rocks Bar & Grille and Rocky Bottom; homemade fudge and delicious treats from Sweetshop Landing confectionery; 29,000 square-foot conference center and fine dining facility including The Beacon (for the parents). Overnight packages start at $200. For a little more, try the nautical themed KIdAquarium Bunk Suite. This room also includes patio or balcony, microwave, mini-refrigerator, coffee maker, hair dryer, iron and ironing board, complimentary high-speed wireless Internet, in-room safe and access to pay-per-view movies and pay Nintendo Game Cube.

KOHLER-ANDRAE STATE PARK

1020 Beach Park Lane **Sheboygan** 53081

- ☐ Phone: (920) 451-4080 http://dnr.wi.gov/topic/parks/name/kohlerandrae/
- ☐ Admission: A vehicle admission sticker is required. Daily $8.00-$11.00. Annual passes available.

924-acre park on the shore of Lake Michigan with wooded campsites and 2.5 miles of sandy beach. Open daily 6:00am-11:00pm with overnight camping. KOHLER DUNES CORDWALK - The Dunes Cordwalk is just north and south of the nature center in the state natural area. Hikers walk on a 2 1/2 mile "cordwalk" (boards and rope) through the dunes with three lookout points and benches overlooking Lake Michigan and a rare interdunal marsh area.

HIGH CLIFF STATE PARK

N7630 State Park Road **Sherwood** 54169

- ☐ Phone: (920) 989-1106   http://dnr.wi.gov/topic/parks/name/highcliff/
- ☐ Hours: Daily 6:00am-11:00pm.
- ☐ Admission: A vehicle admission sticker is required. Daily $8.00-$11.00. Annual passes available.

High Cliff, overlooking the largest inland lake in Wisconsin, is situated on limestone cliffs once sacred to Native Americans. History and geology buffs will enjoy the park's effigy mounds, lime kiln and quarry. Camp atop the park's 200-foot bluffs offers terrific lakeside views. Swimming, boating, hiking & nature trails. Boating and fishing on Lake Winnebago are popular activities with access to the big lake easy via four harbors and eight public boat landings between the park and town. You'll also find concessions, nature center, seasonal naturalist programs, lookout tower, vistas, shoreline with marked beach area, canoeing, boating, fishing, 2.3 miles of nature trails, 5.2 miles of hiking trails, 8.2 miles of horseback trails, 9.7 miles of off- road bicycle trails, 5 miles of snowmobile trails, 4.2 miles of cross- country ski trails. Open 6:00am-11:00pm with overnight camping.

WINTERFEST

Sherwood - High Cliff State Park. Dog-sled racing, fur trader rendezvous and snowshoe demos. Saturday evening candlelight ski/hike. (late January)

AL JOHNSON'S SWEDISH RESTAURANT

Sister Bay - 10698 N. Bay Shore 54234. www.aljohnsons.com. Phone: (920) 854-2626 Hours: Daily 6:00am-9:00pm (summer), Monday-Saturday 6:00am-8:00pm (winter). Sunday 7:00am-8:00pm. Follow your morning or afternoon hikes immediately with a hearty meal at Al Johnson's Swedish Restaurant. It's not just about the fabulous and authentic Swedish food (order the Swedish pancakes with Lingonberries or Swedish Meatballs). It's about the Scandinavian uniformed wait staff, the gift shop and, most notably, the goats grazing on the grass sod roof! They have a big Kids Menu with prices ranging $7.00-1$1.00. To keep it authentic, try the Swedish Meatballs, applesauce and mashed potatoes Lunch - for $11.00.

CORNER OF THE PAST / OLD ANDERSON HOUSE MUSEUM

10310 Fieldcrest Rd (located at the intersection of State Highway 57 and Fieldcrest Road) **Sister Bay** 54234

- Phone: (920) 854-7680 **www.sisterbayhistory.org**
- Hours: Weekends 10am-3pm (June-September). Farm Market, Heritage programs and demonstrations every Saturday, 8:00am-Noon (late-June to mid-October). See website for a complete events schedule.
- Tours: Wednesday-Saturday 11:00am-2:00pm at half hour intervals. $10 per person for guided tour of buildings.

Tour an 1875 farmhouse, restored farm buildings, log cabins, sawmill and more featuring turn-of-the-century furnishings, farm implements, tools and historic photos. Local artisans volunteer to demonstrate their skills in weaving, rug hooking, painting, carving, blacksmithing, chair caning, bead working, spinning, egg painting, and Norwegian embroidery as part of the summer Saturday Heritage Programs. These programs take place in conjunction with the popular Saturday morning Farmer's Market open from 8 to 12 noon late June through early October. The market includes numerous vendors who bring their locally-grown produce, flowers, and honey. Best time to visit is during festivals, programs and the seasonal Saturday Farmers Market.

DOOR COUNTY MARITIME MUSEUM
120 North Madison Avenue Sturgeon Bay 54235

- ☐ Phone: (920) 743-5958 **www.dcmm.org**
- ☐ Hours: Daily 10:00am-4:00pm (winter), 9:00am-5:00pm (May-October), 10:00am-5:00pm (Nov-Dec).
- ☐ Admission: $15.00 adult, $12.00 senior (65+) & military, $7.00 youth (5-17).
- ☐ Tours: Tug John Purves - Tours on the half hour, 10:30am-3:30pm. 30 minutes. Availability of tour is weather permitting. $5.00/person.

Local maritime history, including boats from the early 1900s, shipbuilding, commercial fishing, lighthouses, even a fishing tug. The museum had a number of hands on/interactive exhibits including the pulleys, two touch-screen interactive elements, a fresnel lens experiment, and a real periscope from a submarine. Ever been caught in a bad storm? They have a room devoted to storms while at sea. There aren't many more tug boats you can tour so be sure to allow time to tour this one.

POTAWATOMI STATE PARK
3740 County PD (2 miles N of SR 57, 2 miles NW of Sturgeon Bay)
Sturgeon Bay 54235

- ☐ Phone: (920) 746-2890 **http://dnr.wi.gov/topic/parks/name/potawatomi/**
- ☐ Admission: A vehicle admission sticker is required. Daily $8.00-$11.00.

On a clear day, the view from the park's observation tower reaches 16 miles across Green Bay. Features cabin for people with disabilities, 123 campsites, 25 electric sites, winter camping, showers, a dumping station, handicap-accessible picnic area and campsites, seasonal naturalist programs, lookout tower, vistas, 2 miles of shoreline, canoeing, boating, fishing, 1/2-mile of nature trails, 6.3 miles of hiking trails, 4 miles of off- road bicycle trails, 8.3 miles of snowmobile trails, 13.2 miles of cross- country ski trails. There is a boat launch on Lake Michigan. Open 6:00am-11:00pm with overnight camping.

THE FARM
4285 Hwy 57 Sturgeon Bay 54235

- ☐ Phone: (920) 743-6666 **www.thefarmindoorcounty.com**
- ☐ Hours: Daily 9:00am-5:00pm (Memorial Day Weekend - Labor Day) 10am-4pm (Sept to mid October)

◻ Admission: $9.50 adult (13+), $6.00 child (4-12).

The Farm is a delight for people of all ages. As a living museum of rural America, it is a blending of cultural, historical, agricultural, ecological, recreational and educational values. Every year, The Farm virtually explodes with newborn and new-hatched creatures. For about 25 cents you can buy a bottle of milk and feed the babies. Goat kids, piglets, foals, calves and lambs are born throughout the season; chicks hatch everyday in the observation incubator. Be sure to check the stork report in the lobby.

You learn about farm life and what tools were used in the old days. Each animal type has its own fenced yard of barn so the farm is huge. Take your time and go back to favorites. And, here's something you don't see every day - fainting goats. Yes, they have goats that faint. They are a breed known as fainting, nervous or stiff goats. When frightened they will stiffen and fall over. Fainting is normal for this breed and is not an ailment. Just so you know before your child thinks they hurt one…

WHITEFISH DUNES STATE PARK
3275 Clark Lake Road (8 miles E of SR 42, 10 miles NE of Sturgeon Bay)
Sturgeon Bay 54235

◻ Phone: (920) 823-2400   **http://dnr.wi.gov/topic/parks/name/whitefish/**
◻ Admission: A vehicle admission sticker is required. Daily $8.00-$11.00.
Annual passes available.

Set aside to protect the fragile dune environment, Whitefish Dunes has more visitors than any other day use park in Wisconsin. Whitefish Dunes offers rugged Lake Michigan shoreline, sand beach and huge sand dunes. Enjoy strolling along Lake Michigan, watching waterfowl at Clark Lake, using the boardwalk to discover the wetlands or relaxing on one of the many trails throughout the forested sand dunes and beech forest. Trails are open year round and 8 miles are groomed for skiing in winter. In addition, the nature center offers displays on ecology, geology and human history of the park. Programs for all ages are presented year round at the park. Many features for people with disabilities. Features handicap- accessible picnic area, concessions, nature center, seasonal naturalist programs, lookout tower, shoreline, fishing, 1.5 miles of nature trails, 13 miles of hiking trails, 1.5 miles of off-road bicycle trails, 13 miles of cross- country ski trails. Open 6:00am-11:00pm with no overnight camping.

HISTORIC WASHINGTON HOUSE

1622 Jefferson Street **Two Rivers** 54241

- ☐ Phone: (920) 793-2490 **https://www.tworivers-history.org/historic-washington-house/**
- ☐ Hours: Wednesday-Sunday 9:00am-5:00pm.
- ☐ Admission: FREE.

Two Rivers takes pride in being the birthplace of the ice cream sundae – invented here in 1881. For a taste of that frozen treat, stop at the Washington House – part museum and part soda fountain. 18 different sundae flavors are offered at this replica of Ed Berners' Ice Cream Parlor where he invented the Ice Cream Sundae.

How did it happen? One day a customer asked to top a dish of ice cream with chocolate sauce vs. the usual chocolate sauce in ice cream sodas. The concoction cost a nickel and soon became very popular, but was only sold on Sundays. Later, the confection was sold every day in many flavors. Learn why we spell it: Ice Cream Sundae vs Sunday.

LONDONDAIRY ALPACAS & FIBER STUDIO

6827 State Hwy 147 (8 miles east of I-43 exit 154, just north of Manitowoc) **Two Rivers** 54241

- ☐ Phone: (920) 793-4165 **www.londondairyalpacas.com**
- ☐ Tours: Summer scheduled Farm Tours are typically once daily 10:30am $6.00-$8.00/person, guided. Call to be included. No walk-ins.

Tour a century old family farm that now raise exotic, soft alpacas. Get up close and personal with over 80 gentle alpacas. Enjoy the unique gift store adorn with teddy bears, capes, mittens, sweaters and scarves made from the alpaca's warm, non-allergenic, durable fiber. Learn the history of these creatures, sort their fiber, and feed them treats. Touring visitors please call for availability. Advance appointments made for group tours.

POINT BEACH STATE FOREST

9400 County Highway O **Two Rivers** 54241

- ☐ Phone: (920) 794-7480 **http://dnr.wi.gov/topic/parks/name/pointbeach/**
- ☐ Admission: A vehicle admission sticker is required. Daily $8.00-$11.00. Annual passes available.

Located on a point jutting into Lake Michigan, this forest's 6-mile beach is a great place to catch a wave or walk in the sand. Features indoor and outdoor group campsites,

127 campsites, 66 electric sites, winter camping, showers, a dumping station, handicap- accessible picnic area and campsites, concessions, nature center, seasonal naturalist programs, shoreline, fishing, 1 mile of nature trails, 12 miles of hiking trails, 4 miles of off- road bicycle trails, 11 miles of cross-country ski trails. 5 miles of sandy beach, and the 113' Rawley Point Lighthouse. Open 6:00am-11:00pm.

ROGERS STREET FISHING VILLAGE & MUSEUM

2102 Jackson Street, East Twin River **Two Rivers** 54241

- Phone: (920) 793-5905 **www.rogersstreet.com**
- Hours: Weekdays 10am-7pm, Weekends Noon-4pm (Memorial Day- mid October). Closed all Tuesdays.
- Admission: $2.00-$5.00

Five historic buildings chronicle commercial fishing on Lake Michigan. View an 1886 lighthouse, Lifesaving Service and Shipwreck exhibit, plus a new exhibit on commercial fishing in the LeClair Fishing Shed.

The 1886 Lighthouse was the first Lighthouse for the City of Two Rivers. Made almost entirely of wood, it is one of few original wooden structures left on the Great Lakes. Two Rivers' North Pier lighthouse is a type of lighthouse known as a pierhead light. This means that its primary duty was to mark a harbor entrance and serve as a navigation aid to ships entering the harbor. Shipwrecks are always interesting - be sure you learn about the famous Christmas Tree Ship.

This site is more of an open-air museum district. Summertime and festival weekends are good bets when this fishing village buildings are open.

WASHINGTON ISLAND FERRY LINE

(Northport Pier Mainland Dock - 125 Highway 42 and Death's Door, Ellison Bay) **Washington Island** 54246

- Phone: (920) 847-2546 **www.wisferry.com**
- Hours: Daily (year-round) but schedule varies with season. Call or visit website for most current schedule.
- Admission: Roundtrip - $15.00 adult, $8.00 child (6-11). Ferry charges (passengers not included), $28.00 auto $6.00 bicycle.

The Washington Island Ferry Line offers daily year-round service from Northport Pier to Detroit Harbor on Washington Island. Ferry rides in the winter through the ice are definitely more of an adventure.

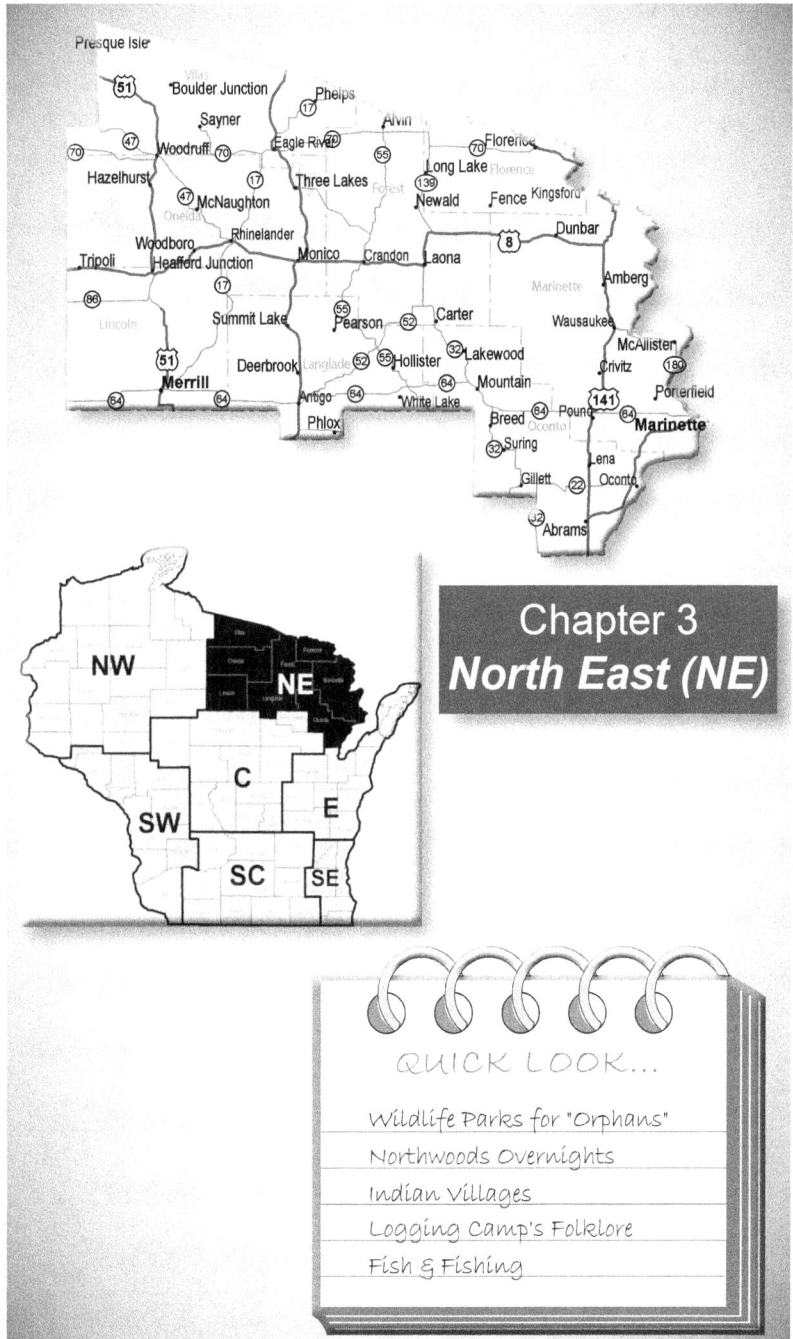

Chapter 3
North East (NE)

QUICK LOOK...

Wildlife Parks for "Orphans"

Northwoods Overnights

Indian Villages

Logging Camp's Folklore

Fish & Fishing

Antigo

- Mepps / Sheldon's Inc Factory Tour

Eagle River

- Cranberry Fest
- Northwoods Children's Museum
- World Championship Snowmobile Derby

Eagle River (St. Germain)

- Snowmobile Hall Of Fame

Hazelhurst

- Hazelhurst Inn Bed & Breakfast

Lac Du Flambeau

- Ojibwe Museum & Cultural Center, George W. Brown
- Waswagoning Recreated Ojibwe Indian Village

Laona

- Lumberjack Steam Train, Camp 5 Museum & Ecology Complex

Merrill

- Council Grounds State Park

Minocqua

- Northwoods Wildlife Center
-

- Wildwood Wildlife Park & Nature Center

New London

- Wolf River Trips & Campground

Oconto

- Copper Culture State Park

Oconto Falls

- Springside Cheese

Rhinelander

- Holiday Acres Resort
- Rhinelander Logging Museum Complex

Rhinelander (Monico)

- Kovac Planetarium

Rock Island

- Rock Island State Park

Woodruff

- Art Oehmcke Hatchery
- Hillestad Pharmaceuticals Vitamin Factory Tour

For updates & travel games visit: **www.KidsLoveTravel.com**

Sites and attractions are listed in order by City, Zip Code, and Name. Symbols indicated represent: 🍽 Restaurants   ⛵ Lodging

MEPPS / SHELDONS' INC FACTORY TOUR
626 Center Street (just off Hwy 45 North) **Antigo** 54409

- Phone: (715) 623-2382 **www.mepps.com/about_us/#plant-tours**
- Admission: FREE
- Tours: Monday-Thursday, 9:15am, 10:15am, 11:15am, 1:30pm, 2:30pm (May-December). Monday-Thursday, 10:15am & 2:00pm (January-April). Tours last about 1/2 hour. Groups of 10 or more please call ahead.

It's like a beading co-op gone wild. The world's largest producer of lures employs locals who sit at a station and produce maybe 1,000 lures in one shift. Watching these ladies work is something to see - especially their ease of looping and winding small objects. Do you know that they use real squirrel tails in some of their lures? See all of the 4000-plus lures Mepps manufacturers. They also have an impressive trophy room you won't want to miss…unless you don't like to fish.

NORTHWOODS CHILDREN'S MUSEUM
346 W Division Street **Eagle River** 54521

- Phone: (715) 479-4623 **www.northwoodschildrensmuseum.com**
- Hours: Monday-Friday 10:00am-5:00pm, Saturday 10:00am-3:00pm.
- Admission: General $9.00 (age 1+)
- FREEBIES: Kid Konnection Crafts are described on their online link - like make potato stamps.

This Northwoods Children's museum has 23 exhibits all in one room. There are unique things to the northwoods area, like fishing and a ranger tower, as well as dressup clothes, and ambulance, and other creative areas. Crawl through a Badger mine and see if you can find gold or gems. Step inside a bubble or run your own cranberry bog. You can watch a tornado swirl without the worry of destruction and test your storm chasing abilities. Craft projects add to many exhibit themes. Seasonally, they have live baby critters visit the museum in the mini-barnyard. Since there isn't a lot for kids to do in this remote area, the museum is just enough to stave off those "I'm bored blues." Events are their specialty.

WORLD CHAMPIONSHIP SNOWMOBILE DERBY

Eagle River - *Highway 45. The World Championship Snowmobile Derby is the NASCAR for snowmobilers. More than 300 professional snowmobile racers, some from as far away as Japan, and 30,000 spectators converge in Wisconsin's northwoods for one the largest gatherings of "sledders" in the world. Their speeds can top 100 mph. Vilas County is where the snowmobile was invented. Wear warm long johns and extra socks. Concessions w/ chili and hot chocolate are available. Admission.* **https://derbycomplex.com/** *(mid-January weekends)*

CRANBERRY FEST

Eagle River - *Vilas County Fairgrounds, Downtown, and Derby Track. More than 40,000 cranberry lovers descend on Eagle River for its annual tribute to the cranberry, where the "World's Largest Cranberry Cheesecake" is served. Visitors can eat, drink, wear, bake and decorate with cranberries; tour the cranberry marshes and area winery; and visit different exhibits. A sampling of the cranberry-related foods available includes: fresh cranberries, cranberry cheesecake, craisins, cranberry beer, hot spiced cranapple drink, cranberry meatballs, cranberry chili, cranberry mustard, lots of fresh baked goods and even cranberry bratwurst. Weekend activities and entertainment include farmers, antique and flea markets, a craft show, walk/run/bike tour, and musical entertainment.* **www.cranberryfest.org.** *(first weekend in October).*

SNOWMOBILE HALL OF FAME

8481 West Hwy 70 (1 mile west of the Chamber office & one mile East of the Whitetail Inn) **Eagle River (St. Germain)** 54558

- ☐ Phone: (715) 542-4HOF (4463) **www.snowmobilehalloffame.com**
- ☐ Hours: Thursday-Friday 10:00am-5:00pm. Saturday 10:00am-3:00pm. (longer hours in season).
- ☐ Admission: Donation box.

Dedicated to preserving and showcasing the rich and exciting history of snowmobiling at both the recreational and competitive levels, this newly expanded museum has nearly 100 vintage machines on display. They also showcase historic racing snowmobiles through the years, uniforms, trophies and biographies of inductees. View racing videos in their theater. Visitors to the HOF may take advantage of a public viewing area to watch the team and see a professional race shop in action.

HAZELHURST INN BED & BREAKFAST

Hazelhurst - *6941 Highway 51 (off Hwy 51) 54531*. **www.hazelhurstinn.net**. *Phone: (715) 356-6571. It doesn't get much quieter or relaxing than staying at the Hazelhurst Inn. Surrounded by 18 acres of woods in a secluded area, Hazelhurst offers a comfortable stay in Wisconsin's Northwoods. A short walk down a path from Hazelhurst will lead you to the Bearskin State Trail, an 18 mile former railroad passageway gives guests a great place to take a morning walk or jog. Minocqua is not far from here, so the opportunity exists for entertainment and activities there. There are also plenty of cross-country ski trails near Hazelhurst for those looking for winter exercise. They offer four (4) guest rooms for your comfort, each unique with its own charm. Awake to the aroma of fresh coffee brewing and homemade muffins baking. Guests who stay for three nights claim you won't have the same breakfast twice. Amenities include air conditioning, full breakfast, private bath (most attached to rooms), patio dining, guest refrigerator, and a TV/DVD and Fireplace in the common area. Hazelhurst is pet and children friendly. Regular nightly rate is $110.00 and includes breakfast.*

OJIBWE MUSEUM & CULTURAL CENTER, GEORGE W. BROWN

603 Peace Pipe Road (just south of the Indian Bowl)
Lac du Flambeau 54538

- Phone: (715) 588-3333   **www.ldfmuseum.com**
- Hours: Monday-Friday 10:00am-4:00pm (March-October), Tuesday-Thursday 10:00am-2:00pm (November-February).
- Admission: $4.00 adult, $3.00 senior, child (5-15).

The museum celebrates Ojibwe culture with a four seasons diorama and other exhibits, including a 24-foot Ojibwe dugout canoe, smaller birch-bark canoes, Ojibwe arts and crafts, traditional clothing, a French fur trading post, and a world-record sturgeon taken from a local lake. Offering visitor tours, living history presentations, videos, and a beautiful diorama. Enjoy the lake side setting located in historic downtown. Year-round programs and classes are available as well as special events.

WASWAGONING INDIAN BOWL & CENTER
2750 County Road H Lac du Flambeau 54538

- ☐ Phone: (715) 588-3560 www.facebook.com/indianbowl
- ☐ Hours: Tuesday-Saturday 10:00am-4:00pm (mid-June - August).
- ☐ Admission: $8.00 adult, $6.00 senior (65+) & child (5-12).

This place is a re-created Ojibwe village with birchbark lodges and canoes. It is a wonderful place to learn the history of the people, also called the Chippewas, indigenous to northern Minnesota, Wisconsin, and Michigan. You get to see how people lived 200 years ago in encampments based on the cycle of the four seasons. Before contact with Europeans, the Ojibwe, like other Native American tribes, practiced a seasonal cycle of hunting, fishing, and gathering in order to survive. The tour guides (from the Lac du Flambeau Ojibwe tribe) do an excellent job of showing you how their people lived during that time. The folktales they told also made their culture come alive as the tour progressed. How is the summer and winter camp different? The Bowl hold lots of authentic Pow Wows.

LUMBERJACK STEAM TRAIN, CAMP 5 MUSEUM & ECOLOGY COMPLEX
5064 US 8 (The Depot is about 3/4 mile West of Laona on US 8) Laona 54541

- ☐ Phone: (715) 674-3414 www.lumberjacksteamtrain.com
- ☐ Hours: Open Tuesday-Saturday (summer) plus September Saturdays. Train departs Laona at 10am, 11:00am, Noon, 1:00pm. Last train returning to Laona departs at 3:00pm. Visitors are encouraged to stay a minimum of 2 hours to enjoy all the Lumberjack Camp Museum activities.
- ☐ Admission: $20.00 adult, $18.00 senior, $8.00 child (3-16), $60.00 family.
- ☐ Note: Choo-Choo Cafe. Cracker Barrel Store. Visitors can bring their own picnic coolers.

At this logging camp and farm established by a lumber company in the late 1890s, the Lumberjack Steam Train is the big family attraction. This is not your typical train ride through the countryside. The vintage steam engine takes you to an actual site of a Northwoods logging camp. The camp itself (formerly the Camp Five Museum) is now a historic site where you can visit an operating farm, a blacksmith shop, a forestry museum, a nature center and more. A simulated logging camp bunkhouse with archaeological artifacts gives visitors an idea of what life was like in a real logging camp in the early

20th Century. The Animal Barn is lined with enclosures now holding smaller, cuddlier animals, and the Corral is alive with shy calves, frisky little goats, quacking ducks, plodding turtles, parading pheasants, and honking geese.

COUNCIL GROUNDS STATE PARK
N1895 Council Grounds Drive **Merrill** 54552

☐   Phone: (715) 536-8773 **http://dnr.wi.gov/topic/parks/name/ councilgrounds/**
☐   Admission: A vehicle admission sticker is required. Daily $8.00-$11.00.

Located along the Wisconsin River near the site of an ancient Native American village, Council Groups is a favorite of water enthusiasts. Features a physical fitness trail, 55 campsites, 19 electric sites, showers, a dumping station, handicap- accessible picnic area and campsites, concessions, nature center, seasonal naturalist programs, shoreline with marked beach area, canoeing, boating (electric motors only), fishing, 0.8 miles of nature trails, 3.1 miles of hiking trails, 2.5 miles of off- road bicycle trails, 5.3 miles of cross-country ski trails. A scenic 1/3-mile-long self-guided nature trail connects the campground and the beach.

NORTHWOODS WILDLIFE CENTER
8683 Blumenstein Road (Highway 70 West) **Minocqua** 54548

☐   Phone: (715)-356-7400 **www.northwoodswildlifecenter.com**
☐   Tours: Tuesday-Saturday 9:00 am-4:00pm (May-September). suggested $5.
☐   Admission: Fees based on type of tour and amount of activities.
☐   Tours: Guided tours of permanent residents leave every 1/2 hour.
☐   FREEBIES: coloring pages and wildlife projects here: http:// northwoodswildlifecenter.org/kids-corner.html

Learn how to better coexist with our wild neighbors at this real wildlife hospital. The center is a not-for-profit organization which cares for injured and orphaned wild animals while educating the public about their plight. They offer outdoor, guided tours of a wildlife hospital caring for injured and orphaned wild animals. Visitors will have the ability to view various animals including birds of prey, reptiles, and amphibians. We can only tell you to look for one resident, Orson, as most of the creatures they host are only here to get better and move on. So, every visit means someone new to meet.

WILDWOOD WILDLIFE PARK & NATURE CENTER

10094 Hwy 70 West (2 miles west of US 51 on US 70) **Minocqua** 54548

- ☐ Phone: (715) 356-5588 **www.wildwoodwildlifepark.com**
- ☐ Hours: Daily 9:00am-4:30pm (Spring & Fall), 9:00am-5:30pm (summer).
- ☐ Admission: $24.99 adult, $16.99 child (2-11).
- ☐ Note: Adventure Boat Ride $4.00 per person and Pedal Zoo-Indy Race Cars $5.00 per persons. Go fishing in the trout pond or ride the oval track Safari Train Ride $4.00 per person. Food and concessions available on the grounds at the Wild Den Snack Stand.

Families have been visiting Wildwood for generations. More than 750 animals and birds including wallaby, zebra, bear, tiger, white-tail deer, bobcat, lynx, reptiles, lemur, wolf, coyote, fox, and skunk reside here. Meet Toby and Tenzin, the spotted leopard couple who hope to have little cubs when they get older. Pet a porcupine, kiss a pig, feed a deer, bottle feed a baby goat, cuddle a bunny and see hundreds of other woodland animals.

Budgie Encounter. This exhibit allows visitors to get up-close and personal with 500 parakeets. Roam among the parakeet aviary while the birds free fly throughout the space. You can also feed the birds with "feeding sticks". Hold out a feed stick and you may have a budgie (parakeet) eating right out of your hand. The center has a Baby nursery, daily amphitheater programs, musky pond, picnic area & nature boardwalk.

The otters have their own space full of playful pools and slides. They especially like to show off so be sure to clap and squeal. There's a trout pond with fee fishing - bait & equipment, catch cleaned and iced. OH, and don't forget to feed the bears "Bear Juice" before you leave.

WOLF RIVER TRIPS & CAMPGROUND

E8041 County Road X **New London** 54961

- ☐ Phone: (920) 982-2458 **www.wolfrivertrips.com**
- ☐ Hours: Office Hours - Monday-Thursday 9:00am-9:00pm, Friday & Saturday 8:00am-11:00pm, Sunday 8:00am-8:00pm (summer).
- ☐ Admission: Rentals start at $11.00 per person.

The clear water, gentle rapids, and breathtaking scenery of the Little Wolf River make tubing a fun and relaxing recreational activity for all ages. Trips start at the campground, where a shuttle bus takes you to the drop-off point on the beautiful Little Wolf River. From there, the river takes you through rocks, rapids and quiet drifting areas. Along the way, stop for a swim at one of the smooth sandy spots or stay in your tube and relax. Allow the river to take you on a leisurely trip back to the main campgrounds. Once you're back on land, they have a restaurant and recreation hall with over 25 games to play.

COPPER CULTURE STATE PARK

(just west of the Highway 22 / Highway 41 interchange) **Oconto** 54153

- ☐ Phone: (920) 826-7304 **http://dnr.wi.gov/topic/parks/name/copperculture/**
- ☐ Admission: Vehicle admission sticker not required.

A National Historic Landmark, a state park, and a museum demonstrates what was found at this oldest copper burial ground. Small day-use park features 2,000-year-old Indian burial mounds. Locally owned park museum offers a detailed look at Copper Culture life and time (open seasonally - long weekends only). Also enjoy the 15-acre short-grass prairie or fish the Oconto River. Open 6:00am-11:00pm.

SPRINGSIDE CHEESE FACTORY

7989 Arndt Road (Cty B, 8 miles north) **Oconto Falls** 54154

- ☐ Phone: (920) 829-6395 **www.springsidecheese.com**
- ☐ Hours: Monday, Wednesday, Friday and Saturday 8:30am-4:30pm.

Their specialties are cheddar, colby, monterey jack, farmers, and low sodium. This retail outlet also gives prearranged tours, and has an observation window.

HOLIDAY ACRES RESORT

4060 South Shore Drive **Rhinelander** 54501

- ☐ Phone: (715) 369-1500 or (800) 261-1500
  http://holidayacres.com

An authentic Northwoods vacation (w/ clean, no fuss amenities) still exists! This resort is run by one family - mostly for families. You can rent a cabin in the woods with one bedroom up to six bedrooms or rent a basic lodge room. Rates start around $99.00/night but it's the activities that will catch you. Winters you can come for cross country skiing, sledding or snow shoeing but summers are grand. Mornings you'll see folks out walking, boating, beaching it, fishing or swimming in the lake or in the indoor pool. Fishing boats, kayaks, sailboats, pontoons and bikes are available to rent.

They offer waterski instruction for beginners up to advanced and the Zambon family are known for that. They have a good program for geocachers - you may even find some unique spots in town you never noticed before. Hungry? They have a simple coffee shop with light food service and the 3 Coins Restaurant that always gets rave reviews. Try the pan-fried walleye. The wood and stone interior is just the way you picture the northwoods should be. You also don't go hungry here as they provide a lot of the extras of the supper club era. Their Sunday brunch and Friday Fish buffet are very popular. Their Kids Menu has seven selections averaging $6.00.

RHINELANDER LOGGING MUSEUM COMPLEX

705 Martin Lynch Drive (Located in Pioneer Park, on Business US 8 - Oneida Avenue) **Rhinelander** 54501

☐ Phone: (715) 369-5004 **https://rhinelanderpphc.com/**
☐ Hours: Daily 10:00am-5:00pm (Memorial Day-Labor Day).
☐ Admission: No admission charge, but donations are greatly appreciated.

This complex is a full-scale reproduction of a 19th-century logging camp with a narrow gauge railroad. On the museum grounds, visitors will see a variety of early logging equipment, including Thunder Lake's No. 5 narrow gauge locomotive, President Jack Mylrea's private car, one of the few steam-powered snow snakes used to hauls sleds of logs over iced highways, a turn table, Big Wheels to haul logs to stream or rails, and a road icer.

• LOGGING MUSEUM - These buildings represent a true-to-life replica of a lumber camp of the 1870's, consisting of a bunkhouse, a cook shanty, and a blacksmith shop. It is the most complete display of its kind in the area, housing a collection of artifacts pertaining to the early logger: all kinds of tools and equipment, including peavies, pike poles, cant hooks, and cross-cut saws, as well as an extensive file of photographs covering the life and work of the old time logger. By the way, is the "hodag" real or a mythological critter?

•

•

KOVAC PLANETARIUM

2401 Mud Creek Road (look for the flags and small white arrow sign)
Rhinelander (Monico) 54501

- Phone: (715) 487-4411 **https://frankkovacplanetarium.com/**
- Hours: Open daily.
- Admission: $12.00 adult, $10.00 senior, $8.00 child (6-12).

The world's largest mechanical globe planetarium, 22-feet in diameter. It displays all the stars in the northern hemisphere visible to the unaided eye. Open daily by reservation only. Call for seating and show times.

ROCK ISLAND STATE PARK

(accessible only by ferry or private boat) **Rock Island** 54246

- Phone: (920) 847-2235 **http://dnr.wi.gov/topic/parks/name/rockisland/**
- Hours: (Memorial Day - Columbus Day).
- Admission: A vehicle admission sticker is required. Daily $3.00-$11.00. Annual passes available.

Take the ferry (Memorial Day weekend through Columbus Day) to this primitive island off the tip of the Door County peninsula in Lake Michigan. Stone buildings, built by a wealthy inventor who owned the island between 1910 and 1945, house exhibits. The ferry carries people, vehicles, bicycles, and freight. Take County Highway W to the opposite end of Washington Island. There are fees for ferries. Cars and even bikes are not allowed on the 912-acre island, making for an experience unlike any other Wisconsin state park. There are 10 miles of hiking trails, including a one-mile interpretive trail, a naturalist program, and 5,000 feet of beach. Primitive, walk-in camping; no wheeled vehicles allowed.

ART OEHMCKE HATCHERY

8770 County Highway J (2 miles east of town) **Woodruff** 54568

- Phone: (715) 358-9215 **https://dnr.wisconsin.gov/topic/Fishing/ hatcheries/hatcheries.html**
- Hours: Monday thru Friday 8:00am-4:30pm (Mday thru Lday)
- Tours: conducted 11:00am and 2:00pm, weekdays except holidays.
- Miscellaneous: Picnic areas and campgrounds nearby in Northern Highlands-American Legion State Forest.

Large cool-water hatchery specializing in Muskellunge, walleye, lake trout and suckers. There are mounted fish on the walls inside but kids spend most of the time outside watching young fish leap and splash. Called 'Mr. Musky,' Oehmcke knew the fish like no one else; State career lasted 41 years, most of them at Woodruff Hatchery.

HILLESTAD PHARMACEUTICALS FACTORY TOUR

178 U.S. Hwy. 51 N (1/2 mile north of Hwy 47 & 51) **Woodruff** 54568

- ☐ Phone: (800) 535-7742 **www.hillestadlabs.com/factory%20tours.html**
- ☐ Tours: Monday-Friday 9:00am to 3:00pm. Walkins are welcome.

See vitamins, minerals, protein tablets, herbs, skin cremes and lotions manufactured using natural source nutrients. Take a peek in the warehouse where they store 5,000 different kinds of natural raw ingredients. Notice the ingredients for a specific "recipe" are then weighed, mixed and blended. Now you have a bunch of powder and need to form it into tablets. In the tableting department the powder is pressed into tablets - that's the secret, pressing. The presses create 10,000 pounds of pressure per square inch to create tablets. After the tablets are pressed they are coated to seal the tablet. This locks in the potency and eliminates any odor or aftertaste. Why do some tablets have noticeable layers?

Travel Journal & Notes:

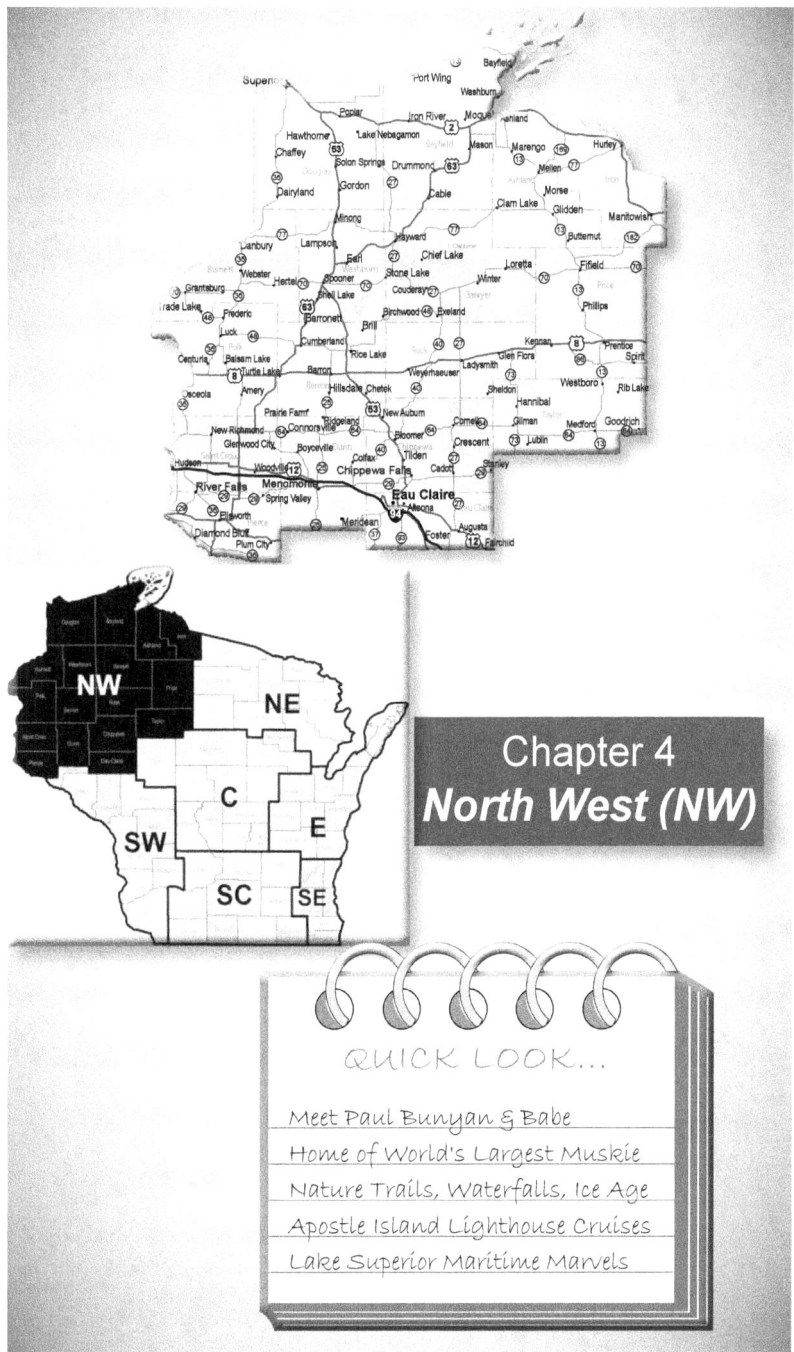

Chapter 4
North West (NW)

QUICK LOOK...

Meet Paul Bunyan & Babe

Home of World's Largest Muskie

Nature Trails, Waterfalls, Ice Age

Apostle Island Lighthouse Cruises

Lake Superior Maritime Marvels

Apostle Islands (Bayfield)

- Apostle Islands Cruise Service
- Apostle Islands National Lakeshore
- Applefest
- Bayfield Maritime Museum
- Lake Superior Big Top Chautauqua

Apostle Islands (Devils Island)

- Devils Island Lighthouse

Apostle Islands (La Pointe)

- Big Bay State Park
- Madeline Island Ferry Line
- Madeline Island Historical Museum

Ashland

- Northern Great Lakes Visitor Center

Cable

- Cable Natural History Museum

Cable To Hayward

- American Birkebeiner Ski Race
- Chequamegon Fat Tire Festival

Chippewa Falls

- Chippewa Falls Museum Of Industry & Technology
- Lake Wissota State Park
- Olson's Ice Cream Parlor & Deli

Cornell

- Brunet Island State Park

Danbury

- Forts Folle Avoine Historical Park

Duluth, MN

- Great Lakes Aquarium
- Great Lakes Floating Maritime Museum

Duluth, MN (cont.)

- Lake Superior Maritime Visitor Center
- Vista Fleet Harbor Cruises

Eau Claire

- Chaos Waterpark & Action City
- Paul Bunyan Logging Camp Museum

Glidden

- St. Peter's Dome

Grantsburg

- Crex Meadows Wildlife Area

Hayward

-
- Honor The Earth Pow-Wow
- Lumberjack World Championships
- National Fresh Water Fishing Hall Of Fame & Museum
- Scheer's Lumberjack Shows & Village
- Wilderness Walk Zoo & Recreation Park

Hudson

- Hot Air Affair
- Octagon House & America's First Kindergarten
- Willow River State Park

Manitowish Waters

- Manitowish Waters Skiing Skeeters

Medford

- Perkinstown Outhouse Race
- Perkinstown Winter Sports Area

Mellen

- Copper Falls State Park

Menomonie

- Caddie Woodlawn Historical Park
- Wayside

New Auburn
- Chippewa Moraine Ice Age Interpretive Center

Osceola
- Osceola & St. Croix Valley Railway

Park Falls
- Northern Wisconsin Maid Sugarbush

Phillips
- Wisconsin Concrete Park

Prescott
- Great River Road Visitor Center

Rice Lake
- Red Barn Summer Theatre

River Falls
- Kinnickinnic State Park

Shell Lake
- Museum Of Woodcarving

Spooner
- Governor Thompson State Fish Hatchery
- Heart Of The North Rodeo
- Wisconsin Great Northern RR

Spring Valley
- Crystal Cave

St. Croix Falls
- Fawn-Doe-Rosa Animal Park
- Interstate State Park
- St. Croix National Scenic Riverway Center

Superior
- Amnicon Falls State Park
- Pattison State Park
- Richard I. Bong Veterans Historical Center
- S.S. Meteor Museum

Taylors Falls, MN
- Taylor Falls Princess
- Wild Mountain Recreation

Wilson
- Cady Cheese Factory

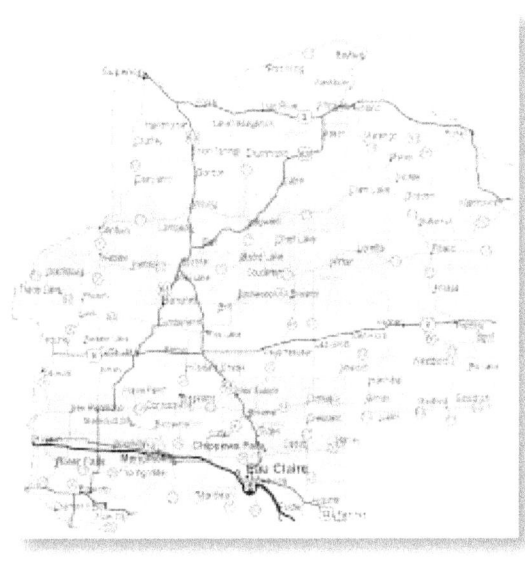

Sites and attractions are listed in order by City, Zip Code, and Name. Symbols indicated represent: 📷 Restaurants   🛏 Lodging

APOSTLE ISLANDS CRUISE SERVICE

City Dock **Apostle Islands (Bayfield)** 54814

- ☐ Phone: (800) 323-7619 **www.apostleisland.com**
- ☐ Admission: $51.95 adults, $30.95 child (6-12).
- ☐ Tours: Reservations are highly recommended for all cruises. Boarding begins 1/2 hour prior to cruise departure. *Want more adventure? Try a glassbottom boat tour of shipwrecks below the waters of Lake Superior!* (3 hour tours each summer departs at 2pm). Grand Tour takes 2.5 to 3 hours.

Their most popular cruise, the Grand Tour takes you on a narrated, informative, 55-mile, scenic cruise aboard ISLAND PRINCESS. Throughout this memorable cruise, you'll pass extraordinary natural scenics, beautiful historic Raspberry and Devils Island Lighthouses, standing rocks, extensive sea caves and marine wildlife. Learn the rich history of centuries of human interaction with Wisconsin's "Crown Jewels" on majestic Lake Superior. Tours daily May - mid-October.

Cruises to many of the Apostle Islands and their lighthouses, too. For example, the RASPBERRY ISLAND LIGHTHOUSE TOURS - giving insight into the lives of those who lived and worked in this secluded setting. The Wisconsin Park Service Interpretive fees apply ($3.00/person or $8.00 family) to tour this newly renovated lighthouse and Keepers home.

APOSTLE ISLANDS NATIONAL LAKESHORE

715 Washington Avenue (one block off Wisconsin Route 13 in Bayfield)
Apostle Islands (Bayfield) 54814

- ☐ Phone: (715) 779-3397 **www.nps.gov/apis/index.htm**
- ☐ Hours: The mainland portion and the islands of the Apostle Islands National Lakeshore are open to visitors year round. Bayfield Visitor Center: Daily 8:00am-4:30pm (late May - mid-October). Closed weekends (mid-October - late May). Open summers until 6:00pm.
- ☐ Admission: $5.00 per vehicle for beach. Optional recreation fees apply.
- ☐ Note: Cuisine ranges from home cooking to gourmet, and area chefs take inspiration from Bayfield's harvest of berries, fish and apples. Educators: Lighthouse Curriculum at the bottom of the page titled: For Kids.

APOSTLE ISLANDS NATIONAL LAKESHORE - The windswept beaches and cliffs formed by centuries of Lake Superior waves crashing against ancient shores is captured and preserved in the 21 islands and 12 miles of mainland that comprise this treasure that is now part of the National Parks Service. The area is a unique blend of cultural and natural resources, where the original Native Americans and pioneering settlers grew together in peace, awe and respect of nature's beauty. Called one of North America's "Virtually Pristine" national parks by National Geographic Traveler, the 22 gem-like Apostle Islands offer lighthouses, hiking trails, shipwrecks and terrific blue-water sailing. However, they are perhaps best known for their red sandstone sea caves. The town has an APPLE FESTIVAL in October showcasing the many breeds of apple grown here (blueberries rule here, too). Madeline Island is the only Apostle Island not managed by the National Park Service. Bayfield is known as the "Gateway to the Apostle Islands."

VISITORS CENTER - Enjoy a brief film on the history of the Apostle Islands and take advantage of the gift shop with a Lighthouse Fresnel lens on display. The Hokenson Brothers Fishery Museum has preserved the buildings, tools, and craft used by the brothers in their fishery operation. Tours are conducted by the Park Service staff.

BAYFIELD'S WINTER RECREATION: The famous sea caves become magical sparkling cathedrals of ice, creating a popular destination for hikers. Even those who prefer not to get out into the elements can admire the dramatic ice formations on the lake from the comfort of their cars on a drive along the shoreline.

Snowshoers will discover 100 miles of snowshoe trails and skiers will find 130 miles of groomed cross country ski trails. You can also find challenging snowboarding and alpine skiing at Mt. Ashwabay, where 13 runs and a chairlift await. With rare exception, Lake Superior freezes deep enough to allow them to fashion the famous "Ice Road", allowing you to drive, hike or ski back and forth to Madeline Island. Ice fishing hotspots also.

Up for a real backcountry experience? Join a guided dog sledding expedition to experience the snowy solitude of the surrounding landscape (Sled Dog Races early February). Or take a brisk hike or walk along one of the many area trails through the woods, made even more tranquil by the stillness of the season.

WINTER FESTIVAL

Apostle Islands (Bayfield) - *Activities are scheduled all weekend long, including "Run on Water," a family race across the frozen "ice road" to Madeline Island, the "Polar Bear Plunge," where brave volunteers don festive costumes and jump into the icy waters of Lake Superior, and the Egg Toss "Pajama" Breakfast Buffet. (first full weekend in March)*

LAKE SUPERIOR BIG TOP CHAUTAUQUA
32525 Ski Hill Rd **Apostle Islands (Bayfield)** 54814

☐   Phone: (888) 244-8368 **www.bigtop.org**

On summer nights, Lake Superior Big Top Chautauqua stages unique cabaret entertainment and national music acts under a big tent just outside of town. A summer season of 70 shows - historical musicals, variety shows, top national entertainers – all under the "Big Top." Performances June-September, see Web site for schedule.

APPLEFEST

Apostle Islands (Bayfield) - *(on the shores of Lake Superior). Phone: (800) 447-4094. https://www.bayfield.org/bayfield-apple-festival/. A festival featuring more than 40 orchard and food booths with traditional festival foods, as well as apple desserts is fun for all ages. More than 100 artists and crafters, and a grand parade. Visitors enjoy ongoing stage entertainment, a traditional fish boil, carnival rides and games, and an evening dance on the waterfront. Other attractions include orchard visits (free shuttle), apple pie and peeling contests, an evening boat parade, and the Apple Dumpling Gang prize drawing. (first long weekend in October)*

DEVILS ISLAND LIGHTHOUSE
(Lake Superior) **Apostle Islands (Devils Island)** 54814

☐   Phone: (715) 779-3397 **http://www.nps.gov/apis/historyculture/devils-light.htm**
☐   Hours: Daily, 9:00am-4:00pm (June - Labor Day). National Park Service volunteers provide guided tours. Tours per person are $3-$5.00 per person.

Built in 1898. 82-foot tower and two Queen Anne-style keepers' dwellings can be viewed May through October. Devils Island (the northernmost point in Wisconsin) has a dock at its south end and a rock landing near the lighthouse which is accessible to boats in calm weather.

BIG BAY STATE PARK

(located on Madeline Island) **Apostle Islands (La Pointe)** 54814

- Phone: (715) 747-6425 **http://dnr.wi.gov/topic/parks/name/bigbay/**
- Hours: Daily 6:00am-11:00pm with overnight camping.
- Admission: A vehicle admission sticker is required. Daily $8.00-$11.00. Annual passes available.
- Note: No launching facilities are available at the park, but boats can be launched at the public landing in Bayfield or at a privately operated landing on Madeline Island.

Madeline Island, the most southern island of the Apostle Islands, is a great weekend or week long retreat for families who love the outdoors but still want a few urban comforts. It is located on a peninsula 7 miles from the village of La Pointe where there are restaurants, ice cream parlors, gift shops, etc. The State Park offers camping, swimming, a 1.5 mile sand beach, and a one-mile boardwalk. Water sports, fishing and hiking are also popular and most offer a view of Lake Superior. Connecting with the Bay View Trail near the tip of the point, this 1.7-mile trail includes a loop with both inland and shoreline segments, plus a trail that winds through the woods between the outdoor group camp and regular campground and beach area. The Cut-Across Trail, a short self-guided nature trail, also serves as a shortcut through the Point Trail loop. This shortcut trail is the most kid-friendly. Bike rentals are available in La Pointe.

MADELINE ISLAND FERRY LINE

(Ferry Line docks are located at the northeast end of Bayfield.
Turn east unto Washington Avenue off of Highway 13)
Apostle Islands (La Pointe) 54850

- Phone (715) 747-2051 **www.madferry.com**
- Hours: Call or visit website for complete schedule that varies by weather. As soon as the ice is out, the Madeline Island Ferry begins running 4 times a day from Bayfield to the village of La Pointe. After May 7th, its schedule increases to 11 daily trips, in June and July even more frequent.
- Admission: Ferry charges $8.50 OW $17.00 RT. Child $3.50-7Autos $31.00 RT.
- Notes: While taking your car or RV to the island is a neat experience, you can see quite a lot by walking around town. If you want to go further around the island, you can rent a bike.

The Madeline Island Ferry crosses the bay on a 3-mile trip to Madeline Island. The Island is home to Big Bay State Park and the Madeline Island Museum, located on the historic site of the former American Fur Company trading post.

MADELINE ISLAND HISTORICAL MUSEUM

226 Colonel Woods Avenue (located in Lake Superior 2.5 miles offshore from Bayfield) **Apostle Islands (La Pointe) 54850**

- ☐ Phone: (715) 747-2415
  http://madeineislandmuseum.wisconsinhistory.org/
- ☐ Hours: Daily 10:00am-4:00pm (late May-Labor Day). Wednesday-Sunday only (September-late October). Closed Mondays during the school year.
- ☐ Admission: $10.00 adult, $8.00 students & seniors (65+), $5.00 child (5-12).
- ☐ Note: School field trips are available. Contact for details.

Madeline Island, the most southern island of the Apostles, is steeped in history - both for the Ojibway-Anishinabe peoples and Europeans who later founded trading posts, missionary outposts, and eventually the town of La Pointe. The Ojibway occupied the area for several hundred years prior to encountering French explorers in the 1600s. The first European trading post was founded in 1693 by Pierre Le Sueur on the south end of the island which he operated until 1698. More than a century later the American Fur Company built their post at essentially the same spot. That building is adjoined to an old barn, the former La Pointe town jail, and the Old Sailor's Home, which had been built as a memorial to a drowned sailor. It also includes Logging Camp tools and items used in boat building and fishing industries. Lifestyle focus is on a settlers cabin and a Ojibwa dugout canoe.

NORTHERN GREAT LAKES VISITOR CENTER

29270 County Highway G (south shore of Lake Superior on Hwy 2)
Ashland 54806

- ☐ Phone: (715) 685-9983 **http://nglvc.org/**
- ☐ Hours: Daily 9:00am-5:00pm.
- ☐ Admission: FREE.

Everyone enjoys a good story and this museum's aim is to bring area stories alive. Assistants can tell you how to retrace routes of the native peoples, old voyageurs, immigrants, or the fur traders' far flung travels along nearby lakes and rivers. Most every exhibit has a short story, joke, riddle or music associated with it. Besides that, they have a theater and a five-story observation tower offering a panoramic view of Lake Superior and the Apostle Islands Region. Outside, they offer a 3/4 mile boardwalk interpretive trail. This dynamic center is a must stop before you head north to explore Apostle Islands.

CABLE NATURAL HISTORY MUSEUM
13470 County Highway M **Cable** 54821

- ☐ Phone: (715) 798-3890 **www.cablemuseum.org**
- ☐ Hours: Tuesday-Saturday 10:00am-4:00pm.
- ☐ Admission: $5.00 per adult over 18. FREE on Tuesdays.

A small, but excellent museum with wildlife displays, a summer lecture and field trip series, and a Junior Naturalist program. All of the exhibits at the Cable Natural History Museum are focused on the environment and natural history of the region - taxidermied fish, birds, mammals and reptiles. Many kids like the squirrel and the animal skulls. Regulars to the area like the Museum's blog, updated with current info on creature citings.

AMERICAN BIRKEBEINER SKI RACE

Cable to Hayward - *Downtown for spectators. Fondly known as the "Birkie," the Subaru American Birkebeiner is the nation's largest and most prestigious cross-country ski marathon. Literally thousands of skiers from all over the world strive to conquer the 51-kilometer course from Cable to the city of Hayward each February. Now much more than the central race itself, the Birkie is a winter event including a shorter course race the Kortelopet, the Jr. Birkie for teenagers, a children's and a noncompetitive ski events. Almost everyone but the very young and the very old can actually compete.* **www.birkie.com** *(last Saturday in February)*

CHEQUAMEGON FAT TIRE FESTIVAL

Cable to Hayward - *Dirty fun and grueling gear grinding action as thousands of fat tire cycling enthusiasts from around the world visit Wisconsin's famed Northwoods for one of the countries largest and esteemed off-road biking adventures. 2,500 riders make their way to the forested trails to test their endurance in the Chequamegon 40 mile and Short & Fat races. The weekend also includes a bicycle orienteering event, Criterium closed-circuit races, live entertainment, the "klunker" bike toss, hill climb competition, children's bicycle rodeo and miles of riding trails for all ages. Sunday Funday events are FREE.* **www.cheqfattire.com** *(third weekend in September)*

CHIPPEWA FALLS MUSEUM OF INDUSTRY & TECHNOLOGY

21 E Grand Street **Chippewa Falls** 54729

- ☐ Phone: (715) 720-9206 **www.cfmit.org**
- ☐ Hours: Thursday-Saturday 10:00am-3:00pm.
- ☐ Admission: $5.00 adult $3.00 child (through 18).

The Museum interprets a rich, varied history of manufacturing and processing that began in Chippewa Falls in the 1840's and continues today. Exhibits include the Supercomputer Collection, an interactive learning area and photographs and documents of historic industries. Cray Inc. resides in Chippewa Falls and is a global leader in supercomputers for government, industry and academia. This town is also known for shoes, Mason shoe company employs a lot of folks. That fire engine screaming down the street may be a Darley fire truck. The Great Northern Corp. makes custom containers and displays and Hubbard Scientific is known for making those skeletons you see in almost every science classroom. Every weekend the museum offers family activities.

LAKE WISSOTA STATE PARK

18127 County Highway O (2 miles E of Cty S, 5 miles NE of Chippewa Falls) **Chippewa Falls** 54729

- ☐ Phone: (715) 382-4574 **http://dnr.wi.gov/topic/parks/name/lakewissota/**
- ☐ Admission: A vehicle admission sticker is required. Daily $8.00-$11.00. Annual passes available.
- ☐ FREEBIES: "Wonder Walk" packs may be checked out at the park office. These backpacks are full of activities for children and adults alike to learn more about the nature and environment surrounding Lake Wissota.

Located on a 6,300-acre man-made lake, this park attracts anglers after walleyes, muskies and bass. Features 81 campsites, 17 electric sites, showers, a dumping station, handicap- accessible picnic area and campsites, nature center, seasonal naturalist programs, vistas, shoreline with marked beach area, canoeing, boating, fishing, 1 mile of nature trails, 17.5 miles of hiking trails, 6.5 miles of horseback trails, 0.4 miles of surface bicycle trails, 11 miles of off-road bicycle trails, 4.8 miles of snowmobile trails, 7 miles of cross-country ski trails.

Chippewa Falls - *611 N Bridge St, 54729. Phone: (715) 723-4331. Homemade ice cream, sandwiches and yummy soups served at this store in the heart of historic downtown Chippewa Falls.* **www.olsonsicecream.com**

BRUNET ISLAND STATE PARK
23125 255th S. (2.5 miles west of SR 27) **Cornell** 54732

☐ Phone: (715) 239-6888 **http://dnr.wi.gov/topic/parks/name/brunetisland/**
☐ Admission: A vehicle admission sticker is required. Daily $8.00-$11.00.
Annual passes available.

Framed by the Chippewa and Fisher Rivers, this island park's bays and lagoons offer a quiet respite. Features 69 campsites, 24 electric sites, showers, handicap- accessible picnic area and campsites, seasonal naturalist programs, shoreline with marked beach area, canoeing, boating, fishing, 0.8 miles of nature trails, 5 miles of hiking trails, 4 miles of cross- country ski trails. The Jean Brunet Nature Trail is a self-guided walking trail with signs along the trail describing the history and nature of the area. This .8-mile trail dramatically demonstrates the incredible variety in nature that we sometimes take for granted. This trail starts near the main bridge to the island.

FORTS FOLLE AVOINE HISTORICAL PARK
8500 County Road U (4 miles north of Webster, off Hwy 35) **Danbury** 54830

☐ Phone: (715) 866-8890 **www.theforts.org**
☐ Hours: Wednesday-Sunday, 10:00am-4:00pm. (Memorial Weekend - Labor Day Weekend). Saturday & Sunday 10:00am-4:00pm (September).
☐ Admission (Tours): $10 adult (13+), $8 senior, $6 child (5-11), $28.00 family.
☐ Tours: Start at 10:00am, 11:00am, Noon, 1:00pm, 2:00pm and last 2 hours. Guides take visitors through Fur Trade Posts and the Ojibwe Indian Village.
☐ Note: Wintertime, the grounds serve as x-country ski trails.

History comes to life at Forts Folle Avoine, where bartering between fur traders and the Ojibwe Indians is portrayed as it actually happened almost 200 years ago! The complex includes a reconstructed 1800s fur trading post, an Indian village and an indoor museum.

Inside the Visitors Center you'll find Archeology displays, maps and fur trade artifacts that paint a picture of life along the Yellow River two hundred years ago. Most of these artifacts were actually found on the property.

Outside, during the summer, tours of the historical site and a representation of a Woodland Indian Village are led by traditionally-dressed interpreters. The Indian Village is an accurate reflection of the close relationship that existed between the European fur traders and their Native American trading partners. Many bands of Ojibwe, Odawa, Cree, Dakota, Fox and Sauk lived in and frequented the area for hundreds of years. Why were trading posts similar to Indian villages? Moving on...After the last season of trading in 1805 with the local Ojibwe, they loaded their canoes and pushed off into the Yellow River and never returned. The forts were abandoned and at some unknown time the structures were burned and stayed hidden for 165 years.

THE GREAT FOLLE AVOINE FUR TRADE RENDEZVOUS

Danbury - Forts Folle Avoine Historical Park. Over 150 fur trade camps fill Sayer's Field and Trader's Row, representing the many unique characters that gathered after a winter of trapping to trade goods, stories and a good time. Enjoy demonstrations of period skills, black powder, archery and tomahawk competitions and food preparation. Visit with participants to learn the history of this important era of commerce and exploration in North America. Admission. (last full weekend in July)

GREAT LAKES AQUARIUM
353 Harbor Drive Duluth, MN 55802

- ☐ Phone: (218) 740-FISH **www.glaquarium.org**
- ☐ Hours: Daily 10:00am-6:00pm.
- ☐ Admission: $17.99 adult, $14.99 senior (62+), $13.99 child (13-17), $11.99 child (3-12). Parking is available in the Aquarium parking lot for $5.00.
- ☐ Educators: Online resources/curriculum - https://glaquarium.org/education/k-12-learning/teacher-resource-center/

The Great Lakes Aquarium unveils the secrets and wonder of Lake Superior. Dive in to America's only ALL-freshwater aquarium! Discover what's in and under Lake Superior through 70 species of fish and exhibits from the Great Lakes and other freshwater lakes and rivers of the world. Many of the spaces bring the underwater or remote scapes larger than life like towering waterfalls or cold water flowing over steep volcanic rock. Why is it important that some rivers move fast and others, slowly? Most exhibits allow viewing from above and below the water line. See dive feedings, touch a stingray, enjoy otter antics and more. Go online to find out when their divers will sink into two-story tanks loaded with sturgeon, salmon, trout and other freshwater fish.

Even more entertaining is the river otter program, when handlers bring in buckets of snow filled with hidden treats such as anchovies and worms. Otters have got to be the most playful to watch. Ever "pet" a fish? The "Critter Corner" features two touch tanks: a warm water stingray tank and a cold water sturgeon tank. These fresh water stingrays are found in the Amazon River while the lake sturgeon are native to the Great Lakes. Be sure to stop and see what these fish feel like! Other hands-on areas involve the Wow of Water and a "play" water table complete with ships and locks and dams to navigate. Freshwater isn't always as pretty as tropical, but it definitely is large and mysterious.

GREAT LAKES FLOATING MARITIME MUSEUM

350 Harbor Drive, waterfront Convention Center (just over bridge from Superior, WI) **Duluth, MN** 55802

- Phone: (218) 727-0022 **www.decc.org/william-a-irvin**
- Hours: Thursday-Sunday 10am-5pm. (May- mid September) Summers open daily.
- Admission: $20.00 adult. 15.00 Students and $10.00 seniors.
- Note: The Duluth Omnimax Theatre is in the same complex and tickets can be ordered on the DECC website. Combo tickets for the boat tour and movie. available.

The Great Lakes Floating Maritime Museum consists of a retired Coast Guard Cutter (a ship that breaks up ice so that other craft can pass through the water) and a freighter that once hauled iron ore throughout the Great Lakes and into the ocean. For more than 40 years the S.S. William A. Irvin carried iron ore and coal to Great Lakes ports, often crashing through ferocious storms to reach her destinations. Still, she also provided comfort and elegance to passengers. You can tour the SS William A Irvin. So c'mon aboard! Visitors are treated to stories of the ship by knowledgeable tour guides. Whether you're interested in a 2,000 horsepower steam turbine engine or delicate antique fixtures, you'll find them both in shipshape!

LAKE SUPERIOR MARITIME VISITOR CENTER

600 South Lake Ave, Canal Park waterfront district (Located adjacent to the Aerial Lift Bridge, just over the river from Superior, WI) **Duluth, MN** 55802

- ☐ Phone: (218) 727-2497 **www.lsmma.com**
- ☐ Hours: Thursday-Monday 10:00am-4:30pm (Spring thru Fall). Weekends only each winter.
- ☐ Admission: FREE

Visit the Lake Superior Maritime Visitor Center in the Canal Park waterfront district. The Duluth-Superior Harbor is the world's largest, most inland seaport, bringing ships 2,432 miles across the Great Lakes from the Atlantic. Intriguing exhibits about the Great Lakes shipping industry and life aboard the giant freighters. The museum provides information about the commercial shipping and port development of the upper Great Lakes, and hundreds of Lake Superior shipwrecks. Which great storms wiped out giant steel ships? What was it like to work aboard a Great Lakes ship? How can a heavy steel ship float, with more than 60,000 tons of cargo?

CANAL PARK & LAKEWALK – a variety of restaurants to choose from. Stroll the boardwalk, shop, watch ships as they enter the harbor. The 3-mile Canal Park gives visitors a great view of Lake Superior and the lighthouse that lies at the northern breakwater. Watching ships go under the lift bridge is one of many free attractions. The Duluth News Tribune prints a daily Shipping News column, or call the Boatwatcher's Hotline at (218) 722-6489 for approximate arrival and departure times.

VISTA FLEET HARBOR CRUISES

323 Harbor Drive (dock is located on the harbor side of the Duluth Entertainment & Convention Center) **Duluth, MN** 55802

- ☐ Phone: (218) 722-6218 **www.vistafleet.com**
- ☐ Hours: Daily @ 10:30am & 3:00pm (3rd weekend of June - Labor Day). Spring/Fall tours are available, check website for schedule.
- ☐ Admission: Sightseeing - $32.00 adult, $15.00 child (3-12).
- ☐ Tours: Sightseeing 1 hour cruise. Boarding time begins 15 minutes prior to departure. Reservations recommended.
- ☐ Note: Event cruises sail on holidays such as Mother's Day, Father's Day, July 4th.

Take in all the activity and spectacular scenery in the hard working Duluth and Superior Harbor. Learn about the Harbor, Duluth's history, the science and ecology of Lake Superior and enjoy the panoramic views of the North Shore and the largest freshwater lake in North America. Dine or just cruise and enjoy the sights and sounds of Lake Superior. Dinner, lunch, brunch or sightseeing cruises are available - narrated. Want to view the harbor aerial bridge online? Check out the Duluth Harbor Cam: http://vistafleet.com/view-our-harbor/

CHAOS WATERPARK & ACTION CITY
5150 Fairview Drive Eau Claire 54701

- Phone: (888) 861-6001 **www.metropolisresort.com**
- Hours: (Waterpark) When open, generally Noon-9:00pm. Please check the resort calendar for days and times of operation as hours may change. (Action City) Monday-Thursday 10:00am-9:00pm, Friday & Saturday 8:00am-11:00pm, Sunday 8:00am-9:00pm.
- Admission: Waterpark is included with overnight stays. (Action City) Prices are per attraction with prepaid Fun License, or unlimited packages are available. New Trampoline Park has many pricing package levels. 2 hr Tramp only is $20.00.

Chaos Waterpark is the world's only Comic Book Playground. Each zone is designed for different ages and play types. The park has 3 slides (one goes outside and has mood lighting), a lazy river and other water sports.

Action City has Laser tag, mini-golf, batting cages, a climbing wall, indoor bumper cars & go-carts and a super-sized arcade.

The METROPOLIS RESORT (adjacent) is a designer hotel where no two rooms are alike. Some rooms are super modern, others are old-fashioned. Some are just colorful and fun. Each morning from 6:00am-10:00am guests are greeted with a robust continental breakfast including, made-to-order eggs and omelets, hot waffles, cold cereal, bagels, jam & toast, fresh fruit, juice, yogurt, milk and soda. Overnight rates start at $149.00

EAU CLAIRE CHILDREN'S MUSEUM
126 N. Barstow St **Eau Claire** 54703

- ☐ Phone: (715) 832-5437 **www.childrensmuseumec.com**
- ☐ Hours: Monday-Saturday 10:00am-4:00pm
- ☐ Admission: $10.00 general admission

Eau Claire Children's Museum features a total of 24 exhibits and a brand-new early childcare and 4K preschool program open year-round. The building runs on 100% renewable energy and features a musical instruments room, a life-sized game bubble from the game "Trouble" and a climbing wall. Experience what life was like in an 1890s logging camp when you visit this authentic reproduction of camp in Carson Park.

EAU CLAIRE SCULPTURE TOUR
Eau Claire 54703

- ☐ **https://www.visiteauclaire.com/sculpture-tour/**
- ☐ Hours: Daily Daylight hours
- ☐ Admission: $10.00 general admission

What better way to get a taste of the local art scene than to walk along a free public art display? The Eau Claire Sculpture Tour is one of the largest sculpture tours in the nation with over 150 sculptures that you can view while strolling along these Midwest Indie streets. The tour features more than 70 sculptures and allows visitors to vote for their favorites to be crowned Sculpture of the Year. The winning sculpture gets to stay as new sculptures get installed every year. The route is lined with spots to stop for sweet treats, cold drinks and perfect patches for picnic blankets. There's a google map on the website or you can download a pdf map and print it off. Really cool idea!

PAUL BUNYAN LOGGING CAMP MUSEUM
1110 Half Moon Drive (look for Carson Park entrance and follow signs - next door to the Chippewa Valley Museum) **Eau Claire** 54703

- ☐ Phone: (715) 835-6200 **www.paulbunyancamp.org**
- ☐ Hours: Wednesday-Sunday Noon-5:00pm and Tuesdays 5:00-8:00pm (June-September).
- ☐ Admission: $12.00 adult, $10.00 senior, $5.00 child (up to age 17). Combo discounts available with Chippewa Valley Museum.

☐ Note: Baseball fans will want to take their picture at Hank Aaron's statue also located in Carson Park where he began his professional career.

Experience what life was like in an 1890s logging camp when you visit this authentic reproduction of camp in Carson Park. You can't miss it while driving through Carson Park thanks to the life-size statues of legendary lumber guy Paul Bunyan and his blue ox, Babe, standing out front. Paul Bunyan was the imaginary hero of the lumberjacks that felled the trees of the great North Woods of America. Begin your tour with a short film in the theatre. Then browse the exhibits depicting rugged camp life. Can't you just imagine the loggers sitting around a campfire in those cold winters weaving a tale or retelling the legends of Paul Bunyan? Kids of all ages will want to run to Paul's Tall Tales Room to play games and check out the interactive exhibits. Outside you'll find the replica of a camp complete with the giant logs, heavy equipment, a jammer and a blacksmith shop. Their gift shop has lots of goofy souvenirs but the kids may gravitate to a Bunyan and Babe storybook to read on the way home.

ST. PETER'S DOME

(Located in the Chequamagon-Nicolet National Forest) **Glidden** 54527

☐ **https://dnr.wisconsin.gov/topic/statenaturalareas/StPetersDome**

Have a hearty hiking family? The hike to St. Peter's Dome is 3.6 miles round trip. The trail has moderately steep climbs. Carrying drinking water is recommended. The trail to the dome becomes narrower as you walk across much steeper slopes. There is a lake sized beaver pond on your left. As you continue east, the trail drops in elevation and crosses a rocky stream bed. Beyond the stream the trail becomes steeper and rockier. After a short distance the grade becomes more gentle; you cross a snowmobile trail. At the base of the granite outcrop you will find a jumble of large broken rock from a quarry. The trail follows the old road for a hundred feet and then turns left off the road and begins to climb in earnest. Continue on the trail and climb to the overlook and shear drop on the north face of St. Peter's Dome. On a clear day, you can see Chequamegon Bay of Lake Superior and the Apostle Islands.

CREX MEADOWS WILDLIFE AREA
102 East Crex Avenue Grantsburg 54840

- ☐ Phone: (715) 463-CREX (2739) **www.crexmeadows.org**
- ☐ Hours: Visitor's Center - Weekdays 8:00am-4:30pm. Weekends 10:00am-4:00pm. (April-October).
- ☐ Tours: Printable 24-mile self-guided auto tour available on website. Guided tours available - The fee per person for tours depends on the length of the tour and the number of staff needed per group. These tours are dependent on staff availability. A wildlife biologist and interpretive naturalist also work with schools and youth groups. Please call (715) 463-2739 for more information.

Inside the Center you will find a "History of Crex Meadows" exhibit including museum-quality artifacts, two Blue-ray DVDs featuring Crex Meadows and its wildlife, a habitat diorama, a replica of a 1930's era hunting shack complete with items that would be found in a hunting shack, mounts of ducks, owls, and other wildlife that may be found in the area. Outside, there are many trails where you may just spot a number of endangered and threatened species. Crex has breeding populations of osprey, eagles, trumpeter swans, Karner blue butterflies, Blandings turtles, and red-necked grebes. Timber wolves have used the property on a regular basis in recent years and a pack has recently been designated the "Crex pack". Non resident endangered and threatened species include the peregrine falcon, common and Caspian tern, and great egret. We'd recommend bringing the kids for the Full Moon Series every month during the full moon. Along with revealing the science and folklore of moon phases, the indoor presentations will briefly describe seasonal changes of the flora and fauna at Crex Meadows. The group also goes outside for an exploration of the rising moon during a hike along the Crex Meadows Interpretive Trail, and end the evening by enjoying a full moon-related snack.

NATIONAL FRESH WATER FISHING HALL OF FAME & MUSEUM
10360 Hall of Fame Drive Hayward 54843

- ☐ Phone: (715) 634-4440 **www.freshwater-fishing.org**
- ☐ Hours: Daily 9:30am-4:30pm (June-August), Daily 9:30am until 4:00pm (mid-April, May, September, October). Last admittance 30 minutes prior to close.

- Admission: Nominal gate fee.
- Note: The grounds also include picnic areas, a fishing pond, and a series of colorful – but smaller – fiberglass fish perfect for photo ops with the kids - some you can make look like you've caught one big fish! FREEBIES: if you're a fishing fanatic, you might love their free page of icards - custom ecards you can send to fishing buddies you know.

There is so much to do here but, honestly the most memorable image that will stay with you is driving up and seeing the humongous muskie shaped building before you. *Hayward is the home of the largest muskie in the world*, a four-story replica that houses the Freshwater Fishing Hall of Fame surrounded by a delightful array of larger-than-life freshwater fish. The structure is one-half city block long and four and one-half stories tall, constructed of concrete, steel and fiberglass, hand sculpted into the likeness of a leaping muskellunge. Inside is the museum and its gaping open jaw is an observation platform. You and your family can actually climb inside all the way up to the fish's mouth!

The adjacent four-building museum complex displays fishing artifacts, housing an inventory of more than 50,000 vintage and historical lures, rods, reels and angling accessories. Additionally there are about 300 mounted fresh water fish and about 1,000 vintage outboard motors, including Evinrude's first production outboard from 1909.

DID YOU KNOW? The state fish is a muskellunge or "muskie."

SCHEER'S LUMBERJACK SHOWS & VILLAGE
(One mile south of Hayward on Hwy. B) **Hayward** 54843

- Phone: (715) 634-6923 **www.scheerslumberjackshow.com**
- Hours: Shows - Tuesday, Thursday, Saturday at 2:00pm, Occassional Mondays and Saturdays at 7:30pm (late June - late August). Other shows vary by season - visit website for details.
- Admission: $18.95 adult (12+), $14.95 senior, $12.95 child (4-11).
- Note: Shows travel and have locations throughout the state.

This family fun show features log rolling, chopping, sawing & climbing. Although the show is a bit cheesy with corny, predictable jokes, it is funny and fun to watch.

Lumberjack Village has the Hayward Arena, The Lake Café and eight specialty shops. The specialty at the café - pancakes, of course - every fine lumberjack lives on pancake breakfasts.

WILDERNESS WALK ZOO & RECREATION PARK

9503 North SR 27 (Hwy. 27 - 3 Miles South of Hayward) **Hayward** 54843

- ☐ Phone: (715) 634-2893 **https://www.wildernesswalkzoo.com/**
- ☐ Hours: Daily 10:00am-4:00pm, park closes at 5:00pm (Memorial Day weekend-Labor Day).
- ☐ Admission: $16.95 adult (12-65), $14.95 senior (65+), $11.95 child (2-11).

Wilderness Walk Zoo is a 35-acre animal farm and recreation park with wild and domestic animals, walking trails and a petting zoo. The children's petting zoo is plentiful and they allow several animals to roam free which is fun for the kids. The baby animal nursery is so fun...especially getting to feed them. They also have a Mystery House, Panning for Gold, a Farmyard and a maze activity. The price is higher than other small zoos in Wisconsin so be sure to plan to spend at least a few hours to get your money's worth.

HONOR THE EARTH POW-WOW

Hayward - *LCO Pow Wow grounds. The annual Lac Courte Oreilles Tribe celebration provides an opportunity to gain a greater appreciation of this Chippewa tribe's culture. Young Native American children, dressed in brightly colored traditional costumes and feathers, dance alongside their elders. This celebration also welcomes many other Native Wisconsin's American tribes and nations, speakers, sports, games, drumming, arts and crafts displays, and traditional Native American foods. (mid-July weekend)*

LUMBERJACK WORLD CHAMPIONSHIPS

Hayward - *Professional male and female lumberjacks and logrollers from around the world compete for the largest purse in lumberjack competition at this quintessential Wisconsin event. More than 12,000 spectators watch as participants compete in speed sawing, chopping events, pole climbing and logrolling. Saw-carving demonstrations add to the visual display, and spectators can get in on the fun by trying their hand at pole climbing and logrolling at the Paul Bunyan training camp. Admission.* **www. lumberjackworldchampionships.com** *(last long weekend in July)*

OCTAGON HOUSE & AMERICA'S FIRST KINDERGARTEN

919 Charles Street **Hudson (Watertown)** 53094

- ☐ Phone: (715) 386-2654 **https://www.octagonhousemuseum.org/first**
- ☐ Hours: Wednesday-Monday Noon-3pm (june-August). Weekends only (May, September-October).

☐   Admission: $10.00 adult, $5.00 student (6-17).

The first Kindergarten in the United States was opened in 1865 by Margarethe Meyer Schurz in the town of Watertown. German educator, Friedrich Frobel, is considered the founder of kindergarten in Europe around 1837. Mrs. Schurz was a pupil of Mr. Frobel. The home has five stories and visitors are treated to fully guided tours, hourly. Most kids comment about the cantilevered staircase as it rises 40 feet through the center of the home. Visitors to the Octagon House can also tour the First Kindergarten in America and the Plank Road Barn, both of which are located on the museum grounds.

WILLOW RIVER STATE PARK

1034 County Highway A (just W of Cty A, 4 miles NE of Hudson)
Hudson 54016

☐   Phone: (715) 386-5931   **http://dnr.wi.gov/topic/parks/name/willowriver/**
☐   Admission: A vehicle admission sticker is required. Daily $3.00-$11.00.
    Annual passes available.

Two dams, two lakes, a trout stream, sandy beach, prairie remnants, and a nature center are featured on 3,200 acres of rolling countryside. Spectacular views of the historic Willow Falls and the Willow River Gorge. The Nature Center, located near the main picnic area, features exhibits on animal and plant life, and park naturalists host many interpretive programs there throughout the year. A gift shop is in the Nature Center. Features 72 campsites, 19 electric sites, winter camping, showers, a dumping station, handicap- accessible picnic area and campsites, nature center, seasonal naturalist programs, vistas, shoreline with marked beach area, canoeing, boating, fishing, 1.6 miles of nature trails, 8.6 miles of hiking trails, 8 miles of cross- country ski trails. Open daily 6:00am-11:00pm with overnight camping.

HOT AIR AFFAIR

Hudson - *along St. Croix River. Come celebrate Hudson's spectacular winter ballooning event. Torchlight parade with kazoo marching bands on Friday in downtown historic Hudson. On Saturday, balloons light up the dark for approximately one hour, bring your camera. Other features include a marketplace and craft fair, pancake breakfast, smooshboarding, volleyball in the snow, dances and other winter activities. Some activities have a small fee.* **www.hudsonhotairaffair.com** *(first full weekend in February)*

MANITOWISH WATERS SKIING SKEETERS

Cty. Hwy. W (Rest Lake Park) **Manitowish Waters** 54545

- ☐ Phone: (715) 543-8488 **https://manitowishwaters.org/things-to-do/waterski-show-skiing-skeeters/**
- ☐ Hours: Wed & Saturday performances at 7:00pm (mid-June - late August).
- ☐ Admission: FREE. Donations collected from the shows help with the club's operating costs.

Free water ski shows performed by one of the oldest amateur ski clubs in the country. Did you know Manitowish is the "Barefoot Capital of the Midwest"? - barefoot skiing, that is. Bring a blanket or lawn chair for your comfort, or watch from your boat on Rest Lake.

PERKINSTOWN WINTER SPORTS AREA

N4168 Winter Sports Rd (Located just 16 miles west of Medford on Highway 64 then right (north) on FR 119 4.4 miles to the chalet) **Medford** 54451

- ☐ Phone: (715) 465-0118 **www.facebook.com/perkinstownwintersportsarea/**
- ☐ Hours & Admission: Saturday 11:00am-2:00pm for $8.00 and 2:00pm-5:00pm for $8.00 or all day pass for $13.00., Sunday 12:00pm-2:00pm for $6.00 and 2:00pm-4:00pm for $6.00 or all day pass is $9.00. Ski, snowshoe, and snowboard rentals available.

A very popular outdoor winter getaway spot for everyone offering downhill tubing with a rope tow and stairway and cross-country ski trails. The warming chalet is available for those who want to cozy up to the fireplace or satisfy their hunger with warm food and hot or cold beverages.

COPPER FALLS STATE PARK

36764 Copper Falls Road (2 miles northeast of Mellen in Ashland County) **Mellen** 54546

- ☐ Phone: (715) 274-5123 **http://dnr.wi.gov/topic/parks/name/copperfalls/**
- ☐ Hours: Daily 6:00am-11:00pm with overnight camping.
- ☐ Admission: Daily $8.00-$11.00.
- ☐ Nearby: Potato Falls: This is one of the most impressive waterfalls in all of Wisconsin, especially if you are looking for adventure. The waterfall is large, easy to find and provides all sorts of opportunities for exploration. Gurney is on Hwy 169, about 12 miles northeast of Copper Falls.

Ancient lava flows, deep gorges and spectacular waterfalls make Copper Falls one of Wisconsin's most scenic parks. The Doughboys' Trail has places for viewing the waterfalls. This 1.7-mile trail starts near the concession building and follows the Bad River and Tyler Forks around the scenic heart of the park, Copper and Brownstone Falls and the cascades. A half mile is accessible for people with disabilities. The part of the Doughboys' Trail west of the Bad River also is part of a loop trail that takes you to an observation tower, where you can get a panoramic view of the area. Try to come during high water seasons. Stone buildings from the 1930s Civilian Conservation Corps (CCC) add a special charm.

Features 55 campsites, 13 electric sites, winter camping, backpack camping, handicap- accessible picnic area and campsites, concessions, seasonal naturalist programs, lookout tower, vistas, shoreline with marked beach area, canoeing, boating, fishing, 1.7 miles of nature trails, 7 miles of hiking trails, 7 miles of off-road bicycle trails, 13.7 miles of cross- country ski trails.

CADDIE WOODLAWN HISTORICAL PARK WAYSIDE

Hwy 25 (9 miles south of town) **Menomonie** 54751

Phone: (715) 232-8685 **www.dunnhistory.org/sitecw.html**
Hours: Tuesday-Saturday 11:00am-5:00pm
Admission: $8.00 adult, $5.00 student, senior.

In 1857 John Woodhouse, with wife Harriet and five children, moved from Boston to Dunn County wilderness. One child was Caroline Augusta, who inspired "Caddie Woodlawn" in a book written by her granddaughter, Carol Ryrie Brink. The book is a classic and is read by children throughout the world. The house in which Caroline Woodhouse lived has been moved to the park from a nearby farm. The wayside includes a covered picnic area, fresh water, and restrooms. Open during daylight, Spring thru Fall.

CHIPPEWA MORAINE ICE AGE INTERPRETIVE CENTER

13394 County Highway M (7 miles east of New Auburn and 1.9 miles east of State Highway 40 on County Highway M) **New Auburn** 54757

- ☐ Phone: (715) 967-2800 **http://dnr.wi.gov/topic/parks/name/chipmoraine/**
- ☐ Admission: A vehicle admission sticker is required. Daily $3.00-$11.00.

Situated along the Ice Age Trail, visitors enjoy unspoiled beauty with kettle lakes and many glacial features. The interpretive center sits atop a hill that was once a glacial lake bottom. Display boards around the observation window explain the geology and topography of the trail. The interpretive center is generally open daily from 8:30am-4:30pm year-round. The park also features handicap- accessible picnic area, naturalist programs, vistas, shoreline, canoeing, boating nearby, fishing, 0.7 miles of nature trails, 6 miles of hiking trails. The park is open 6am-11pm year round.

OSCEOLA & ST. CROIX VALLEY RAILWAY

114 Depot Road **Osceola** 54020

- ☐ Phone: (715) 755 3570 **http://trainride.org**
- ☐ Hours: Weekends & Holidays (May-October). Various trips depending on season. See website or call for current schedule. Wed & Sat 10am-4pm.
- ☐ Admission: Wednesday $13 adult, $11 senior (62+), $10 child (5-15), $8 toddler (2-4), $35 family. Saturday $16 adult, $13 senior (62+), $11 child (5-15), $8 toddler (2-4), $50 family.

Ten and twenty-mile excursions along the sandstone bluffs of the St. Croix River aboard a diesel-powered train with vintage cars. Travel along the sandstone bluffs of the St. Croix River valley, cross over the Cedar Bend Draw Bridge, journey through William O'Brien State Park and on to Marine on the St. Croix, Minnesota. At Marine, the engine will do a run around and bring you back to Osceola. While onboard, visit the postal clerk in the mail car to learn how mail was caught "on the fly" and be sure to visit the concession car where you can purchase a railroad trinket, soda or snack.

WISCONSIN CONCRETE PARK

N8236 South Hwy 13 (State Route 13 South) **Phillips** 54555

- Phone: (715) 339-6371 **www.friendsoffredsmith.org**
- Hours: Open to the public year round during daylight hours.
- Admission: FREE, donations for site preservation are accepted.
- Tours: Self-guided tour brochures are available on site for a donation.

Not hard to find - just look for cement - lots of cement. More than 200 concrete statues of cowboys and Indians or animals were created by the late Fred Smith, a retired logger. In retirement, Smith began sculpting to occupy his time. Smith's whimsical creations are one of the largest outdoor collections of sculpture. Although concrete itself is pretty bland, Fred added color using pieces of broken glass. Kids like the dogs and dinos. The site is recognized as a folk art masterwork.

GREAT RIVER ROAD VISITOR CENTER

200 Monroe Street, Freedom Park **Prescott** 54021

- Phone: (715) 262-0104 **www.freedomparkwi.org**
- Hours: Monday-Saturday 10:00am-6:00pm, Sunday Noon-6:00pm (Memorial Day - Labor Day). Closes at 5:00pm Spring & Fall, and 4:00pm Winter.
- Admission: FREE
- Educators: A Learning Center is located here with programs on biodiversity and environmental sustainability related to the Mississippi River watershed. Topics are age appropriate. Click on: For Educators for more info.

The Visitor Center is a fabulous introduction to the Upper Mississippi region using interactive exhibits, satellite maps, even an animated eagle to educate and fascinate. Visitors discover and enjoy the unique stories of this region through hands-on, audio-visual exhibits in the Center. From Dakota people who lived along the river's confluence for centuries to steamboats to fishermen and boat builders. Children of all ages can enjoy the fun playground just outside the Center's doors. Take the walking path along the bluffs and picnic while you overlook the line where the blue waters of the St. Croix join the dun-colored Mississippi.

RED BARN SUMMER THEATRE

2247 22nd Street [2 Miles NE of Rice Lake at the corner of Hwy 48 and
County M (22nd Street)] **Rice Lake** 54868

- ☐ Phone: (715) 234-8301 or (888) 686-3770
  www.redbarntheatre-ricelake.com
- ☐ Hours: Call or see website for current season of performances. (late May -
  August). Showtime 7:30pm.
- ☐ Admission: $20.00 tickets.

Summer stock local community theatre with classic tales, family comedies
and modern twists.

KINNICKINNIC STATE PARK

W11983 820th Ave. (8-1/2 miles S of I-94, 7 miles west of town)
River Falls 54022

- ☐ Phone: (715) 425-1129 **http://dnr.wi.gov/topic/parks/name/kinnickinnic/**
- ☐ Admission: A vehicle admission sticker is required. Daily $3.00-$11.00.
  Annual passes available.

Day-use 1,242-acre park featuring a 70-acre sand delta in the St. Croix River.
Boating, fishing, swimming along the beach and hiking. Open 6:00am-
11:00pm with no overnight camping.

MUSEUM OF WOODCARVING

539 Highway 63 (one half mile north of town) **Shell Lake** 54871

- ☐ Phone: (715) 468-7100
- ☐ Hours: usually open daily 9:00am-6:00pm (May-October).

We've all seen paintings and maybe figurines of the Last Supper but have
you ever seen it in full-size wood carving? Here, you will, along with Daniel
and the Lions Den and others that make you feel like you're walking through
a wooden Bible! Years ago, Joseph Barta created the largest collection of
woodcarvings in the world (created by one man) - 100 life-sized carvings
and another 400 miniatures. Barta spent 15 years crafting the works from
laminated pine. The scenes are stark but effective as the gestures of the
characters reveal their intent - and all of the dioramas are pulled from stories
in the Bible. Barta claimed, "God told me to do it." Small admission.

GOVERNOR THOMPSON STATE FISH HATCHERY

951 W. Maple **Spooner** 54801

- Phone: (715) 635-4147 **www.dnr.wi.gov/topic/fishing/hatcheries/ govthompson.html**
- Hours: The visitor center is open from 8:00am-3:00pm on workdays, daily each spring busy season.
- Tours: Groups can arrange tours (min. 8) ahead of time, depending on work schedule. Summer Tuesdays & Fridays at 10am and 2pm.

This is the home of the largest muskie-rearing hatchery in the world! Also, walleye & northern. With 46 rearing ponds it has the capacity to produce 1.5 to 2 million small walleye fingerlings, 100,000 6" walleye fingerlings and 100,000 8"-10" muskie fingerlings. Browse the Visitors Center which has interactive learning stations that are informational and fun for the kids; then have a picnic at The Veteran's Memorial Park while you and your kids wet a line from the handicapped accessible fishing pier at the Yellow River Flowage. In addition, there's a boat launch, bathroom facilities and parking area. Come in and look around on your own or arrange for a guided tour. Did you ever imagine there could be so much science to raising fish?

WISCONSIN GREAT NORTHERN RAILROAD

426 North Front Street **Spooner** 54801

- Phone: (715) 635-3200 **www.spoonertrainride.com**
- Hours & Admission: Tours run Tuesday-Sunday (July-August). Friday-Sunday (May, June, September, October, late November - middle December). Special events trains also. See website for departure times and fares, $27.00-$35.00.
- Tours: Be sure to arrive at least 30 minutes prior to your departure time.
- Note: Thanksgiving and Christmas themed trains.

Tour a 15-mile stretch of the old Chicago & Northwestern track between Spooner and Springbrook, laid more than 100 years ago. Historic diesel locomotives plus vintage Pullman passenger cars take you on the 1.5 to 2.5 hour trips. This family oriented attraction combines historic railroad equipment with exciting special events to entertain and educate all age groups.

Next door is the RAILROAD MEMORIES MUSEUM - Housed in the former Chicago & Northwestern Depot, the museum contains an outstanding collection of vintage railroading memorabilia from around the nation. It is staffed by volunteers, including the retired railroaders who lead guided tours through the old depot's 12 history-packed rooms.

HEART OF THE NORTH RODEO

Spooner - 15,000 spectators are expected to enjoy the excitement of professional rodeo performances, which feature saddle and bareback bronco riding, tie-down roping, steer wrestling, bull riding and barrel racing. Live music follows evening performances. The weekend's events include a parade, barbecue and cowboy church service. Tickets available online. **www.spoonerrodeo.com** *(weekend after July 4th)*

CRYSTAL CAVE

W965 State Road 29 (just west of the village, on the south side of Highway 29)
Spring Valley 54767

- ☐ Phone: (800) 236-CAVE **www.acoolcave.com**
- ☐ Hours: Daily 9:30am-5:30pm (Memorial Day-Labor Day), Weekends 10:00am-4:30pm (April & May), Daily 10:00am-4:30pm (September-October).
- ☐ Admission: $21.98 adult, $14.98 child (3-12).
- ☐ Tours: Tours leave often throughout the day and the last tour leaves 15 minutes before closing. Baby front packs are allowed, back carriers are not.
- ☐ Educators: cave lesson plans - **http://acoolcave.com/lesson.html**.

The longest cave in Wisconsin, this will delight the entire family with its multiple level, hundreds of stalactites and stalagmites and labyrinth passageways. There are friendly cave bats, too. The cave is accessed by a series of steps and ramps that allow you to descend over 70 feet underground where your journey follows well-lit, graveled trails. The cave temperature hovers near 50 degrees. A sweatshirt is recommended. Above ground, you can take the self-guided nature trail or purchase the gem panning activity. The Sinkhole Nature Trail is a 20-30 minute walk over gentle slopes shaded under a swaying canopy of leaves. Along the trail you will find numerous signs with information regarding the many types of trees you will find.

DID YOU KNOW? This cave was discovered in 1881 by a teenage boy.

FAWN-DOE-ROSA ANIMAL PARK

2131 Hwy 8 **St. Croix Falls** 54024

- ☐ Phone: (715) 483-3772 **www.fawndoerosa.com**
- ☐ Hours: Monday-Friday 10:00am to 5:00pm (mid-May - Labor Day). Weekends 10:00am to 5:00pm (September/October).
- ☐ Admission: $10.50 adult, $9.50 child (2-12). Pony rides $5/child.

This animal park is really designed for education. They have petting and feeding areas, pony rides, bears and other forest animals, and farm animals. Walk through the wooded park and take time to enjoy the animals. The deer are a big hit when they come up and eat out of your hand. Don't worry, many of the animals you encounter have been hand-raised by park employees. Fawn-Doe-Rosa has a release program where they try to return animals back to their natural homes. However, some animals are unable to be released. These animals become members of the Fawn-Doe-Rosa family. Because it's costly to care for these disabled animals, try to make a half-day of it to get your money's worth - or, just know you're contributing to your favorite animal's care.

INTERSTATE STATE PARK

851 S State Road 35 **St. Croix Falls** 54024

- ☐ Phone: (715) 483-3747
  http://dnr.wi.gov/topic/parks/name/interstate/
- ☐ Admission: A vehicle admission sticker is required. Daily $8.00-$11.00. Annual passes available.

A deep gorge called the "Dalles of the St Croix" is the scenic focus of this - Wisconsin's oldest - state park. The Ice Age Interpretive Center includes photographs, murals and other information about the great glaciers. The park is actually two parks with 1,330 acres on the Wisconsin side of the river, and 298 acres on the Minnesota side. In addition to being Wisconsin first state park, it is also the nation's first interstate park. The park's geological heritage is so important, it is one of just nine units included in the Ice Age National Scientific Reserve. Tours are held in the summer, with the rangers providing plenty of background on this geological phenomena. The park also offers 85 family campsites, a swimming beach, boat launch, and ten miles of hiking trails with spectacular views from the bluffs.

ST. CROIX NATIONAL SCENIC RIVERWAY CTR

401 North Hamilton Street **St. Croix Falls** 54025

- ☐ Phone: (715) 483-2274 **www.nps.gov/sacn**
- ☐ Hours: Visitors Center - Daily 9:00am-5:00pm (April-October).
- ☐ Admission: FREE. There are fees to enter the adjoining state parks. They require a day pass or a yearly state park sticker.
- ☐ Educators: Curriculum called "Rivers Are Alive" is available as a download on the FOR TEACHERS page, then Curriculum Materials.

The riverway traces the wild St. Croix and Namekagon Rivers for more than 250 miles. Staff will help plan river trips. Beginning as small intimate streams, both the St. Croix and Namekagon Rivers are ideal for canoeing. Easy, Class I, rapids encourage both beginning and novice canoeists to get out and explore. River descriptions can help you decide what stretch to canoe. Touch tables or interactive activities and children's books are available at visitor centers. The rivers provide lots of things to see and areas to explore. Keep your eyes wide open.

AMNICON FALLS STATE PARK

County Highway U (1/3 mile north of US 2) **Superior** 54880

- ☐ Phone: (715) 398-3000 **http://dnr.wi.gov/topic/parks/name/amnicon/**
- ☐ Admission: A vehicle admission sticker is required. Daily $8.00-$11.00.

Amnicon Falls features a series of delightful waterfalls and rapids along the Amnicon River, viewed from a covered footbridge. The park is a place to picnic, camp, walk in the woods, and learn about the Douglas Fault, the geological formation that created the falls. Open May 1 through the first week of October, the park features 36 campsites, handicap- accessible picnic area and campsites, fishing, 0.8 miles of nature trails, 1 mile of hiking trails, and 1 mile of snowmobile trails. On the park trails, you may encounter porcupine, beaver, mink or otter. Tracks, feeding signs, dens, sounds, and other evidence will tell you of an animal's presence even if you don't see it.

PATTISON STATE PARK

6294 S. State Road 35 (16 miles S of US 53/ I-535 and US 61/ I-35, 13 miles E of Superior) **Superior** 54880

- ☐ Phone: (715) 399-3111 **http://dnr.wi.gov/topic/parks/name/pattison/**

☐   Admission: A vehicle admission sticker is required. Daily $8.00-$11.00. Annual passes available.

Pattison is one of Wisconsin's cornerstone parks, with 165-foot Manitou Falls, the highest waterfall in Wisconsin. A pedestrian tunnel takes you from the park's main picnic area under Highway 35 to short trails that give you many views Big Manitou Falls from both sides of the river. Little Manitou Falls are south about a mile on the highway or 1.5 miles on the Nature Trail and Little Manitou Falls Trail. In the Ojibwa language, the Black River is called Mucudewa Sebee, meaning "black" or "dark." The root beer tint of the water (yes, kids think it looks like rootbeer falls) comes from decaying leaves and roots of vegetation along the river. Features 59 campsites, 18 electric sites, backpack camping, handicap- accessible picnic area and campsites, nature center, seasonal naturalist programs, vistas, shoreline with marked beach area, canoeing, boating, fishing, 2 miles of nature trails, 6.1 miles of hiking trails, 4.5 miles of cross- country ski trails. The Gitche Gumee Nature Center in the shelter building houses interpretive displays about the park's colorful history, abundant wildlife, and unique geology. Note: Most trails are paved and have stairs. Sturdy shoes are recommended. Cliffs are steep and somewhat fenced.

RICHARD I. BONG VETERANS HISTORICAL CENTER

305 Harbor View Parkway **Superior** 54880

☐   Phone: (715) 392-7151 or (888) 816-9944 https://www.bongcenter.org/
☐   Hours: Monday-Saturday 9:00am-5:00pm, Sunday Noon-5:00pm (May - October). Tuesday-Saturday 9:00am-5:00pm (rest of year).
☐   Admission: $10.00 adult, $8.00 senior (65+) & student (12-17), $7.00 child (6-11). Guided tours double price.

Richard Bong was the United States highest scoring ace in the air, having shot down 40 Japanese aircraft during WWII. Bong, the son of Swedish immigrant parents, grew up on a farm in Poplar, Wisconsin as one of nine children. He became interested in aircraft at an early age and was a keen model builder. Housed in a structure intended to resemble an aircraft hangar, it contains a museum, a film screening room, and a P-38 Lightning restored to resemble Bong's plane. Divide into squadrons and test your skills using their Squad Training scavenger hunt.

SS METEOR MUSEUM

(Barker's Island) **Superior** 54880

- Phone: (715) 394-5712 **www.superiorpublicmuseums.org**
- Hours: Monday-Saturday 10:00am-4:00pm & Sunday 11:00am-4:00pm. (mid-May - August). Thursday-Saturday 10:00am-4:00pm & Sunday 11:00am-4:00pm. (September - mid-October).
- Admission: Tours - $12.00 adult, $10.00 senior & $6.00 student (6-17), age 5 and under FREE. Exhibit area only - $5.00.
- Tours: Guided tours available daily on the hour, last tour departs at 4:00pm.

The S.S. Meteor is the last remaining of these innovative ships on the Great Lakes (called whalebacks for their rounded hulls). Launched from Superior in 1896, she carried a variety of cargos on the Great Lakes, including iron ore, grain, cars, and oil. Hear the ship's whistle and see the original 1896 steam engine as you tour from pilot house to cargo holds. The Museum also features exhibits on Twin Ports shipbuilding history and Great Lakes shipwrecks.

TAYLOR FALLS PRINCESS

(directly across the St. Croix River in Minnesota) (Entrance near only stoplight in town look for boat parking lot) **Taylors Falls, MN** 55084

- Phone: (651) 465-6315 or (800) 447-4958 **www.taylorsfallsboat.com**
- Hours: Sightseeing Tours: Daily @ 1:00pm & 3pm, also Saturday & Sunday @ 11am (May-October).
- Admission: ~$30 adult, ~$17 child (3-12).
- Tours: 80 minute narrated trip. The 5:00pm trip is 30 minutes and offered at a discounted ticket price. Other tours are available.

On the Minnesota side of Interstate Park, you can board the Taylor Falls Princess for sightseeing, lunch and dinner cruises along this remarkable stretch of the river. The cruises pass all the park's popular rock formations including Holy Cross (for which the river is named"St. Croix") and The Old Man of the Dalles, the most outstanding natural rock face you'll ever see.

WILD MOUNTAIN RECREATION PARK

37200 Wild Mountain Road (directly across the St. Croix River in Minnesota - entrance off CR 16) **Taylors Falls, MN** 55084

☐   Phone: (651) 465-6315 or (800) 447-4958 **www.wildmountain.com**

Summertime is water fun with waterpark slides, chair lift rides to the top, and an Alpine Slide down the mountainside. Taylors Falls Scenic Boat Tours, too. With free parking and being able to bring in your cooler full of treats and beverages, the day trip to the park doesn't break the bank. Wintertime - it's the ski & snowboard slopes plus the wild chutes for snow tubing. They also have go-carts, an RV park and campground for warm weather recreation. Rates and hours vary daily so go to their updated website for details. $26.00 start.

CADY CHEESE FACTORY

126 Hwy 128 (I-94 exit 28 south) **Wilson** 54027

Phone: (715) 772-4218 **www.cadycheese.com**
Hours: Store open daily 9:00am-5:00pm.
Educators: look up the link: www.moomilk.com for Teacher's Resources & games.

With specialties of different varieties and flavors of Longhorn cheese, this retail outlet offers prearranged tours and an observation window. One step is different than other cheese factories you'll visit - the special tube presses used to create cylindrical longhorn cheese. After you've looked around, mosey on up to the "cheese bar" to sample some fresh product.

DID YOU KNOW? It takes 100 pounds of milk to make 10 pounds of cheese.

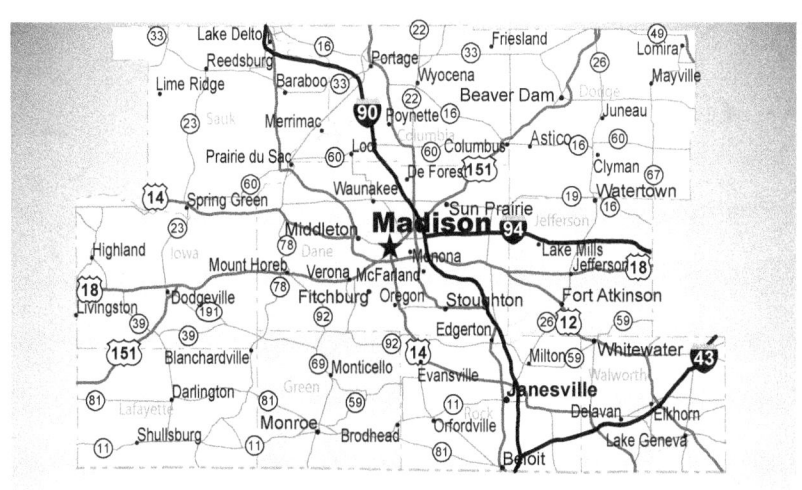

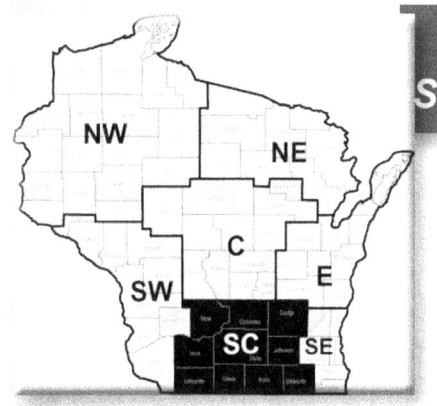

Chapter 5
South Central (SC)

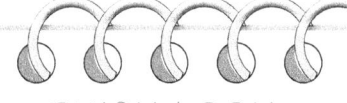

QUICK LOOK...

Circus World & House on the Rock

Nature Centers: Cats, Cranes, Geese

Capitol City and Swiss History

Wisconsin Dells Waterparks

Food Factories & Farms

Arena
- Arena Cheese

Ashippun
- Honey Acres Honey Of A Museum

Baraboo
- Circus World Museum
- Devil's Lake State Park
- Int'l Crane Foundation
- Jayar's
- Leopold Zero Energy Center, Shack And Farm
- Mirror Lake State Park

Baraboo (North Freedom)
- Mid-Continent RR Museum

Belmont
- First State Capitol Hist'l Site

Beloit
- Beckman Mill

Beloit (Brodhead)
- Decatur Dairy

Blue Mounds
- Blue Mound State Park
- Cave Of The Mounds

Browntown
- Browntown-Cadiz Springs State Recreation Area

Cambridge
- Hinchley Dairy Farm

Deerfield
- Schusters Playtime Farm

Dodgeville
- Governor Dodge State Park

Fort Atkinson
- Fireside Dinner Theatre
- Hoard Historical Museum

Horicon
- Horicon Marsh Boat Tours
- Horicon Marsh International Education Center
- Horicon Marsh Wildlife Refuge

Janesville
- Rock Aqua Jays Waterski
- Southern Wisconsin Airfest
- Wisconsin Wagon Company

Janesville (Milton)
- Milton House Museum

La Valle
- Carr Valley Cheese

Lake Geneva
- Big Foot Beach State Park
- Geneva Lake Cruise Line
- Timber Ridge Lodge & Waterpark @ Grand Geneva
- Winterfest & National Snow Sculpting Championships

Lake Mills
- Aztalan State Park

Leland
- Natural Bridge State Park

Madison
- Capitol Building Of Wisconsin & Downtown Exploring
- Crawdaddy Cove Water Park In The Holiday Inn Hotel
- Henry Vilas Zoo
- Madison City Ski Team
- Madison Children's Museum
- Madison Museum Of Contemporary Art
- Olbrich Botanical Gardens
- Old Fashioned Tavern & Restaurant
- Overture Center For The Arts
- University Of Wisconsin - Geology Museum
- University Of Wisconsin Campus Tours
- Vitense Golfland
- Wisconsin Book Festival
- Wisconsin Historical Museum
- Wisconsin Veterans Museum

Madison (Fitchburg)
- Eplegaarden

Madison (Middleton)
- Hubbard Avenue Diner
- National Mustard Museum

Marshall
- Little A-Merrick-A Amusement

Merrimac
- Merrimac Ferry

Monroe
- National Historic Cheesemaking Center

Mount Horeb
- Mount Horeb Trollway

New Glarus
- Chalet Landhaus Inn
- Heidi Festival
- New Glarus Woods State Park
- Swiss Hist'l Village Museum
- Wilhelm Tell Festival

Plain
- Cedar Grove Cheese Factory

Portage
- Cascade Mountain
- Fort Winnebago Surgeon's Quarters

Poynette
- Mackenzie Environmental Education Center

Rock Springs
- Wisconsin Big Cat Rescue & Educational Center

Shullsburg
- Badger Mine And Museum
- Roelli Cheese Haus

Spring Green
- House On The Rock - The Attraction
- Tower Hill State Park

Stoughton
- Lake Kegonsa State Park
- Syttende Mai

Sun Prairie
- Market Street Diner

Theresa
- Widmer's Cheese Cellars

Waterloo
- Trek Bicycles Factory Tour

Waunakee
- Governor Nelson State Park

Wisconsin Dells
- Autumn Harvest Fest
- Big Foot Zipline
- Buffalo Phil's Grille
- Chula Vista Resort Lost Rios Indoor Waterpark
- Dells Boat Tours
- Dells Raceway Park
- Effigy Mounds
- Great Wolf Lodge
- Kalahari Waterpark Resort
- Kiddie Indoor Waterparks
- Noah's Ark Waterpark
- Original Wisconsin Ducks
- Paul Bunyan Cook Shanty
- Pirate's Cove Adventure Golf
- Polynesian Waterpark Resort
- Ripley's Believe It Or Not Museum
- Riverside & Great Northern Railway
- Riverview Park & Waterworld
- Rocky Arbor State Park
- Timbavati Wildlife Park AT Storybook Gardens
- Timber Falls Adventure Park
- Tommy Bartlett's Exploratory Interactive Science Center
- Wilderness Resort Complex
- Wisconsin Deer Park
- Wisconsin Dells Campgrounds
- Wisconsin Dells Go Carting
- Wisconsin Dells Music & Theatre

Sites and attractions are listed in order by City, Zip Code, and Name. Symbols indicated represent: 🍽 Restaurants ⬛ Lodging

ARENA CHEESE

300 US Hwy 14 **Arena** 53503

- ☐ Phone: (608) 753-2501 **www.arenacheese.com**
- ☐ Hours: Daily 8:15am-5:00pm.

Arena Cheese is the home of the original Co-Jack Cheese and is easily recognized by the mouse in front of the cheese and gift store. The retail storefront provides a viewing area so you can watch an artesian cheese maker making different varieties of cheeses. Samples of various cheeses are available for tasting. Don't forget to take home fresh "squeaky" cheese curds made daily. Bus tour groups are always welcome and a narrative of the cheese making process is available with an advance notice.

HONEY ACRES HONEY OF A MUSEUM

N 1557 Hwy 67 (2 miles north of town on Highway 67) **Ashippun (Neoshol)** 53059

- ☐ Phone: (800) 558-7745 **https://honeyacres.com/pages/museum**
- ☐ Hours: Monday-Friday 8:00am-3:30pm. Also open Saturday 10am-4:00pm (June-August).
- ☐ Admission: FREE.
- ☐ Note: there's a nature walk around the property.

Christian Diehnelt moved his family from Germany to Wisconsin in 1852. He brought with him the talent and love of beekeeping that would become the foundation for a honey company that has survived to this day. In the museum you'll witness a live bee tree and watch a 20-minute video about beekeeping. What is the science of bees, pollination and all that bees wax? This 40-acre farm now produces a huge variety of products including: gourmet honey, honey cremes, honey mustards and honey candy. They usually have honey samples (yes, there are different flavors of honey) to try.

CIRCUS WORLD MUSEUM

550 Water St (WI-113) **Baraboo** 53913

- Phone: (608) 356-8341 **www.circusworldbaraboo.org**
- Hours: Open during summer performance season Daily 9:00am-6:00pm. (late May thru late August). Spring/Fall season open weekdays but no performances, 10am-4pm.
- Admission: Performances. $23.00 adult, $20.00 senior (65+), $15.00 child (5-12). Fall/spring season: $5.00-$10.00 per person (age 5+).
- Note: Just like a real circus, The Cookhouse Grill has the traditional cotton candy, hot dogs, popcorn, and sno cones you love while the Ringlingville General Store has candy and some snacks plus a large selection of circus-themed gifts and souvenirs.

Run away and explore the circus – the Greatest Show on Earth. Wisconsin nurtured some of the best known acts under the Big Top, including the seven brothers who created the Ringling Brothers Circus in 1884 in Baraboo. The Circus World Museum preserves the legacy of The Ringling Brothers, with the real stars today being the world's largest collection of antique restored circus wagons and amazing circus posters. But kids really want to see action so you'll spend most of your time watching small acts perform unnatural feats in the Hippodrome or tigers and elephants performing in Circus Animals. Do your kids want to get into the act? Kids create their own circus performance at KidsWorld Circus. Presented twice each day, this popular children's program (held in the original Elephant House) allows kids to learn some tricks and showmanship to be stars of their very own circus.

Before you leave, be sure to get some unique photo ops - like a picture taken inside a gorilla cage.

DEVIL'S LAKE STATE PARK

S5975 Park Rd. (2 miles south of Baraboo) **Baraboo** 53913

- Phone: (608) 356-8301
  http://dnr.wi.gov/topic/parks/name/devilslake/
- Hours: Daily 6:00am-11:00pm. Visitor Center hours: Daily 8:00am-11:00pm (summer) and 8:00am-4:00pm (rest of year).
- Admission: A vehicle admission sticker is required. Daily $8.00-$11.00. Annual passes available.
- Note: This park has Forests Forever ParkPacks to borrow (they include activities, books and fun worksheets).

Devil's Lake State Park is a geologic gem. Created by the glaciers, the park's spring-fed lake is surrounded on three sides by 500-foot high bluffs. One of the biggest draws in this part of the state is the Ice Age National Scenic Trail at Devil's Lake State Park. The Ice Age Trail is part of a 1,000-mile long footpath marking the furthest advance of the last glacier in Wisconsin. The park also offers: swimming areas including 2 large sandy beaches, hundreds of campsites, mountain bike trails, cross country ski trails, great climbs and so much more. Peak visitation is during the late spring, summer and fall, when visitors can swim in or boat on the clear, 360-acre spring-fed lake, hike or bike on over 29 miles of park trails.

Stop in at the Nature Center, near the North Shore entrance road. A three-dimensional landform model of the park will bring the park terrain into sight from a bird's-eye view. A series of panoramas make clear the formation of the valley, once 1,000 feet deep, now half-filled with rock and sediment and topped by the 50-foot-deep Devil's Lake. Children will enjoy the kid's exploration room with quizzes, activities, and mystery boxes of hidden touchy-feely items. Nature Center hours are 9:00am-4:30pm daily in season. Starting mid-October, the Nature Center is closed most days.

INTERNATIONAL CRANE FOUNDATION

E11376 Shady Lane Road (5 miles north of Baraboo on Highway 12)
Baraboo 53913

- ☐ Phone: (608) 356-9462 **www.savingcranes.org**
- ☐ Hours: Daily 9:00am-5:00pm (May - October).
- ☐ Admission: $12.50 adult, $10.00 seniors (65+), $6.00 youth (6-17).
- ☐ Tours: Self guided tours are no charge. Various tour themes and times. All tours begin with an introduction to the history of the International Crane Foundation and multimedia presentation. Guided tours usually last 1-2 hours.

Cranes are the oldest living family of birds on earth and a cultural symbol of fidelity. However, they are also the most endangered species of bird. The world-renowned International Crane Foundation research and refuge facility in Baraboo is the only place in the world where visitors can see all 15 species of cranes. Established in 1973 by two Cornell University graduate students – George Archibald and Ron Sauey – on a farm owned by Sauey's parents, the center is credited for guaranteeing the future of these lovely and rare creatures for future generations. The owners once got lots of news coverage when their staff dressed in crane costumes to help in the reintroduction process of whooping cranes. We'd recommend one of these tours:

- CRANES OF THE WORLD TOUR - (Memorial Day - Labor Day): Daily at 10:00am and 1:00pm (April, May, September and October): Saturday and Sunday at 10:00am and 1:00pm. Featuring all 15 of the world's cranes, the ecosystems they depend on and the conservation projects ICF is leading around the world. See the Whooping crane - the rarest crane on the planet - in a natural Wisconsin wetland from covered theater seating.

- SPIRIT OF AFRICA TOUR - (Memorial Day - Labor Day): Daily at 3:00pm. (April, May, September and October): Saturday and Sunday at 3:00pm. View Africa's fascinating cranes in naturalistic wetland settings. This tour highlights ICF's conservation solutions to protect and restore ecosystems shared by the people and cranes of Africa, including four year-round and two migratory species.

LEOPOLD ZERO ENERGY CENTER, SHACK AND FARM

E13701 Levee Road (15 minutes northeast of Baraboo in Fairfield Twp)
Baraboo 53913

- Phone: (608) 355-0279 **www.aldoleopold.org/Visit/Tours.shtml**
- Hours: Monday-Saturday, 10:00am-4:30pm (May- late October).
- Admission: Varies depending on activity.
- Tours: Basic self-guided tours are $10.00. Guided tours (on Saturdays) are $15.00 adult, $10.00 senior (62+) and child (11-17), FREE (10 or under). Reservations recommended.
- Note: The 300 yard dirt driveway leading to the Shack itself is accessible by wheelchair, but the rest of the trails are not. Tour routes follow rustic trails which may have occasional obstacles such as tree stumps, exposed roots, or downed branches.

Exhibits and signs in the building interpret Aldo Leopold's history and legacy, and the green building techniques applied throughout the facility. Education staff will provide guided tours but, honestly most kids won't last long. We suggest self-guided tours. If there's enough interest, plan to come back for a guided tour. Often at places like this, we just listen in for tidbits from a guided tour walking near us.

Basic Self-Guided Tours - You can also watch two short welcome videos that give a nice overview of Leopold's history, life, and legacy. The most "green" members of your party may want to rent the mp3 42-minute audio tour. There is no charge for basic self-guided tours of the Leopold Center. Self-guided tours of the Shack are permitted from May through October, during public open hours. Self-guided visitors explore the site with a brochure that includes a trail map, historic photos of the land, and background information on Aldo Leopold's history and legacy. The trail loop at the property is approximately one mile in length. A side trail leads to the banks of the Wisconsin River through beautiful floodplain forest, where bald eagles, cranes, and other wildlife are frequently spotted. The Shack itself is shuttered and locked during self-guided tours.

MIRROR LAKE STATE PARK

E 10320 Fern Dell Rd (1-1/2 miles W of US 12, 3 miles SW of Lake Delton)
Baraboo 53913

☐   Phone: (608) 254-2333
     http://dnr.wi.gov/topic/parks/name/mirrorlake/
☐   Admission: A vehicle admission sticker is required. Daily $8.00-$11.00.
     Annual passes available.

A picturesque lake surrounded by sandstone bluffs. Wooded campsites and boat, bike and canoe rentals make this an ideal spot for a weekend vacation. Features 147 campsites, cabin for people with disabilities, 28 electric sites, winter camping, handicap- accessible picnic area and campsites, concessions, seasonal naturalist programs, shoreline with marked beach area, canoeing, boating, fishing, 1.2 miles of nature trails, 19.5 miles of hiking trails, 9.2 miles of off-road bicycle trails (State Trail Pass required), 17.8 miles of cross-country ski trails. In February, the state parks' cross-country ski trails are lighted by thousands of candles for night time light. Open daily 6:00am-11:00pm with overnight camping.

MID-CONTINENT RAILWAY MUSEUM

E8948 Diamond Hill Road **Baraboo (North Freedom)** 53951

☐   Phone: (608) 522-4261 or (800) 930-1385 **www.midcontinent.org**
☐   Hours: Museum grounds open 9:30am-5:00pm when train is running.
     Daily train departures at 11:00am, 1:00pm, and 3:00pm. (late May - early

September). Weekends only early - late May & mid-September - late October).

- [ ] Admission: Fares $24.00 adult, $22.00 senior (62+), $13.00 child (3-15). Train fare includes admission to museum grounds and displays in the depot and the coach shed.
- [ ] Note: All trains are diesel powered. Picnic area and vending machine beverages. FREEBIES: they have a great Kids Page full of online and printable games, coloring and picture books for kids.

Mid-Continent is an outdoor living history museum and operating railroad where visitors can take a seven-mile, 50-minute round-trip ride on a former branch line of the Chicago & North Western Railway through the scenic Baraboo Hills. Restored coaches dating back from 1915 depart from an historic wooden depot built in 1894. The train ride is on the same historical tracks that were laid 100 years ago from North Freedom to the Iron Mines in LaRue. The journey is through some scenic areas and you stop in LaRue and disembark and watch as they switch the engine around to head back (usually kids favorite part).

SNOW TRAIN

Baraboo (North Freedom) - Mid-Continent Railway Museum. Mid-Continent's oldest special event. Travel through the winter wonderland of the scenic Baraboo Hills on the 35th annual Snow Train. All cars are kept comfortably warm using the 100-yr-old tradition of steam heating or coal-fired stoves. First class dining services are available; reservations requested. Admission. (second weekend in February)

FIRST STATE CAPITOL HISTORICAL SITE

19101 County Highway G (on CR-G, near the city of Belmont and US-151)
Belmont 53510

- [ ] Phone: (608) 987-2122 **http://firstcapitol.wisconsinhistory.org/**
- [ ] Hours: Friday-Sunday 10:00am-4:00pm (late May - early September).
- [ ] Admission: FREE.
- [ ] Educators: Printable activity packets (pdf format-questions focused on discussion and writing) are available.

This 1836 Capitol of the Wisconsin Territory formed the rugged origins of the first framework of law and order in this region. Legislatures met from October 25 to December 9, 1836, put 42 laws on the books, established a judicial system, called for roads and railroads, and, most significantly, established Madison as the permanent capital city.

In the Council House guests examine the first laws, discuss the fight for the capitol, and learn about early purchases of the territory. In the lodging house students can try to imagine Wisconsin as a place of beginnings and dig into the everyday lives of its citizens.

BECKMAN MILL

11600 S County Road H (6 miles west of town) **Beloit** 53511

- ☐ Phone: (608) 751-1551 **www.beckmanmill.org**
- ☐ Hours: Weekends 1:00-4:00pm for guided tours (May-October). The park is open year-round from 5:00am-10:00pm.
- ☐ Admission: $3.00/person (age 7+).
- ☐ Tours: Please register at the visitor center prior to going to the mill for the tour. The visitor center is located west of the parking lot.

Beckman Mill is one of Wisconsin's few restored, working gristmills. The operational 1868 grist mill is surrounded by a mill pond, fish ladder, foot bridge, sawmill display, 1840s cooperage, visitor center, blacksmith shop, creamery, picnic area and nature trail. The Visitor Center serves as a gift shop and includes a creamery display (modeled after the original creamery building near the road), a blacksmith shop display and modern rest rooms. The unique fish ladder incorporates a curved 140-foot long series of "pools" and "riffles". The pools, of which there are seven, act as miniature holding ponds while the eight riffles slow the flow of water to allow small species of fish to navigate the route from the stream below the dam to the pond. When mature the Redfin Shiner is less than 4 inches in length and the Starhead, less than 2.5 inches. Little fishies.

DECATUR DAIRY

W1668 Hwy F (3 miles west of town) **Beloit (Brodhead)** 53520

- ☐ Phone: (608) 897-8661 **www.decaturdairy.com**
- ☐ Hours: Retail Outlet - Monday-Saturday 9:00am-5:00pm.
- ☐ Tours: Reservations necessary, Monday-Saturday 9:00-11:00am.

Brick, Muenster, Farmers, Havarti, Swiss, Swiss/Colby, and cheese curds are their mainstay. In 2007 they swept the U.S. Contest and the Green County Fair taking 1st, 2nd and 3rd in Havarti at both contests.

BLUE MOUND STATE PARK

4350 Mounds Park Road **Blue Mounds** 53517

- Phone: (608) 437-5711
  http://dnr.wi.gov/topic/parks/name/bluemound/
- Admission: A vehicle admission sticker is required. Daily $8.00-$11.00.
  Annual passes available.

Blue Mound State Park is on the tallest hill in southern Wisconsin, about 25 miles west of Madison. Because of its elevation, the park offers two observation towers to view the geological formations and valley below. Observation towers are at the far east and far west ends of the picnic area. Each tower is 40 feet high and equipped with a landmark locator to help pinpoint the location of various cities and geologic features. The park also offers a seasonal swimming pool. Blue Mound maintains nearly 13 miles of multipurpose trails. All are open to hiking and many of them for cross-country skiing, mountain biking and snowshoeing. Blue Mound also has a hill for sledding. Open daily 6:00am-11:00pm with overnight camping.

CAVE OF THE MOUNDS

2975 Cave of the Mounds Road (off U.S. Highways 18 and 151 between Mount Horeb and Blue Mounds) **Blue Mounds** 53517

- Phone: (608) 437-3038 **www.caveofthemounds.com**
- Hours: Daily 9:00am-6:00pm (Summer). Weekdays 10:00am-4:00pm, Weekends 9:00am-5:00pm (Spring & Fall). Weekends 10:00am-4:00pm (Winters).
- Admission: $21.99 adult, $12.99 child (4-12). Gem mining extra fee.
- Tours: 1 hour. Cave temperature is 50 degrees F. year-round so please dress appropriately. Depart every 20-30 minutes most seasons.
- FREEBIES: Cave, Rock and Fossil activities are online - **https://www. caveofthemounds.com/blog-cave-of-the-mounds-wisconsin-destination/ blog-family-fun/**. Why not sing the Rock Cycle song on your way home!

Head underground into the Cave of the Mounds where the temperature is always 50 degrees. Guided tours of this natural limestone cave take visitors past illuminated stalactites, stalagmites, columns and other formations over thousands of years old. Can you find Polly the Parrot? Why do they call one passage the Narrows? Tours are offered daily throughout the year, even during the winter months. Their Education pages really make this attraction a good deal to visit with purpose and pre-and-post activities to follow up.

CADIZ SPRINGS STATE RECREATION AREA

Pine Tree Road (1 mile east of Browntown and 8 miles west of Monroe on State Highway 11) **Browntown** 53522

- Phone: (608) 966-3777
  http://dnr.wi.gov/topic/parks/name/cadizsprings/
- Admission: A vehicle admission sticker is required. Daily $8.00-$11.00. Annual passes available.

Browntown-Cadiz Springs includes two spring-fed lakes and a 600-acre wildlife refuge. Day-use only. 644 acres. Features handicap- accessible picnic area, shoreline with marked beach area, canoeing, boating (electric motor only), fishing, 1 mile of nature trails, 7.6 miles of hiking trails, 7.6 miles of cross- country ski trails.

HINCHLEY DAIRY FARM

2844 Hwy 73 **Cambridge** 53523

- Phone: (608) 764-5090 **www.dairyfarmtours.com**
- Hours: Open April thru October. Tours from 10:00am-2:00pm by reservation only. Sorry, Drop-in visits are not allowed for safety and biosecurity reasons. Family outings are on weekends.
- Tours: By reservation only - last 1-3 hours. Single families may be asked to be added to another tour. Fee: $15.00-$25.00 per person (ages 2+). Tours may be affected by weather or other conditions related to harvests or raising animals.

Take a beautiful drive in the country and visit the Hinchley Dairy Farm, a real dairy farm open for tours. The educational farm tours are guided and run from April 1st through October 31st. The main attraction of the farm is the cows, but there is so much more. Tours spotlight farm animals, food production, and farm life. Plan on hand-milking a cow, gathering eggs from the hen house, going on a hayride into the fields and petting or feeding farm animals. With over 230 cows to view, nothing beats being able to squirt milk from a cow. In the milk house, you will see how the milk is stored before it is hauled by the milk truck to be processed. See baby animals in the spring and pick pumpkins in the fall.

FALL TOURS & CORN MAZE

Cambridge - *Hinchley Dairy Farm. Enjoy a day at the farm, milk a cow, gather eggs, hold, pet and feed farm animals, and then head to the hayride to pick a FREE pumpkin from the 6 acre pumpkin patch. Your hayride will go through the fields, past silly scare crows, and stop at the pumpkin patch. Family Hayrides are available. CORN MAZE: It is family friendly with silly prizes throughout. They have found after many visitors with small children; a corn maze can not be too long, too tricky, or too boring. SO they make them short, with educational information, and PRIZES. All corn maze visitors also get a hayride and a FREE PUMPKIN! Tour admissions apply. (weekends in October, weekdays by reservations.*

SCHUSTERS PLAYTIME FARM

Deerfield - *1326 Hwy 12/18. Centennial round barn, cornmaze, beautiful hayrides, pumpkin patch, awesome animals, haunted forest, and fantastic farm fun! Admission.* **https://schustersfarm.com/fall-fun/** *. (Open daily late September- October)*

GOVERNOR DODGE STATE PARK

4175 Highway 23 N (The park entrance is 3 miles north of Highway 18)
Dodgeville 53533

☐   Phone: (608) 935-2315
     http://dnr.wi.gov/topic/parks/name/govdodge/
☐   Admission: A vehicle admission sticker is required. Daily $8.00-$11.00.
     Annual passes available.

Governor Dodge State Park offers a pair of man-made lakes and 5,000 acres of fun. 5,000 scenic acres of steep hills, bluffs and deep valleys, plus two lakes each with pet swim areas adjacent to swimming beaches. Features 267 campsites, 77 electric sites, winter camping, backpack camping, handicap-accessible picnic area and campsites, concessions, nature center, seasonal naturalist programs, vistas, shoreline with marked beach area, canoeing, boating (electric motor only), fishing, 2 miles of nature trails, 26.6 miles of hiking trails, 24.7 miles of horseback trails (State Trail Pass required), horse- riders' campsites, 10.3 miles of off- road bicycle trails (State Trail Pass required), 15 miles of snowmobile trails, 18.1 miles of cross-country ski trails. Two designated hiking trails begin at the Enee Point Picnic Shelter - the self-guided Pine Cliff Nature Trail and the 4.5-mile White Oak Trail. Open daily 6:00am-11:00pm with overnight camping.

FIRESIDE DINNER THEATRE

1131 Janesville (Hwy 26 S Fort Atkinson) **Fort Atkinson** 53538

- ☐ Phone: (800) 477-9505 **www.firesidetheatre.com**
- ☐ Admission: Varies depending on performance. All shows are lunch/dinner shows ONLY. See website for schedule of performances and ticket prices.

The Fireside Dinner Theatre is one of the Midwest's most popular professional theatres and a favorite destination for couples, families and tour groups alike. Live Broadway musicals and dining in a unique entertainment complex, including lovely dining rooms, state-of-the-art theatre-in-the-round, and five gift shops. A menu and show time to fit any itinerary, with nine shows Wednesday-Sunday. Musical reviews covering toe-tapping, swinging 50s or a family show like Cinderella are typical of their yearly productions.

HOARD HISTORICAL MUSEUM & DAIRY SHRINE

401 Whitewater Avenue **Fort Atkinson** 53538

- ☐ Phone: (920) 563-7769 **www.hoardmuseum.org**
- ☐ Hours: Tuesday-Saturday 9:30am-4:30pm.
- ☐ Admission: FREE. Donations gratefully accepted.

Former Governor of Wisconsin, W.D. Hoard, is considered the father of dairy farming in the state. His 1869 mansion now houses a museum and dairy shrine. Your family can learn the health benefits of milk plus see some crazy ways early dairies operated (ex. Check out the dog-powered treadmill used to churn butter). Here you'll also meet the Sauk warrior Black Hawk and hear the story of the 1832 Black Hawk War. Find out what kind of soldier young Abraham Lincoln was and learn how "Fort Atkinson" came to be. And how about those floor-to-ceiling walls of "stuffed" animals and birds. A great small town museum with big stories.

HORICON MARSH BOAT TOURS

311B Mill Street **Horicon** 53032

- ☐ Phone: (920) 485-4663 **www.horiconmarsh.com**
- ☐ Admission: Sightseeing Tour - $25.00 adult, $14.00 child (4-13).
- ☐ Tours: One hour, narrated Sightseeing Tour Daily 1:00pm with video 30 minutes prior. (May-September). Monday-Friday 1:00pm, Weekends at 10:00am, 1:00 & 3:00pm with video 30 minutes prior. (until late October).

Reservations Highly Recommended. Other tours/themes available at various costs and times. See website or call for details.

☐ Note: Canoe / Kayak rentals available at additional cost.

Spring, summer and fall, the marsh is a hive of activity as its inhabitants go about their normal activities. Enjoy the birds and animals in their natural habitat on these environmentally friendly pontoon boats. Join a one-hour narrated "Sightseeing Tour" (best for kids), 1 1/2 half hour "Sunset Cruise" or two-hour "Birding Adventure" of the inner marsh. If you have a sunny day, look for turtles "sunning" on the fallen trees and rocks near the banks of the marsh.

HORICON MARSH EXPLORIUM

N7725 Highway 28 **Horicon** 53032

☐ Phone: (920) 387-7860 **www.horiconmarsh.org**
☐ Hours: Monday-Friday 9am-4pm, Weekends 10am-4pm.
☐ Admission: $6.00 adult, $4.00 student (5-17).

Dodge County's Horicon Marsh is a 32,000-acre complex of open water, wetlands, prairie and woods. To some, the name Horicon Marsh has almost become synonymous with Canada geese. Each fall the largest migratory flock of Canada geese in the world migrates through Horicon Marsh with peak numbers reaching more than 200,000! The geese begin to arrive in mid-September, but for many the most popular time to see this fall spectacle is in mid-October as numbers approach the fall peak, other wildlife is still abundant, and fall colors paint a perfect background.The marsh is also home to one of the widest arrays of plants, animals and birds in the Midwest and is one of the most important wetland habitats in the country. There are a number of ways to explore the marsh, including canoeing, kayaking, auto tours, guided boat tours, hiking trails or a stroll on the popular floating boardwalk located in the northwest corner of the marsh. Stop at the marsh's all-new Explorium for maps and area information. The center has an observation deck, displays and trails. The indoor Marsh Viewing Area has three-sided glass walls aimed out onto the marsh and the Children's Discovery Room was developed to provide hands-on activities that change with the seasons.

HORICON MARSH WILDLIFE REFUGE
N7728 Hwy 28 (Hwy 151 to Hwy 49 to Hwy Z) **Horicon** 53032

- Phone: (920) 387-7860 **www.fws.gov/midwest/horicon/**
- Hours: Visitor Center open year round, Monday-Friday 9:00am-4:00pm and Saturdays (April-November). Closed Wednesdays each fall.
- Admission: no entry fees.
- Tours: Guided Pontoon Boat Tours & canoe/kayak rentals depart from Blue Heron Landing 800-414-4474.
- Note: The Horicon refuge visitor center is located on County Road Z, 3.5 miles south of State Highway 49 on the east side of the refuge and has many educational exhibits and the Coot's Corner bookstore.

Often called the "Everglades of the North," Horicon Marsh is the nation's largest freshwater cattail marsh. The 32,000 acre march, which is part national wildlife refuge and part state wildlife refuge, is home to more than 300 species of animals and birds. Although fall is prime time at Horicon Marsh (as many as one million ducks and Canadian geese migrate through it every year), spring and summer bring their own spectacles and nature-watching opportunities.

Located in the northern part of the Marsh. Trails are open year-round for hiking, snowshoeing, and wildlife observation. The Auto Tour Route and Dike Road, conditions permitting, are open from dawn to dusk year round. Old Marsh Road open for hiking and biking Saturday & Sunday during June, July, and August. Fishing available at selected sites. Tours, special events, and educational programs.

AUDUBON DAYS FESTIVAL - SPECTACLE OF THE GEESE
Horicon - *Horicon Marsh Wildlife Refuge. Tours, hayrides and other harvest activities celebrate this resting spot of more than 200,000 geese as they fly south for the winter. Backed by beautiful fall colors, visitors will enjoy a myriad of activities including: music, food court, run/walk, bicycle tours, a parade, car show and arts and crafts fair. www.audubondays.com. (first long weekend in October)*

ROCK AQUA JAYS WATERSKI SHOWS
(RAJ Stadium on the Rock River at Traxler Park) **Janesville** 53547

- Phone: (800) 487-2757 **www.rockaquajays.com**
- Hours: Shows Wednesday & Sundays at 7:00pm (June & July), 6:30pm in

August & early September. Special events also throughout the season.
☐ Admission: FREE. Donation buckets are available and "drops" are appreciated.

One of the top waterski show teams in the nation, well-known for their star doubles, barefoot skiing and pyramid acts. Each year, they prepare a new theme - usually a spoof of a retro TV show. Although they have traveled all over the world and hold records at many events, they still perform FREE shows for the public (and to hone their competition skills). They use more than 8 miles of tow rope per show and burn more than 2,500 gallons of gasoline per season so donations are appreciated.

WISCONSIN WAGON COMPANY
507 Laurel Avenue (I-90 exit 171A, Hwy 26 - will need directions from here)
Janesville 53548

☐ Phone: (608) 754-0026 **www.wisconsinwagon.com**
☐ Tours: Monday, Tuesday & Thursday tours by appointment only. 15 person minimum. Approximately 1 hour, charge $5/person. (February thru October)

This company makes hand-crafted Janesville Coaster Wagons and other solid wood toys for little girls and guys patterned after quality products of past generations. The story starts in 1978 when a retired businessman seeking a special gift, a wooden wagon, for his first grandson, realized that the Janesville coaster wagon that he remembered was no longer being produced. He then dissected the remains of an original wagon discovered in a friend's garage and from those remains and sketches, built what was to become the first "Wisconsin Wagon Company's" Janesville Coaster Wagon. The series II wagons produced here use current, safe materials and each is registered and has a numbered nameplate under the dashboard so future generations can determine the age of their heirloom. For an extra fee, you can order a wagon with your child's name on it.

MILTON HOUSE MUSEUM
18 S Janesville Street (Hwy 26) **Janesville (Milton)** 53563

☐ Phone: (608) 868-7772 **www.miltonhouse.org**
☐ Hours: Daily 10:00am-4:00pm (Memorial Day-Labor Day). Wednesday-Friday 10:00am-2:00pm only (rest of year).
☐ Admission: $12.00 adult (13+), $10.00 senior (62+), $8.00 child (6-17).
☐ Tours: First tour begins at 10:00am, last tour 4:00pm.

A man named Goodrich built the Milton House, a stagecoach inn, in 1844. Prior to the Civil War, runaway slaves were given safe haven in the basement of the Milton House. Runaways entered through the cabin to the rear of the inn and then through a trap door in the cabin's floor to the dirt tunnel that led to the basement of the inn. He cared for them quietly in the basement of the inn where they could eat and rest and get ready for the next stage of their journey. But if the alarm were sounded, his method of helping the slaves to escape was to have them crawl back through his tunnel. Then they could get away down to Storrs Lake and go on up through Bowers Lake to the Otter Creek area and get out to Lake Koshkonong and keep on their northward journey to Fort Atkinson or where they were going next. Milton's underground tunnel is also unique in the nation for being the only segment of the Underground Railroad that was actually underground and has retained its identity and is open to the public. Just tell your kids you get to find the secret tunnel and they'll can't wait to tour!

CARR VALLEY CHEESE

S3797 County G (off SR 58) **La Valle** 53941

- ☐ Phone: (800) 462-7258 **www.carrvalleycheese.com**
- ☐ Admission: FREE
- ☐ Tours: Viewing window self-guided tours are random. Self-guided tour hours are Monday - Saturday from 8:00am-4:00pm.

Carr Valley Cheese is one of America's finest specialty cheese plants and the company is over 100 years old. Their skilled cheesemakers turn milk delivered fresh from local dairy farms into more than 100 delicious cheese varieties.

At the La Valle plant, cheddar is made six days a week. They actually begin making cheese in the middle of the night and may finish by 9:00am when the store opens. Waxing cheese (wax coating the block of cheese) can be watched also and that usually happens between 9:00am-Noon. The tour starts with a short video to orient you to curds and whey and the simple process of creating cheese. The secret's in the milk. The video allows you to imagine what the stainless steel tubs and vats look like in the process (especially because most cheese-making is done before the store opens). If you get there at opening (8:00am), you get to see the process live. These cheeses include Black Sheep Truffle, Cave Aged Marisa, and Smoked Ba Ba Blue made from sheep's milk;

Baraboo Blue, Chevre au Lait, Cocoa Cardona, and Goat Cheddar made from goat's milk; Bread Cheese, Jenny Eye Reserve, Sid's Bahl Baby Swiss made from cow's milk; and Canaria, Menage, Mobay, and Shepherd's Blend made from mixed milk. Cheese from goat milk may sound yucky but it's not. Don't you love how they name their cheeses?

Besides the viewing windows, guests will be tempted to try some free samples available throughout the retail store. Pick up some cheeses and some locally made Wisconsin products (ginseng, honey, milled grains) to make cheesehead snacks when you get home.

BIG FOOT BEACH STATE PARK

1550 S. Lake Shore Drive **Lake Geneva** 53147

☐ Phone: (262) 248-2528 **http://dnr.wi.gov/topic/parks/name/bigfoot/**
☐ Admission: A vehicle admission sticker is required. Daily $8.00-$11.00. Annual passes available.

Big Foot Beach, on the shores of Lake Geneva, offers wooded campsites, a sand beach and picnic areas. Lake Geneva is known for its clear, clean water. A 100-foot swimming area is about a 10 minute walk and across Highway 120 from the campground. Share in family fun fishing in Ceylon Lagoon. You can reel them in from the pier, two bridges or the lagoon bank. Fishing equipment is loaned free of charge at the office. Open mid-May through October. 271 acres. Features picnic areas, 100 campsites, showers, a dumping station, handicap- accessible picnic area and campsites, shoreline with marked beach area, canoeing, boating, fishing, 1/2 mile of nature trails, 5.3 miles of hiking trails, 1 mile of snowmobile trails, 4.3 miles of cross- country ski trails.

GENEVA LAKE CRUISE LINE

812 Wrigley Drive (Riviera Docks) **Lake Geneva** 53147

☐ Phone: (262) 248-6206 or (800) 558-5911 **www.cruiselakegeneva.com**
☐ Hours: Various tours and tour times available. Call or see website for most current schedule. (mid-April into early winter)
☐ Admission: (Sightseeing 1 hour) $39.00 adult (18-64), $37.00 senior (65+), $25.00 child (4-17). Prices increase with length of tours and options selected.

Narrated cruises on beautiful Geneva Lake include US Mailboat delivery, luncheon & Dixieland dinner cruises, and 1 & 2-hour sightseeing tours.

The sight-seeing tours cover a great many of the mansions on Lake Geneva that were built by Chicago businessmen around the turn of the century. You'll pass sprawling estates such as the one owned by the Wrigley family. The Captain and carrier provide lots of stories of the Chicago/Milwaukee industrial age history, too.

U.S. MAIL BOAT TOUR - While all mail carriers must deliver the mail in the rain, snow and dark of night, none face quite the same challenge as the mail carrier who has the Lake Geneva route. Mail carriers must leap off the deck of a moving boat, place the mail in the box on the pier, grab outgoing mail, and jump back on board. All while the ship never stops. Extra fee.

TIMBER RIDGE LODGE & WATERPARK @ GRAND GENEVA RESORT

7020 Grand Geneva Way (US 12 to Hwy 50 East/Lake Geneva, the second exit) **Lake Geneva** 53147

- ☐ Phone: (866) 636-4502 **www.timberridgeresort.com**
- ☐ Packages: Timber Ridge offers midweek and weekend "Water Ski" packages, features all suite accommodations, and includes access to both The Mountain Top and Moose Mountain Falls Waterpark through mid March. The 'Midweek Ski Package' is available Sunday-Thursday (excluding holidays) and features overnight accommodations for one night, four lift tickets and half-price ski and snowboard equipment rental for up to two children, ages 11 and under. Overnight packages start at $159. DAY PACKAGES: Spend just the day at Timber Ridge Lodge with waterpark passes and a hotel suite for changing, eating or just hanging out. Rates starting at $129 and includes 5 waterpark passes. Hang out for an afternoon or make a day of it.

Timber Ridge offers a 50,000-sq. ft. indoor/outdoor waterpark experience, while The Mountain Top is a family friendly, full service ski and snowboard facility capable of churning out its own snow. Guests can also enjoy all the amenities of Grand Geneva, including miles of hiking/biking, a full service spa and sport center, and two championship 18-hole golf courses. Smokey's Bar-B-Que House is the restaurant on the property.

MOOSE MOUNTAIN FALLS WATERPARK - Designed as a shallow water entertainment complex to appeal to children and adults of all ages, Moose Mountain Falls features a 50,000-square foot indoor/outdoor waterpark complete with two giant slides which begin three stories above ground and wind their way 300-feet before finishing at ground level. A winding "lazy river" inner tube float area is also featured plus numerous play areas and slides for all age levels. For guests who've spent the day on the slopes or just wanting to relax more, refuge can be sought in either of the two giant whirlpools, one of which offers indoor-to-outdoor accessibility.

WINTERFEST & NATIONAL SNOW SCULPTING CHAMPIONSHIPS

Lake Geneva - *Riviera Park. A one-of-a kind event. Activities include snow sculpting, music, children's activities, helicopter rides and horse drawn carriage rides. These works are amazing to see created - not quite knowing what will turn out until near the end.* **https://www.visitlakegeneva.com/winterfest/** *(week in early February)*

AZTALAN STATE PARK
(County Highway Q, east of Lake Mills, 2 miles off I-94) **Lake Mills** 53551

- Phone: (920) 648-8774
  http://dnr.wi.gov/topic/parks/name/aztalan/
- Hours: Daily, 6:00am-11:00pm.
- Admission: A vehicle admission sticker is required. Daily $8.00-$11.00. Annual passes available.

Does the name sound Mexican? Well, this site was settled by Native Americans who were believed to have links with the Aztecs in Mexico. This is Wisconsin's most important archaeological site as it showcases an ancient civilization Middle-Mississippian village. The people who settled Aztalan built large, flat-topped pyramidal mounds and a stockade around their village. They hunted, fished, and farmed on the floodplain of the Crawfish River. The prime attraction for the kids is the rebuilt stockade, similar to one that stood from 1075 to 1175.

The AZTALAN MUSEUM, operated by the Lake Mills-Aztalan Historical Society, Inc., is just north of the park. It includes two pioneer church buildings and other structures from the 19th century and displays of pioneer life. The Princess Mound (girls, why is it called that?) is on location here. The museum is open from noon to 4:00pm Thursdays through Sundays from mid-May through late September. Fees are $5.00 for adults, $3.00 for children, free for those under age 5. **www.orgsites.com/wi/aztalan**.

The Aztalan Historical Society sponsors a festival on the museum grounds each year on the Sunday closest to July 4, celebrating Aztalan's pioneer past.

NATURAL BRIDGE STATE PARK

(County Highway C, 3/4 mile northeast of Leland) **Leland** 53913

- ☐ Phone: (608) 356-8301
- ☐ **http://dnr.wi.gov/topic/parks/name/naturalbridge/**
- ☐ Admission: A vehicle admission sticker is required. Daily $8.00-$11.00. Annual passes available.

See a breathtaking natural sandstone arch created by the eroding effects of wind and water. This weathered formation, located in Wisconsin's Driftless Area, was missed by the glaciers during the last Ice Age. No, to protect the natural area, you can not climb onto the bridge itself. Near the bridge is a rock shelter used by people when the glacier was melting. Open for day use from spring through autumn. 530 acres. Features handicap- accessible picnic area, 1.1 miles of nature trails, 2.5 miles of hiking trails, 0.7 miles of snowmobile trails. Open only during daylight hours with no camping allowed.

CAPITOL BUILDING OF WISCONSIN & DOWNTOWN OUTDOOR EXPLORING

2 East Main Street **Madison** 53702

- ☐ Phone: (608) 266-0382 **http://tours.wisconsin.gov/**
- ☐ Hours: For general viewing Monday-Friday 8:00am-6:00pm, Weekends & Holidays 8:00am-4:00pm.
- ☐ Admission: FREE.
- ☐ Tours: Tours start at the information desk Monday-Saturday at 9:00, 10:00, 11:00am and 1:00, 2:00, 3:00pm, Sundays at 1:00, 2:00, 3:00pm. A 4:00pm tour is offered weekdays (Monday-Friday), excluding holidays, during Memorial Day through Labor Day. The sixth floor museum and observation deck are open during the summer months.

Built on an isthmus between two lakes, the center of downtown is dominated by the State Capitol, which was modeled after the Capitol in Washington, D.C. Completed in 1917, the Capitol building features the only granite dome in the nation. The interior contains 43 varieties of stone from around the world, decorative murals, glass mosaics and hand-carved furniture. The tours allow access to the senate and assembly chambers, the Hearing room, the Supreme court chamber and the governor's conference room. We'd recommend taking the one hour guided tours as the friendly guide's interpretation adds flavor to the ornate rooms. At the end, you go up on the observation deck and have a great view of downtown Madison and the lakes surrounding it. One way to keep the younger set engaged - have them look for stone badgers peeking out from secret nooks and crannies.

Saturday mornings from early spring to late fall, area farmers transform the Capitol Square into the largest producer's only farmer's market in the nation (DANE COUNTY FARMERS MARKET- **www.dcfm.org**). Shoppers here can find everything from artisan cheeses and organic oregano to 20 different varieties of bean sprouts or freshly made German-style summer sausage.

The University of Wisconsin campus is a pleasant stroll away, linking the Capitol and campus with a pedestrian mall.

MAD CITY SKI TEAM

1 John Nolen Drive (Law Park at the corner of John Nolen Drive and Williamson Street right next to the Monona Terrace - Downtown)
Madison 53703

- Phone: (608) 663-TEAM **http://madcityskiteam.com/**
- Hours: Ski shows nearly every Sunday from Memorial Day to Labor Day weekend at Law Park. The Junior Team show starts at 5:30pm and the main show follows it starting about 6:00pm. Please check website for dates and times. There are also a few smaller Wednesday shows.
- Admission: FREE. Donation buckets available to contribute after the show.

Jumping, swiveling, trick skis, skiing backwards barefoot and more! Every Sunday at 6:00pm just east of the Monona Terrace and Convention Center on John Nolen Drive. Bleachers available, but feel free to bring your lawn chairs or beach blankets. This team wins State Show Ski Tournaments practically every year as they hone their skills for you. Can you believe their pyramids!

MADISON CHILDREN'S MUSEUM

100 N. Hamilton Street (Capitol Square) **Madison** 53703

- Phone: (608) 256-6445 **www.madisonchildrensmuseum.org**
- Hours: Tuesday-Sunday 9:30am-5pm. Open daily summers.
- Admission: $12.00 general, $11.00 senior, $1.00 public assist. members.

This three-story museum is targeted to children up to age 12 and features an art studio, rooftop terrace and a café. Exhibits include the Log Cabin and Possible-opolis, a city of art and science where anything can happen. More surprises tucked away in unusual places are found in the Concourse. They have a Wildernest area for the younger set too.

MADISON MUSEUM OF CONTEMPORARY ART

227 State Street **Madison** 53703

- ☐ Phone: (608) 257-0158 **www.mmoca.org**
- ☐ Hours: Thursday-Sunday Noon-6:00pm.
- ☐ Admission: FREE.

MMoCA encompasses 51,500 square feet of interior space, including highly flexible gallery space and a rooftop restaurant and sculpture garden. The permanent collection features nearly 5,000 works of art, including a vast selection of American paintings, prints, photographs, drawings, and sculptures. Ok, but what's there to do with the kids?

- ARTPACK - Stop by the reception desk in the lobby and ask for the MMoCAkids ArtPack, the museum's hands-on discovery kit for exploring art. Designed for family members to use together, the ArtPack contains a variety of activities that promote observation and imaginative thinking about visual art. The kit is designed with flexibility in mind, allowing families to choose which activities to use and what to look at in the galleries.

- LET'S LOOK - These fun, interactive hand-outs help children to think imaginatively about what they are seeing while learning about art and artists. Let's look handouts are designed for families to use together and are available free of charge at the entrance to MMoCA's exhibitions.

- LEARNING CENTERS - MMoCAkids Learning Centers are developed with families in mind. Learning Centers include children's books on art and artists and innovative, easy-to-use discovery activities that encourage families to be creative together. MMoCAkids Learning Centers are located within galleries and available to use on a drop-by basis.

- KIDS' ART ADVENTURES invites families to make art together inspired by the MMoCA's current exhibitions. Activities are planned for 6 to 10 year olds, but younger siblings are welcome. Kids' Art Adventures are offered free of charge on the second Sunday of the month, September through May, unless otherwise noted.

-

OLD FASHIONED TAVERN & RESTAURANT

Madison - _23 N. Pinckney St. (in the shadow of the State Capitol building, downtown)
53703. Phone: (608) 310-4545_ **www.theoldfashioned.com** _Hours: Lunch and Dinner
(weekdays). Brunch and early dinner (weekends). Menu: sandwiches avg $12.00,
entrees range from $13.00-$18.00...most big enough to share (served Lazy Susan
style). Nightly specials are great deals. Inspired by the traditions of Wisconsin taverns
and supper clubs. The Old Fashioned exists to pay tribute to the foods that made
Wisconsin famous...in a classic family get-together set up. The "buy local" mentality
features produce and local specialties from small Wisconsin producers. Here, that
means so much more than beers, brats, and cheese. There is mostly tame foods like
Grilled Cheese, Mac n Cheese, chicken and salmon on the Children's Menu but the
parents might want to try a side of House-made fresh Wisconsin beer-battered cheese
curds, followed by locally made brats on a local bakery bun or a salad prepared
with Door County cherries and Wisconsin blue cheese. Did you know some cheeses
are cave aged in Wisconsin. Ask your waiter about that. Also, if you've never tried
Braunschweiger, this is the place to add it to any sandwich (maybe ask for it on the
side?). Real casing hot dogs, ring bologna and rainbow trout can be sampled here,
too. And, the most common condiments used around here? Mustard._

OVERTURE CENTER FOR THE ARTS

201 State Street, downtown **Madison** 53703

Phone: (608) 258-4141 **www.overturecenter.com**

Every Saturday from fall through spring, Overture Center offers free arts programs called Kids in the Rotunda, designed for children and families at 9:30am, 11:00am and 1:00pm. Performances feature storytellers, jugglers, magicians, puppeteers, theater troupes, and multicultural artists. The 1:00pm performances are sign language interpreted.

The center also presents internationally acclaimed jazz, classical, opera, musicals, dance, world music, family entertainment and more.

WISCONSIN HISTORICAL MUSEUM

30 North Carroll Street (Capitol Square) **Madison** 53703

- ☐ Phone: (608) 264-6555 **www.wisconsinhistory.org/museum/**
- ☐ Hours: Tuesday-Saturday 9:00am-4:00pm.
- ☐ Admission: $5.00 adult, $3.00 child (5-17) $10.00 family.
- ☐ Educators: click on Field Trips, then Educational Resources. Click for teaching games and activities for elementary-and-secondary aged students.

Explore Wisconsin's distinctive heritage and a variety of other American history topics through artifacts, photographs, full-scale dioramas, audio-visual presentations, and interactive multimedia programs. Look for the comedic politician, "Fighting Bob" or an original diary from the Lewis and Clark expedition. Odd Wisconsin has a monster knife and a pink flamingo - both oddly important to Wisconsin history. The second floor has a marvelous history of the woodland Indians, complete with pottery, crafts, beadwork, and a reproduction of an adobe-like house. On the third and fourth floor, explore themes unique to Wisconsin history from settlement days to the present. Discover a frontier lead mine, track immigration routes to the state, explore work and play in a lumber camp, and examine Wisconsin's political heritage. The fourth floor has a large window with a view of the state Capitol building.

WISCONSIN VETERANS MUSEUM

30 W. Mifflin Street, Capitol Square **Madison** 53703

- ☐ Phone: (608) 267-1799 **https://wisvetsmuseum.com/**
- ☐ Hours: Tuesday - Saturday 10:00am-5:00pm (Year-round), also, Sunday Noon-5:00pm (April-September).
- ☐ Admission: FREE.

The museum honors Wisconsin's citizen-soldiers through large-scale exhibits, displays and presentations. The 10,000-square-foot museum contains two main galleries, a gift shop, and exhibit space for displays that change periodically. Walk through times of war from the Civil War to Desert Storm.

Learn why Wisconsin regiments marched off to war in the wrong color - and what problems that caused. Why did some vets have blistered skin? Is the USS Wisconsin still in use?

OLBRICH BOTANICAL GARDENS

3330 Atwood Avenue (located on the Capital City Bike trail about 3 miles from downtown) **Madison** 53704

- Phone: (608) 246-4550 **www.olbrich.org**
- Hours: Outdoor Gardens - Daily 10:00am-6:00pm (April-September), 10:00am-4:00pm (October-March). Conservatory - Monday-Sunday 10:00am-4:00pm.
- Admission: Outdoor Gardens is FREE. Conservatory - $2.00 for age 6+.
- Note: Holiday Express-Flower and Model Train Show.

Enjoy a tropical paradise year-round in Olbrich's Bolz Conservatory, a glass pyramid filled with exotic plants, bright flowers, a rushing waterfall, fragrant orchids and free-flying birds. Each season, even winter in the tropical greenhouse, features a different theme. The Rock Garden has two streams running through it and the water sounds like a waterfall.

UNIVERSITY OF WISCONSIN - GEOLOGY MUSEUM

1215 West Dayton Street (located in Weeks Hall - corner of Charter and Dayton streets) **Madison** 53706

- Phone: (608) 262-2399 **http://geoscience.wisc.edu/museum/**
- Hours: Monday-Friday 8:30am-4:30pm, Saturday 9:00am-1:00pm.
- Admission: FREE.
- Tours: guided tours are $2.00.
- FREEBIES: ask for the 4th to 8th grade scavenger hunts before you begin your self-guided tour.

Reconstructed dinosaurs, huge mastodon skeleton, colorful mineral samples, a six-foot diameter rotating globe and a walk-through model of a Wisconsin limestone cave. On your visit you can touch rocks from a time when there were volcanoes in Wisconsin; see corals, jellyfish and other sea creatures that used to live and swim where we now walk; and stand under the tusks of a mastodon while imagining yourself in the Ice Age. They even have real meteorites on display. Kids like the rocks that glow in the dark and the touchable large piece of copper. They also like peering through the window into the Paleo Lab where scientists are prepping new specimens. Can you tell the sedimentary, metamorphic and igneous rocks apart?

UNIVERSITY OF WISCONSIN CAMPUS TOURS

21 N. Park Street, Welcome Center **Madison** 53711

☐ Phone: (608) 262-4636 **http://info.wisc.edu/campus-tours/**
☐ Hours: Monday-Friday 9:00am-4:30pm.

Explore the University of Wisconsin – Madison through a guided walking tour. These 75-minute tours of campus are led by experienced tour guides and highlight campus life, academics and the history of the university. They are offered at 3:00pm, Monday through Friday, and at noon, Saturday and Sunday, throughout the year. Reservations are recommended. Tours leave from the Campus Information Center in the Red Gym, 716 Langdon St. No tours on home football Saturdays, state holidays and the day after Thanksgiving.

Campus Walking Tour booklets are also available. Here are some self-guided tour spots you'll want to check out:

- BABCOCK DAIRY STORE. 1605 Linden Drive. (608) 262-3045. Stop for ice cream and watch it being made.

- UW SPACE PLACE. 2300 S Park Street. (608) 262-4779. This is a vibrant public education center with professionally designed exhibits, classroom space, lecture room, and a roof top deck for sky viewing. The Space Place provides hands-on activities, lively presentations, and informative lectures by UW researchers. Space Place is only open during scheduled events so visit their event calendar. www.spaceplace.wisc.edu/index.shtml.

- UW INTERCOLLEGIATE ATHLETICS (Year-round) In addition to the fast-paced action on the gridiron, UW-Madison athletes compete in a wide range of sports including: basketball, cross country, golf, hockey, rowing, soccer, softball, tennis, track and volleyball. Please check www.uwbadgers.com for a complete schedule of great collegiate competitions.

- CHAZEN MUSEUM OF ART. 800 University Ave. 608/263-2246 or www.chazen.wisc.edu. The art museum of the University of Wisconsin. Exhibitions of national and international art and artists. Open Tuesday-Friday 9:00am-5:00pm, Saturday & Sunday 11:00am-5:00pm, closed Monday.

- UNIVERSITY OF WISCONSIN ARBORETUM. 1207 Seminole Hwy. 608/263-7888. uwarboretum.org. An oasis in the heart of the city, the Arboretum embraces part of Lake Wingra and 1200 acres of shore, stream, marsh and prairie. Contains native and cultivated shrubs and trees, restored prairie grasses and wildflowers, and over 200 varieties of lilacs. Feel free to walk the nature trails on your own or join one of the guided walks. Arboretum trails open year round 7:00am-10:00pm. Visitor Center open Monday-Friday 9:30am-4:00pm, Saturday & Sunday 12:30-4:00pm.

UW MADISON FOOTBALL FAMILY FUN DAY

Madison - Camp Randall Stadium. The Badgers take a break from fall camp and take the opportunity to catch up with some family and friends at Camp Randall Stadium. Here's your chance to meet the team so bring your UW gear and get autographs from your favorite players. 1440 Monroe Street, (800) 462-2343.

VITENSE GOLFLAND

5501 W. Beltline Hwy at Whitney Way **Madison** 53711

- Phone: (608) 271-1411 **www.vitense.com**
- Hours: Daily opens at 8:00am, closes 9:00pm or later.
- Admission: Tokens start at $1.00 and games range from $5.00-$12.00 Unlimited play packages available. Golf Range - $8.00-$20.00 buckets.

Vitense offers batting cages, water games, a climbing wall, junior golf and The Green Tree Grill. At the Indoor 18-hole "Madison" landmark mini golf course you have to see the Capitol Building and "Rhythm & Booms" in black light - awesome! The Indoor Mini Golf, remote controlled boats game and Heated outdoor golf range are open year round. Most other activities are only open summers.

HENRY VILAS ZOO

702 South Randall Avenue (corner of Randall Avenue & Drake Street) **Madison** 53715

- Phone: (608) 266-4732 **www.vilaszoo.org**
- Hours: Grounds - Daily, 9:30am-5:00pm. Buildings - 10:00am-4:00pm.
- Admission: FREE. Donations accepted.

One of the nation's only free zoos, Vilas Park Zoo is open year-round and boasts a state-of-the-art Tropical Forest Aviary. See a wide variety of wild animals, birds, reptiles and fish, including a children's zoo during the summer months. The Zoo also has the Exotic Frog Exhibit with three new state of the art terrariums that contain native South American plants and have individual life support systems. Have you met the meerkats - Stan and Groucho? There are areas to grab a snack or bring-your-own picnic. Each season, different animals seem to be more active - ex. Mountain goats love winter. Bears tend to hibernate then.

CRAWDADDY COVE WATER PARK IN THE HOLIDAY INN HOTEL & SUITES MADISON

Madison - *1109 Fourier Drive (US 12/14 exit 252 or 253) 53717. Phone: (608) 826-0500.* **https://www.ihg.com/holidayinn/hotels/us/en/madison/msnbh/hoteldetail.** *This family-friendly full-service hotel features Madison's only indoor waterpark (three pools), 158 rooms including oversized deluxe suites, on site restaurant & two lounges. Each room offers complimentary hi-speed internet and a microwave and frig in every room. Best of all...as always, Kids Eat FREE. Promo family packages start as low as $129.00 a night.*

Even if you are not staying at the Hotel you can enjoy the indoor waterpark Kiddie Waterslides and Adventure Pool. All ages will love the SS Crawdaddy Shrimp Boat and the unique atmosphere of the Louisiana Bayou Adventure.

WISCONSIN BOOK FESTIVAL

Madison - *Stories come to life at the Wisconsin Book Festival, a public celebration of the written word. Featuring numerous authors from across the nation including novelists, poets, children's writers, book artists, editors and critics, the four-day festival treats readers of all ages to a variety of events including children's events, storytelling, readings, lectures, discussions, exhibits and book signings. Events are free to the public and held at locations throughout the capital city including the Orpheum Theatre, Overture Center for the Arts, the Madison Public Library, as well as local museums, libraries and local bookstores. FREE.* **https://www. wisconsinbookfestival.org/** *(first weekend in November)*

EPLEGAARDEN

Madison (Fitchburg) - *2227 Fitchburg Road.* **www.eplegaarden.com**. *Eplegaarden is an old fashioned orchard featuring selv plukk (U-Pick) apples, raspberries and pumpkins for lots of old fashion rural farm fun. It's the home of the Wisconsin Sesquicentennial Barn and "Ole & Lena", and "Bakke and Dal". During fall fest weekends: horse drawn hayrides around da orchard, da pumpkin patch, old barn loft and silo play, folk music and a themed self-guided playground. Admission for some activities. Daytime hours daily except closed Mondays.*

HUBBARD AVENUE DINER

Madison (Middleton) - *7445 Hubbard Avenue (US 12/14 exit 251) 53562. Phone: (608) 831-PIES.* **www.hubbardavenuediner.com**. *The ultimate classic American diner in an award-winning 1940's design. Serving diner classics like meatloaf and mashed potatoes, as well as innovative sandwiches, salads and entrees. They have a big Kids Menu (ages 12 and under) with games on it to play while eating. Most kids dinners are well under $6.00, drinks extra. Have a Cuppa Dirt for dessert. The dessert case will make your eyes pop! Famous for pie - but which to choose?*

NATIONAL MUSTARD MUSEUM

Hubbard Avenue in downtown Middleton (US 12 / 14 exit 251 to downtown)
Madison (Middleton) 53562

- ☐ Phone: (608) 831-2222 **www.mustardmuseum.com**
- ☐ Hours: Daily from 10am-5pm except winter holidays.

Yellow, stadium, gourmet, brown...not many more varieties, right? This museum will prove you wrong. Tucked on Main Street in this town is a museum store that has shelves lined with several THOUSAND varieties of mustards...from all 50 states and more than 60 countries! Often, there's a video playing in the "MustardPiece Theatre." Samples are offered, and recipes are given out at each station. Have you ever seen so much yellow? FREE.

EXPLORE CHILDREN'S MUSEUM

1433 W Main St. **Madison (Sun Prairie)** 53590

- ☐ Phone: 608-478-5456 **https://www.explorecm.org/**
- ☐ Hours: Monday, Wednesday - Saturday 9am-4pm. Tuesdays 9am-Noon. Sundays 10am-4pm.
- ☐ Admissiond: $8.00 per person

Opened in early 2022, the Sun Prairie Explore Children's Museum is a 4,800-square-foot space with plenty of places for imaginative play and hands-on learning. Exhibits are simply larger versions of many play tables and structures you may have at home. So, it allows "larger imaginations" to foster. The Explore experience is developmentally appropriate for children between the ages of 0-8, offering a wide range of both permanent and rotating exhibits.

LITTLE A-MERRICK-A AMUSEMENT PARK

700 East Main Street **Marshall** 53559

- ☐ Phone: (608) 655-3181 **www.littleamerricka.com**
- ☐ Hours: Most days, Noon-6:00pm (June-August). Call or see website for current schedule.
- ☐ Admission: Park admission is FREE. Single tickets: $2.00. Unlimited ride passes varying in prices from $13.95-$26.95. Each type of pass is good for unlimied rides on certain color-coded rides.

An old fashioned, family owned amusement park, where young and old alike can enjoy an entire afternoon of affordable classic family fun. Little Amerricka is also home to one of this country's most extensive premier light railways, keeping the knowledge and passion of a by gone era alive. Plus, you'll find three small coasters, a tilt-a-whirl, kiddie rides, bumper cars & boats, mini-golf, and a Ferris wheel. We like their ingenious color-coded wristband system so you only pay as much as you think you'll want to ride. Less for kiddie/family rides - more for fast rides.

MERRIMAC FERRY
State Road 113 **Merrimac** 53561

☐ Phone: (608) 246-3806
https://wisconsindot.gov/Pages/travel/water/merrimac/default.aspx

Free carferry service across the Wisconsin River on Hwy 113. Ferry operates seasonally from ice-out to ice-in (about April-November), 24-hours a day.

NATIONAL HISTORIC CHEESEMAKING CENTER
2108 6th Avenue (just off State Highway 69 at 21st Street) **Monroe** 53566

☐ Phone: (608) 325-4636 http://nationalhistoriccheesemakingcenter.org
☐ Hours: Thursday-Sunday 10:00am-3:00pm. (May-October).
☐ Admission: $5.00 per person (age 16+).

See the cheese industry explained historically. Take a stroll back in time, to the "beginning" when the new and old worlds met...to when there was a cheese factory at every rural crossroad. Hear voices from the past tell their stories of hardship and joy. It was from this depot that tons of cheese were shipped by rail to eventually reach world markets. The art and business of making cheese has kept the city thriving for more than 100 years. Local cheese factories welcome visitors with samples and retail sales.

Cheese Curds: Invented in the Dairy State, curds are peanut-sized pieces of fresh Cheddar cheese in their natural, random shape before being processed into blocks and aged. In the first few hours, they "squeak" when you bite into them. Purists like them just as they are, although deep-fried in beer batter (but of course) is very popular too. www.eatwisconsincheese.com.

MOUNT HOREB TROLLWAY
125 S First St **Mount Horeb** 53572

☐ Phone: (608) 437-7185 **www.mounthorebtrollway.com**

The Mount Horeb Trollway could easily be explained by the over-active imagination and occasional over-indulgence of the highly skilled (Irish) Troll Meister, Michael J. Feeney, who created them. The Trollway in Mount Horeb is dotted with the whimsical Norwegian gnomes in tribute to their mischievous nature for all to enjoy. The online field guide shows you a picture and name of what to look for and where. One or two have gone missing, but may appear near something related to their namesake from time to time.

CHALET LANDHAUS INN

New Glarus - 801 Highway 69, 53574. www.chaletlandhaus.com. The Chalet Landhaus is built in traditional Swiss style, with a blend of modern convenience & old-fashioned Swiss decor to give you a touch of Switzerland close to home. They have a very clean, modern indoor pool, hot tub and exercise room. For a traditional Swiss meal (or American Cuisine), the Alpine Restaurant is open for breakfast and dinner meals. Be sure to save room for one of their Swiss desserts. A standard room runs $139.00/night (includes breakfast buffet) but they offer some better rates if you purchase a two-night package.

NEW GLARUS WOODS STATE PARK

W5446 County Rd NN (just W of SR 39/69, 1 mile S of New Glarus)
New Glarus 53574

☐   Phone: (608) 527-2335
http://dnr.wi.gov/topic/parks/name/ngwoods/
☐   Admission: A vehicle admission sticker is required. Daily $8.00-$11.00. Annual passes available.

Wooded campsites in quiet solitude close to the Sugar River Bike Trail. Features picnic area, playground, 32 campsites, showers nearby, backpack camping, handicap- accessible picnic area, seasonal naturalist programs, 4.4 miles of nature trails, 7.1 miles of hiking trails. Open daily 6:00am-11:00pm with overnight camping.

SWISS HISTORICAL VILLAGE MUSEUM

612 7th Avenue (west side of New Glarus, along Highway 39)
New Glarus 53574

☐   Phone: (608) 527-2317 **www.swisshistoricalvillage.org**
☐   Hours: Tuesday-Sunday 10:00am-4:00pm (May - mid-October).
☐   Admission: $10.00 adult, $3.00 child.
☐   Note: Nearby on First Street is the ALPINE CORNER STORE with Alpine-themed gifts and MAPLE LEAF STORE w/cheese and chocolates.

Known as "America's Little Switzerland," New Glarus and Green County were settled by Swiss immigrants in the mid-1800s. Here Swiss architecture, customs, and cuisine have been nurtured and preserved. The Swiss Historical Village Museum presents the unique story of the founding of New Glarus in

1845 and traces the Swiss colony's growth into a dairy farming community that continues to keep alive its ethnic heritage. Visit the Hall of History, Settler's Log Cabin (1850s), a Pioneer Cabin from the late 1800s, a small Swiss Cheese Factory and a Sausage Factory, the School House (you can actually sit at the desks), the blacksmith, the local paper's old print shop, and a log church. A typical guided tour lasts about an hour and a half. The tours are continuous and you can join them at any point. And if you happen to Sprechen Sie Schweizer-Deutsches, some of the guides speak Swiss-German.

Right before the village closes for the season, they hold their annual Harvest Festival-it's especially fun to watch them make cheese using 1890s era equipment and methods.

HEIDI FESTIVAL

New Glarus - *Downtown.* **https://www.facebook.com/heidifolkfestival/**. *Each year, the Swiss settlement of New Glarus brings back the beloved characters of the book Heidi. Townsfolk don lederhosen for the street dance complete with polka music, and costumed performers present a dramatized version of the book several times throughout the weekend. Old world traditions Saturday night include yodeling, flag throwing and singing. Saturday is also the Taste of New Glarus with food, discounted merchandise and live music on the streets of New Glarus.*

WILHELM TELL FESTIVAL

New Glarus - *Tell Grounds off Hwy 69.* **https://wilhelmtellfestival.org/**. *More than 200 costumed local volunteers take to the stage to celebrate Swiss Independence with lavish performances of "Wilhelm Tell" in English and German. Visitors are invited to enjoy a family camp-out complete with a campfire full treats and fun. Awake to the sounds of alphorns and goats. The weekend is filled with ethnic fold costumes, outdoor art fair, entertainment and plenty of unique shops. (Labor Day weekend)*

CEDAR GROVE CHEESE FACTORY TOUR

E5904 Mill Road (just east of Hwy 23) **Plain** 53577

- ☐ Phone: (608) 546-5284 or (800) 200-6020 **www.cedargrovecheese.com**
- ☐ Hours: Retail store - Monday-Saturday 8:00am-4:00pm (April-December). Monday-Saturday 10:00am-3:00pm (Jan-March)
- ☐ Tours: Occasionally they take a day off production for repairs, so we recommend groups or large families call ahead. However, the wash water treatment facility is always operational.
- ☐

Cedar Grove Cheese specializes in organic cheese which is made from pasteurized whole organic milk. The process is actually pretty simple: they start with milk, then add rennet, an enzyme produced by bacteria. This makes the milk coagulate into curds and whey. The watery, milky whey is drained off and the curds are pressed into blocks and then aged to form solid cheese. Tour guides share the history and art of cheesemaking and how small-scale production helps the product, the environment and the farmers that bring the milk. Cedar Grove tours also features first of its kind "Living Machine" water treatment system - a greenhouse full of tropical plants and animals that clean their water. Like cheese? Think you'd like to be a cheesemaker? Cheesemaking at Cedar Grove begins around midnight and ends when they finish wrapping and cleaning, about 9:00pm later that day.

DID YOU KNOW? *Once, the rennet was prepared from the fourth stomach of calves. Today it is produced by bacteria that have been altered to produce the enzyme chymosin. This enzyme clots the milk. It is so powerful that it is mixed with milk in a 1:5,000 ratio.*

CASCADE MOUNTAIN
(I-90/94 exit 106) **Portage** 53901

☐   Phone: (608) 742-5588 **www.cascademountain.com**

Ski, snowboard and snow tubing facilities. Kids 12 and under ski free when accompanied by a paid adult. 36 trails for skiing. Ten lifts. Check out the Snow Tube Park with five 800' long chutes.

FORT WINNEBAGO SURGEON'S QUARTERS
W8687 Highway 33 East **Portage** 53901

☐   Phone: (608) 742-2949 **www.fortwinnebagosurgeonsquarters.org**
☐   Hours: Wednesday-Sunday 10:00am-4:00pm (May -October). Last tour starts at 3:30pm.
☐   Admission: $10.00 adult, $8.00 senior (65+), $5.00 student (6-17), child 6 and under FREE. $30.00 family.

The city of Portage marks an ancient overland portage that was a strategic link between the Fox and Wisconsin Rivers. In 1828, Fort Winnebago was built to protect the site. Thirty years later, a two-mile canal was hand-dug joining the two rivers. Today, visitors can tour a restored section of the canal. Tours of the Surgeon's Quarters and the Indian Agency House – all that's left of old Fort Winnebago – are also offered. Surgical equipment of a by-gone day in the Surgeons' Room as well as the fort Surgeon's operating table, furnishings of the Fort Winnebago period in the bedroom, sitting room, and kitchen have made Surgeon's Quarters the most interesting attraction for visitors. A narrow stairway leads from the kitchen to the "Children's Room" on the second floor. There toys and furnishings of the period of the farm families are displayed. The other building of interest to kids is the Garrison School-restored and furnished as an eighth-grade country school with one teacher and supplied with mannequin students using desks and textbooks representing its 110 years of use.

MACKENZIE ENVIRONMENTAL EDUCATION CTR

W7303 County Road CS **Poynette** 53955

- Phone: (608) 635-8105 **https://dnr.wisconsin.gov/education/mackenzie**
- Hours: Open year-round. Grounds dawn-dusk. Exhibits open Daily 8:00am-4:00pm (May-October), Weekdays only rest of year.
- Admission: FREE but donations are appreciated.

The center has many features including a live wildlife exhibit, self guided nature trails, museums, fire tower, large picnic area, lodge and dormitories and so much more. The wildlife exhibit features live animals native to Wisconsin, including bison, bobcat, deer, mountain lions, a wolf, and many raptors including a bald eagle. All of the animals in the exhibit were injured, orphaned, or raised in captivity and cannot be released into the wild. Outdoorsy types will like to climb the observation tower from which one can view the grounds and the surrounding countryside. There's a logging exhibit featuring a 19th century log cabin and sawmill and a maple syrup facility (open for groups and events in March) on the grounds too.

WISCONSIN BIG CAT RESCUE

305 Pine Street (near Hwy 136 and 154) **Rock Springs** 53961

- Phone: (608) 524-LION **www.wisconsinbigcats.org**
- Hours: Daily 10am-5pm (summers). Weekends only (spring, fall)
- Tours by reservation. Minimum donation required: $10.00 adult, $8.00 senior (55+), $6.00 child (6-12). Closed if raining, chance of storms, or extreme heat 90 degrees or higher.
- Educators: They have quick fact sheets on each type of cat online on the Education Page.

This center gives these cats a chance at a peaceful and happy life, and a chance for the public to learn about them, and the abuse that they endure elsewhere in captivity. These animals were not put in nature to jump through hoops or perform tricks, or to pose for pictures. The free-roaming enclosures allow the animals to "play" and they even have giant cylinders for them to hide. The cubs are adorable...and usually plentiful. Hopefully, you'll get to hear the Lion roar. You don't really understand how much bass is in a lion's roar until you're nearby and feel the earth tremble!

BADGER MINE AND MUSEUM

279 W. Estey Street (off of Rte 11, southwest of town) **Shullsburg** 53586

- Phone: (608) 965-4860
  http://badgermineandmuseum.com
- Hours: Wednesday--Sunday 11:30am-4:00pm. (Memorial Day-Labor Day)
- Admission: Museum and Mine Tour Rates: $7.00 adult, Free (4 and under).

Take a tour into the main drift of Badger Mine, a lead mine. With a guide you will descend 51 stairs to the main drift of the early 1900s mine, extending beneath the city. You will marvel at the small side tunnels of the mine and wonder how they worked in such cramped conditions. See how the pioneers did their work as you also get to look at early farm tools, medical equipment, a drugstore, a turn-of-the-century kitchen, a blacksmith shop, and a carpenter's shop. Exhibits focus on some of Shullsburg's most important industries, including mining and cheesemaking, but also on day-to-day life through the decades. Wonder what more modern mines look like? The museum's newest acquisition, a fully functional replica of the Eagle Pitcher Mine. While going into the mine may be the most adventuresome part of the visit, your kids just might learn some early Wisconsin history, too.

ROELLI CHEESE HAUS

15982 State Hwy 11 (a few miles east of town) **Shullsburg** 53586

- Phone: (608) 965-3779 **www.roellicheese.com**
- Hours: Monday-Saturday 8:00am-5:30pm.

Adolph Roelli came to Lafayette County from Switzerland in the 1920s. From that time, four generations of the Roelli family have been in the cheese business at this location. They have a public viewing area with retail cheese sales along with deli, snacks, cheese and ice cream. Cheese making at Roelli Cheese Haus occurs in the early mornings, Monday through Friday.

HOUSE ON THE ROCK - THE ATTRACTION

5754 State Road 23 **Spring Green** 53533

- Phone: (608) 935-3639 or (800) 334-5275 **www.thehouseontherock.com**
- Hours: Daily 9:00am-5:00pm (May-early September). Closes Tuesdays and Wednesdays (spring/fall).
- Admission: Ultimate Experience (all 3 tours) $32.95 adult, $17.95 child (7-17). Children 6 and under $4.95. Each sections may also be purchased as a separate admission ($19.95/$11.95 per section)

Here's a simple guarantee: no matter how long or widely you have traveled, you have never seen anything remotely like The House on the Rock. This house was literally built atop a 60-foot chimney of rock - a 450-foot drop overlooking the Wyoming Valley. Built by Alex Jordan in the early 1940s, the house and grounds are full of stuff - and large amounts. Outside, the landscapers planted 50,000 trees and 100,000 flowers in the garden and front lawns. There's even a Japanese Garden with 14-foot quadruple waterfalls that cascade into the garden pond. If you dare, walk the sky ledge "terrace" to "hang" out over the valley below. Inside, a family favorite is the Infinity Room with its narrow point and mirrors that give the illusion the room corner never ends. That one room also has over 3,000 windows! Look for the 200-foot long whale fighting an octopus in the Heritage of the Sea Building, as well as hundreds of ship models. Count how many suits of armor you can find. Another room displays 250 dollhouses, furnished completely and the house also holds the world's largest carousel - 269 animals and not one a horse. Be prepared for lots of walking, some stair climbing, meandering underneath waterfalls and over bridges. Sounds like a maze? Simply follow the arrows and no one will get lost.

TOWER HILL STATE PARK

5808 County Road C **Spring Green** 53588

- Phone: (608) 588-2116
  http://dnr.wi.gov/topic/parks/name/towerhill/
- Admission: A vehicle admission sticker is required. Daily $8.00-$11.00. Annual passes available.

Visit the park's restored shot tower and melting house to see exhibits on lead shot making from the 1800s. Challenging bluff trails and panoramic views. Open mid-April through October. 77 acres featuring 15 campsites, handicap-accessible picnic areas, vistas, Wisconsin River shoreline, canoeing, boating, fishing, 1/2-mile of nature trails. 1.5 miles of hiking trails. Open May-October daily 6:00am-11:00pm with overnight camping.

LAKE KEGONSA STATE PARK

2405 Door Creek Road (2 miles S of I-90, 3 miles N of Stoughton)
Stoughton 53589

- Phone: (608) 873-9695
  http://dnr.wi.gov/topic/parks/name/lakekegonsa/
- Hours: Daily 6:00am-11:00pm.
- Admission: A vehicle admission sticker is required. Daily $8.00-$11.00. Annual passes available.

Lake Kegonsa State Park is a popular choice; its 80 campsites, 6 miles of trails, boat launch and beach are a great way to beat the summer heat. Lake Kegonsa offers swimming, fishing, water-skiing, sailing, and motor boating. The lake covers 3,209 acres and is more than 30 feet deep. Park visitors enjoy the lake's excellent fishing. Wetland boardwalk. Pet swim area. In the winter the trails are open for crosscountry skiing as well.

SYTTENDE MAI

Stoughton - Downtown, Opera House. The longest-running Norwegian Independence Day festival held outside of Norway. Stoughton honors its Norwegian roots with two parades, folk dancing, arts and crafts, Norwegian costumes, rosemaling exhibitions, Norwegian paintings, a quilt show and authentic Norwegian foods. Don't forget the ugly troll contest. Did you know Stoughten is the self-proclaimed birthplace of the coffee break? **https://www.stoughtonfestivals.com/** *(Weekend closest to May 17th)*

WIDMER'S CHEESE CELLARS
214 West Henni Street **Theresa** 53091

- Phone: (920) 488-2503 **www.widmerscheese.com**
- Hours: The factory store and viewing area are open Monday-Saturday 7:00am-5:00pm (year-round). Also, Sunday 10:00am-3:00pm (June-October).
- Tours: If you would like a guided tour for groups they are available Monday through Friday at 9:30am. Please call in advance to make a reservation. NOTE - Open Toe Shoes and Jewelry are not permitted when taking a guided tour. Video tour is available on website.

The story of Widmer's Cheese begins over 70 years ago, when the founder, John O. Widmer, left Switzerland to come to America. He choose to settle in one of the most famous cheese producing regions of the world, Dodge County, Wisconsin. As did many Swiss immigrants, Widmer became a cheese maker. He worked in various cheese factories as an apprentice before settling in Theresa Wisconsin in 1922. Embracing the manufacturing techniques which have been handed down through generations of cheese makers, Widmer's Cheese Cellars offers a Wisconsin original, Wisconsin Brick cheese. Come and see Wisconsin's only cheese factory still using real bricks to press their brick cheese...the same bricks Gramps Widmer used in 1922. Just a step down from a small retail area sits the "make room," its traditional open vats being carefully tended, curds being stirred or hand-scooped into forms, or the famous Widmer bricks being gently placed atop the forms to press the whey out of the signature Brick cheese. Brick's earthy, sweet flavor and its slice ability make it not only delicious, but easy to use as a table cheese kids like too.

DID YOU KNOW? *United States and France rank as the leading cheese-producing countries. Wisconsin is the leading cheese making state.*

TREK BICYCLES FACTORY TOUR
801 W Madison Street **Waterloo** 53594

- Phone: (920) 478-2191 **www.trekbikes.com/us/en/company/factory_tour/**
- Tours: Wednesdays at 10:00am. Tours last one hour and are open to kids and adults. Wheelchair and stroller accessible. Closed toes shoes must be worn and safety glasses will be provided during the tour.

Trek Factory tours offer the chance to get behind the scenes at Trek and everything that goes into making your Trek. Custom Project One bikes are painted right at Trek's Waterloo, WI factory.

GOVERNOR NELSON STATE PARK

5140 County Road M (2 miles SW of SR 113) **Waunakee** 53597

- Phone: (608) 831-3005
  http://dnr.wi.gov/topic/parks/name/govnelson/
- Admission: A vehicle admission sticker is required. Daily $8.00-$11.00.
  Annual passes available.

Located on Lake Mendota in Governor Nelson Nature And Recreation Area, you can mingle mingle within sight of the State Capitol. Features effigy mounds in the wooded upland, handicap-accessible campsites, seasonal naturalist programs. It has a 500-foot sand beach, bathhouses with solar-heated showers, a four-stall boat launch, a fish cleaning facility, picnic areas, barrier free playground equipment, prairie restorations, 8.4 miles of hiking/cross country ski trails, and a scenic overlook of Lake Mendota. Day use only park.

KIDDIE INDOOR WATERPARKS
Wisconsin Dells

The same four-story waterslides, high-speed vortexes and cavernous wave pools that teens and adults crave may intimidate smaller children. That's why several resorts have created waterparks with whimsical themes and interactive areas geared toward pre-school or younger school-age kids.

The WINTERGREEN RESORT & CONFERENCE CENTER (www. wintergreen-resort.com), and MT. OLYMPUS (www.mtolympuspark.com) welcome kids under 10 with special goodie bags and Kids Club Cards that feature discounts to area attractions. The ATLANTIS WATERPARK HOTEL & SUITES (www.theatlantishotel.com) recently added two-room fanciful King Neptune suites perfect for families who need a little extra room.

WISCONSIN DELLS CAMPGROUNDS
Wisconsin Dells

Wisconsin Dells campgrounds range from back-to-nature tent camping to RV parks to camp cabins. Folks often tell us this is a good place to ease into camping and see where it takes you. Two campgrounds stand out as providing more casual "resort" amenities and backed by national campground company standards:

- **WISCONSIN DELLS KOA KAMPGROUND** (www.wisdellskoa. com) - swim in heated pool, free wi-fi, nightly movies at the outdoor theatre.

- **YOGI BEAR'S CAMP RESORT & WATER PLAYGROUND** (www. dellsjellystone.com) - themed water playground, game rooms, a pool, hot tub, restaurant, mini-golf, and boat rentals.

WISCONSIN DELLS GO CARTING
Wisconsin Dells

- **ADARE GO CARTS** - Put the pedal to the metal at the area's fastest track! A challenging road course that takes drivers over hills, under bridges, around hairpin turns and waterfalls. Families love our kiddie go cart track. $5.00 per ride. Located next to Original Wisconsin Ducks. (608) 253-7170.

- **EXTREME WORLD** - 1/4 mile SuperSpeedway asphalt track - (608) 254-4111

WISCONSIN DELLS MUSIC & THEATRE
Wisconsin Dells

- **RICK WILCOX THEATER** - www.rickwilcox.com. Experience the impossible with master illusionists, Rick & Suzan Wilcox. Open year-round, visit Web site for schedule. 1666 Wisconsin Dells Pkwy. Start $49.00.

BIG FOOT ZIPLINE
1550 Wisconsin Dells Parkway (behind Dells Army Duck Tours)
Wisconsin Dells 53965

- Phone: (608) 244-3668 **www.bigfootzip.com**
- Admission: $99.00 per person. Online discounts.

This Zipline tour is comprised of six lines strung across 30 acres, making it the largest in the nation. Riders can take in scenic "birds-eye" views as they glide over the attraction's four water crossings.

They also have a ropes course, duckboat and jet boat tours for ~ $30.00.

BUFFALO PHIL'S GRILLE

Wisconsin Dells - 150 Gasser Road (next to Tanger Outlet Mall) 53965. Phone: (608) 254-7300 www.buffalophilsgrille.com. At Buffalo Phil's you can enjoy family oriented western dining experience. Enjoy their wings, pizzas, BBQ, rotisserie chicken, and buffalo burgers. Lil' Buckaroos Menu - Each meal is served with western waffle fries & choice of drink served in a complimentary kids' cup–$7.00 Some nights are all-you-can-eat, some offer free bowling. Phil's has added a train depot inside its restaurant. Sit near the tracks and your food will be delivered by miniature train!

CHULA VISTA RESORT LOST RIOS INDOOR WATERPARK

2501 River Road (Hwy 13 North) **Wisconsin Dells** 53965

☐ Phone: (800) 388-4782 or (608) 254-8366
www.chulavistaresort.com

Chula Vista Resort's Lost Rios Indoor Waterpark, home of the world's longest and fastest indoor water coaster, the Fly'n Mayan. 300 themed guestrooms and suites, 3 restaurants, sports bar, indoor & outdoor waterparks, and golf. An underground lighted tunnel leads the way from the resort to the waterpark. Weekends can be very crowded and some days they have teen nights which can be intimidating for little ones. A first grader can go on all the rides and, because this waterpark is more compact, you can keep an eye on your kids from a lounge chair. *Day rates: $49.00*

DELLS BOAT TOURS

107 Broadway (Upper Dells Dock) **Wisconsin Dells** 53965

☐ Phone: (608) 254-8555 **www.dellsboats.com**
☐ Hours: Open (April-early November), Hours: 10am-4:00pm (Spring & Fall), 8:00am-7:00pm (Summer). Tours depart every 20-30 minutes. Call for rates and details.
☐ Admission: Varies by tour ~$36.00 adult (12+), ~ half price child (4-11). Combo tours available.
☐ Note: Several ticket booths are located throughout the area and a Lower Dells dock is at the junction of Highways 12, 13 & 16.

Believe it or not, there's still a way to slow down the pace on vacation in the Wisconsin Dells. The Dells are actually a strip of a dozen or more miles of riverbanks and sandstone cliffs plus nature trails that weave around it. Several companies offer leisurely excursions of the Upper and Lower Dells (the dam split the waterway into the upper and lower portions).

An Upper Dells excursion is available with shore landings at two of the area's most famous sandstone rock formations - Witches Gulch (has mysterious passageways and canyons), and Stand Rock, made famous by photographer H.H. Bennett's photo of his son leaping from one rock bluff to another. Although people aren't permitted to leap those rocks, specially trained jumping dogs leap the five-foot chasm from the main cliff to the rock ledge!

A Lower Dells excursion is available with a more historic note. Guides recount stories about the ghost town of Newport, the once-vibrant logging era, and Native American history.

DELLS RACEWAY PARK

N1070 Smith Road **Wisconsin Dells** 53965

- ☐ Phone: (608) 253-RACE **www.dellsracewaypark.com**
- ☐ Hours: Racing Sat nights at 7:00pm (May - mid-September). Fan Gates Open @ 4:00pm, Green Flags at 6:30pm.
- ☐ Admission: $15.00 adult, $12.00 senior (62+) & student (10-15), Ages 9 and under admitted FREE. Some special events have separate pricing.

1/3-mile asphalt, banked oval with racing in Super Late, Limited Late, Super Stock, Pure Stock and Bandit divisions.

EFFIGY MOUNDS

Kingsley Bend Wayside on Hwy 16 **Wisconsin Dells** 53965

The Wisconsin Dells area has been inhabited by native people for 2,000 years and their legacy is noted in ceremonial and burial mounds. Some 20 burial and effigy mounds, including two 100-foot long bears, a panther with a tail as long as a football field, and an eagle with a 200-foot wingspan are found at this wayside. The Ho-Chunk Sovereign Nation (also known as Winnebago) were once forced west, now have been able to reclaim some of their land.

GREAT WOLF LODGE

1400 Great Wolf Drive (I-90/94 exit 92 (Hwy 12) to Gasser Road. Left)
Wisconsin Dells 53965

- ☐   Phone: (608) 253-2222 **www.greatwolflodge.com**
- ☐   Dining: Bear Paw Sweets & Eats lighter fare; Camp Critter Buffet & casual meals; Loose Moose Bar & Grill for full-service dining.

A Northwoods themed year-round resort with family-sized suite lodging; a huge indoor waterpark (waterslides, lazy river, whirlpools, interactive water fort, kiddie play pool) plus a seasonal outdoor waterplay area. Visitors can ride the world's first enclosed "Howlin' Tornado," a six-story funnel of extreme tubing, or hurtle downward four stories on the nation's first enclosed, head-first mat race slide. This waterpark is exclusively reserved for guests.

- DRY IDEAS: MagiQuest. Young adventurers use a magic wand that they can customize and keep to navigate through this four-story, Renaissance-themed interactive adventure. An arcade fills out the dry fun. Scooops Kid Spa (an ice cream themed spa) is another distraction for girls.

- LODGING: Many unique suite styles that comfortably sleep from two to fourteen guests. The kids … er, cubs … sleep in the wolf den, an in-suite cave-themed area with a bunk bed. They can "rough it" with movies and Nintendo on their own TV. In the main portion of the suite, adults can sprawl out on a queen bed and full-size sleeper sofa. They get their own TV too. This suite also features a private balcony or patio. Consider upgrading to the more spacious and equally charming KidCabin® suite. All rooms come equipped with a microwave and medium frig. Packages start at $129.95. Your stay includes passes to the indoor waterpark, evening storytimes and Cub club activity room. _____ 🍽️ 🛏️

KALAHARI WATERPARK RESORT

1305 Kalahari Drive (I-90/94 exit 92 (Hwy 12) north) **Wisconsin Dells** 53965

- ☐   Phone: (608) 254-5466 **www.kalahariresorts.com/wi/**
- ☐   Admission: Overnight guest packages start at $199.95, complete with admission to Wisconsin's Largest Indoor Waterpark for each registered guest. Most "dry" amusements and rides are extra fees - tokens and all day ride passes ($30). Waterpark day passes only: ~$45.00.
- ☐   Note: Kalahari has a smart "energized System" which automatically conserves heat and turns off lights when guests leave the room. Golf course

on property. For total relaxation, there are five whirlpool spas.

Kalahari's claim to fame is the FlowRider and Master Blaster. Guests can surf standing up or boogie board indoors 365 days a year on the FlowRider or experience the Master Blaster uphill water rollercoaster waterslide. That is clearly why tweens and teens gravitate to this park - the thrills and large scale of the place. You can also choose from a water treehouse, lazy river or water sport pools, but the kids over 10 spend more time in the rides area. Family raft slides are king and the Tidal Wave Pool is the best indoor wave pool around. They have an equally nice outdoor waterpark, too.

Adding to these tweeked thrills - include a six-story Ferris wheel, laser tag, go karts, golf simulators and a sports bar. Dining options are numerous.

Kalahari also features over 750 guestrooms with 10 stand alone five-bedroom suites. Other amenities offered: Spa Kalahari, fitness center, on site restaurants, arcade, pottery pizzazz create station and they have daily craft stations.

NOAH'S ARK WATERPARK

1410 Wisconsin Dells Parkway **Wisconsin Dells** 53965

- Phone: (608) 254-6351 **www.noahsarkwaterpark.com**
- Hours: Daily 9:00am-7:00pm (mid-June - mid-August). Park is open from Labor Day - Memorial Day with shorter hours. Closed for winter.
- Admission: Day Pass ~$39.00 adult, ~$29.00 child (under 48") and senior.

If you've never been to an outdoor waterpark before, then why not start with the country's largest. Noah's Ark, at 70 acres, is huge. They are most noted for their Black Anaconda ride - America's longest water roller coaster and The Point of No Return extreme body slide that is 10 stories high.

"The Scorpion's Tail" is America's first looping tube water slide and the tallest and largest of its kind in the world. Riders drop through a trap door below their feet and speed through a 45-degree loop in an enclosed, gravity-defying slide. Here you'll also find 49 thrilling waterslides, TWO giant wavepools, two Endless Rivers, four children's water play areas, bumper boats, an 18-hole miniature golf course, and a mammoth 4-D Movie Theater.

ORIGINAL WISCONSIN DUCKS

1890 Wisconsin Dells Parkway North **Wisconsin Dells** 53965

- ☐ Phone: (608) 254-8751 **www.wisconsinducktours.com**
- ☐ Hours: Daily 8:00am-7:00pm (summer). 9:00am-5:00pm (spring & fall).
- ☐ Admission: $36.00 adult, $18.00 child (4-11).
- ☐ NOTE: Normally it is customary to tip drivers for a GREAT ride, but remember this is optional and no further purchases are necessary.

This town is home to the world's largest fleet of WWII land-to-water vehicles known as DUCKs. Originally used for covert operations, these vehicle's shining moment in history was D-Day, June 4, 1944, when more than 2,000 of the vehicles were used to deliver troops to the rough shores of Normandy, France. In the mid-1900s, a man brought the first surplus DUCKS (never used in combat) to the Dells and set up a tour company. Now those quacky ducks load up and tour the Lower Dells and Lake Delton. This is one of our favorite ways to see an area and going through canyons, cruising the river, back on land, then splashing into Lake Delton was a neat way to mix it up. One hill gives you the butterflies. The tour guides are known to be corny and goofy but, hey, you're on a silly duck boat anyway. Hope your kids get to co-pilot part of the way - it's a kids thrill.

PAUL BUNYAN COOK SHANTY

Wisconsin Dells - 411 State Hwy 13 (I-90/94 exit 87) 53965. **https://dellspaulbunyans. com/.** *With all those water rides around town, a family gets pretty hungry. Paul Bunyan, a famous lumberjack, knew how to eat well and fill up. For more than 50 years, Paul Bunyan's has been a familiar face in Wisconsin Dells. Since 1958, they've been serving their famous Camp Style Breakfast to hungry patrons at the busiest tourist destination in Wisconsin. This place is open 7am-12:30pm everyday (breakfast only). The décor looks like something right out of a North Woods logging camp so it's comfy casual.* 🍽️

PIRATE'S COVE ADVENTURE GOLF

Downtown on Broadway (Intersection of Hwy 12/13/16/23)
Wisconsin Dells 53965

- Phone: (608) 254-7500 or (608) 254-8336 **www.piratescovewisdells.com**
- Hours: Daily 8:00am-11:00pm (Memorial Day-Labor Day). Open April-October, spring and fall hours vary, call for times.
- Admission: Varies by activity. Just mini golf starts at $8.00-$11.00.

The largest Pirate's Cove in the USA; miniature golf at its best with 90 holes and 17 waterfalls. The grounds crew here maintain 30,000 plants around 90 holes.

POLYNESIAN WATERPARK RESORT

857 N Frontage Road (exit 87) **Wisconsin Dells** 53965

- Phone: (608) 254-2883 or (800) 272-5642 **www.dellspolynesian.com**
- Hours: Waterpark 9:00am-9:00pm, outdoor water park closes at dusk. (Memorial Day-Labor Day). Areas vary by season rest of year. Call or see website for current schedule.

Did you know that owner Stan Anderson's concept for the country's first INDOOR WATERPARK was sketched out on a napkin? Because of long Wisconsin winters with not much to do, Anderson conceived the idea of putting a roof over a water attraction. Today, he's widely considered the "Father of the Indoor Water Park," having turned winter into summer, an idea that caught on like indoor plumbing. The Polynesian Water Park Resort is the best Water Park Hotel for Families with kids 10 and Under. That is why all kids 10 and under stay absolutely FREE! And, come summertime, they do have an outdoor waterpark, too. From Memorial Day through Labor Day enjoy Over 4 Acres of Outdoor Waterpark areas which includes: Waterslides, Lazy River, Interactive Pirate Ship, Basketball & Volleyball Pool, Whirlpool's, Mushroom Waterfalls, and Kiddie interactive water play areas and kiddie water slides.

RIPLEY'S BELIEVE IT OR NOT MUSEUM

115 Broadway **Wisconsin Dells** 53965

- ☐ Phone: (608) 253-7556 **www.ripleysdells.com**
- ☐ Hours: Daily 9:00am-11:00pm (Memorial Weekend-Labor Day weekend). Hours vary by month rest of season. Call or visit website for most current schedule.
- ☐ Admission: $26.99 adult, $16.99 child (3-9).

Ok, those familiar with Ripleys always know to look for the shrunken head or the real mermaid. They're here. Their motto: "Let us put bizarre before your very eyes." Many replicas of famous Ripley artifacts from around the world are on display with quirky signs describing them. There is a 6-legged mounted cow and a goose mounted with shoes on it. The interactive Temple of Discovery is set up like a temple crumbling as the walls shake and the floor vibrates. Note, as with all Ripley's, hallways are dimly lit and confining and some exhibits are downright scary to look at (man with head cut in half) - it may be too scary for young ones.

RIVERSIDE & GREAT NORTHERN RAILWAY

N115 County Road N (1 mile north on Stand Rock Road) **Wisconsin Dells** 53965

- ☐ Phone: (608) 254-6367 **https://www.dellstrain.com/**
- ☐ Hours: (Memorial Day-Labor Day). Please arrive at least 15 to 20 minutes before the hour to allow time for ticketing. Hours vary rest of season - call or see website for Weekends in April, May, September, October, November.
- ☐ Admission: Museum FREE. Train rides $15.00 adult, $12.00 senior (62+), $10.00 child (4+).

The R&GN is an operating 15" gauge live steam railroad, located in Wisconsin Dells. This Railway uses smaller scale trains that are too cute. The 45 minute ride covers 3 miles. This living railroad museum looks back into the history of railroading in Wisconsin. The buildings represent railroad facilities found at railroad terminals at the turn of the 20th century. The staff is very friendly to children, and the small scale of the trains is way more hands on for kids then the average railroad museum. Before or after the ride, your kids will be sure to catch the colorful Museum Store with its wide selection trains, including Thomas the Tank Engine. Bring or purchase some snacks and have a picnic near the depot.

The Learning Center/Museum has an operating train - a train your children can operate. Equipment displays and a theater offering videos about railroad history and trains.

ROCKY ARBOR STATE PARK

N381 US Highway 12 and 16 (1 mile SE of I-90/94, 1-1/2 miles NW of Wisconsin Dells) **Wisconsin Dells** 53965

☐ Phone: (608) 254-8001
http://dnr.wi.gov/topic/parks/name/rockyarbor/
☐ Hours: Daily 6:00am-11:00pm with overnight camping.
☐ Admission: A vehicle admission sticker is required. Daily $8.00-$11.00. Annual passes available.

Camping and hiking among spectacular sandstone cliffs. The 244-acre Park is within 1.5 miles of the popular Wisconsin Dells vacation community. Eighty-nine wooded campsites offer seclusion, while pine trees and sandstone bluffs offer a cool escape to the picnicker or hiker in this summer park. The park has a 1-mile self-guided nature trail. In February, the state parks' cross-country ski trails are lighted by thousands of candles for night time light.

TIMBAVATI WILDLIFE PARK AT STORYBOOK GARDENS

2220 Wisconsin Dells Parkway (Hwy. 12) **Wisconsin Dells** 53965

☐ Phone: (608) 253-2391 **www.timbavatiwildlifepark.com**
☐ Hours: Daily 9:00am-5:00pm.
☐ Admission: $19.95 adult, $16.95 child (2-12). Feed cups extra.
☐ Note: Train and Carousel rides available in the park.

Built in the early 1950's, Storybook Gardens was one of the first tourist attractions in the Wisconsin Dells Area. Parents, imagine a fiberglass fairytale park. Being an older attraction in the Dells, it isn't as glitzy and over-stimulating but may be better for the younger set who only care about the cutesy animals. The animals are all very docile and friendly. The addition of jungle wildlife and some wild Wisconsin creatures engages the elementary-aged kids. You can get pretty close to zebra and kangaroos. Besides the wildlife shows, you can pet and feed a giraffe at one station designed to put you face-to-face with this tall creature. For the best experience, go early and the camels, llamas, deer and goats will welcome you with open mouths and eager attitudes.

TIMBER FALLS ADVENTURE PARK

1000 Stand Rock Road (at the Wisconsin River Bridge)
Wisconsin Dells 53965

☐ Phone: (608) 254-8414 **www.timberfallspark.com**
☐ Hours: Vary by season - call or see website for current listing.
☐ Admission: Most activities are $7.00-$10.00 each.

Roller coasters? The Avalanche, a wood/steel hybrid, has the second steepest drop - at 62 degrees - in North America and banks of 70 degrees. You'll also find bumper boats, log rides and other thrill rides. Visitors can golf around a volcano that erupts every 15 minutes on a 72-holes of miniature golf, or head across the street to their links along the Wisconsin River, the only course with shade.

TOMMY BARTLETT'S EXPLORATORY INTERACTIVE SCIENCE CENTER

560 Wisconsin Dells Parkway **Wisconsin Dells** 53965

☐ Phone: (608) 254-2525 **www.tommybartlett.com**
☐ Hours: Daily 10:00am-9:00pm (summer), Daily 10:00am-4:00pm (rest of year).
☐ Admission: $16.00 general, $13.00 child (5-11).

Packed with interactive family fun, the Exploratory is open daily, featuring exhibits that will boggle your brain and spark your imagination. Quirky exhibits like a piece of Russian space hardware and a replica of an American space capsule coincide in the same building. The Russian MIR (only one on display anywhere) is open to step inside. Be sure you read the plaque describing the story behind an American acquiring a famous Russian vessel. There are 150 hands-on interactive exhibits, with lessons on static electricity, magnetic fields, lasers and optical illusions. Ride the High Wire SkyCycle (seasonal) on a one-inch cable positioned 12 feet in the air. The Virtual Sports Center allows players to participate in games and extreme sports through a computer-created environment. The new GravBall simulates the effects of weightlessness through the futuristic game using virtual reality technology. Computerized touch-screen games, a robotic house, playing with gravity, and other electrical energy experiments round out this science entertainment center. Did your hair stand on end?

WILDERNESS RESORT COMPLEX

511 East Adams Street (I-90/94 exit 92 north) **Wisconsin Dells** 53965

☐ Phone: (608) 253-9729 **www.wildernessterritory.com**
☐ Admission: Waterpark passes are included in the overnight room price. Only resort overnight guests can partake in the waterpark and mini-golf features. Monthly specials run as low as $139.00/night for off peak reservations.
☐ Miscellaneous: Golf. Wi-Fi in rooms. FREEBIES: often they run restaurant specials where kids eat FREE (under 12) off the kids menu or buffet with adult purchase.

WATERPARKS - This resort complex boasts the largest indoor/outdoor waterpark combo in the nation, so large, in fact, they've refer to themselves as a "territory." Their most notable rides? Halley's Comet Racers (outdoors) - four slides where you race headfirst through twists, turns and drops toward the finish line. Or, The Hurricane (indoors) - America's tallest waterslide at 58 feet where you plummet through a dark tunnel before landing in a pool below. The WaterDome has two family raft racing rides, cabanas and the largest indoor wavepool. Lazy rivers, play structures, bucket tipping,

ZIP LINE - Visitors of the resort will find adventure in the new Lost Canyon Zip Line Canopy Tour, a zip line that takes riders over the tree canopy of Lost Canyon behind the resort. The zip line's final run spans 900 feet in length and reaches speeds of 30 mph. Don't be concerned, kids and parents are cautious at first, but once you get the "feel" for flying, you want the speed!

AMUSEMENTS - Outdoor go-kart track,laser tag, two indoor black light mini-golf courses and one outdoor mini-golf course, and indoor bumper boats. Try Big Fish 3-D mini golf & native fish aquariums. Of course, several arcades are on the properties.

SNOW SPORTS - Snow machines and an outdoor snow tube area are adjacent to their massive indoor waterpark.

LODGING - Wilderness on the Lake offers upscale condo resort setting on Lake Delton. 5-bedroom and treehouse cabins are available, too. Noteworthy amenities: A combined indoor/outdoor waterpark featuring an adult lap pool area, indoor/outdoor hot spas, a kiddie area and an outdoor infinity pool with a vanishing edge that appears to empty into Lake Delton; food and beverage service; convenience store; exercise room; three outdoor fire pits, barbecue areas; a deck overlooking Lake Delton; and a sand beach with lake access.

WILDERNESS RESORT COMPLEX (cont.)

In addition, boat piers with slips are available for guests to reserve while they're staying at Wilderness on the Lake.

WILDERNESS HOTEL - four more indoor waterparks, three outdoor waterparks as well as dry play area.

GLACIER CANYON - standard and 2 bedroom rooms.

RESTAURANTS - Field's is a classic supper club and Survivors is a large casual environ known as the place for burgers. Wild Canyon Café offers buffets and a Kids Menu and Sarento's Italian Restaurant & Pizzeria is classic Italian.

WISCONSIN DEER PARK

583 Wisconsin Dells Parkway **Wisconsin Dells** 53965

- ☐ Phone: (608) 253-2041 **www.wisdeerpark.com**
- ☐ Hours: Daily 10:00am-4:00pm (May - October). Extended hours (Memorial Day - Labor Day).
- ☐ Admission: $14.00 adult (12+), $10.00 child (3-11). Small additional charge for deer crackers and feed cups.

Established in 1952, stroll along the 40-acre forest and hand-feed many varieties of wildlife - especially deer. 100 deer are on the property and they come up to you and eat directly from your hand. Other animals in the deer family are American Elk, American Bison, and the dainty Japanese Silka deer. Everybody likes the llamas, piggies and lemurs, too. If you visit late spring, fawns (baby deer) are newborn almost daily. Summertime, the bucks' antlers are full racked. Why do the deer look small here vs. when you see them frightened alongside the road? Be sure you only feed the deer the crackers just for them. Human crackers have an ingredient deer can't absorb and it gives them a bad belly ache.

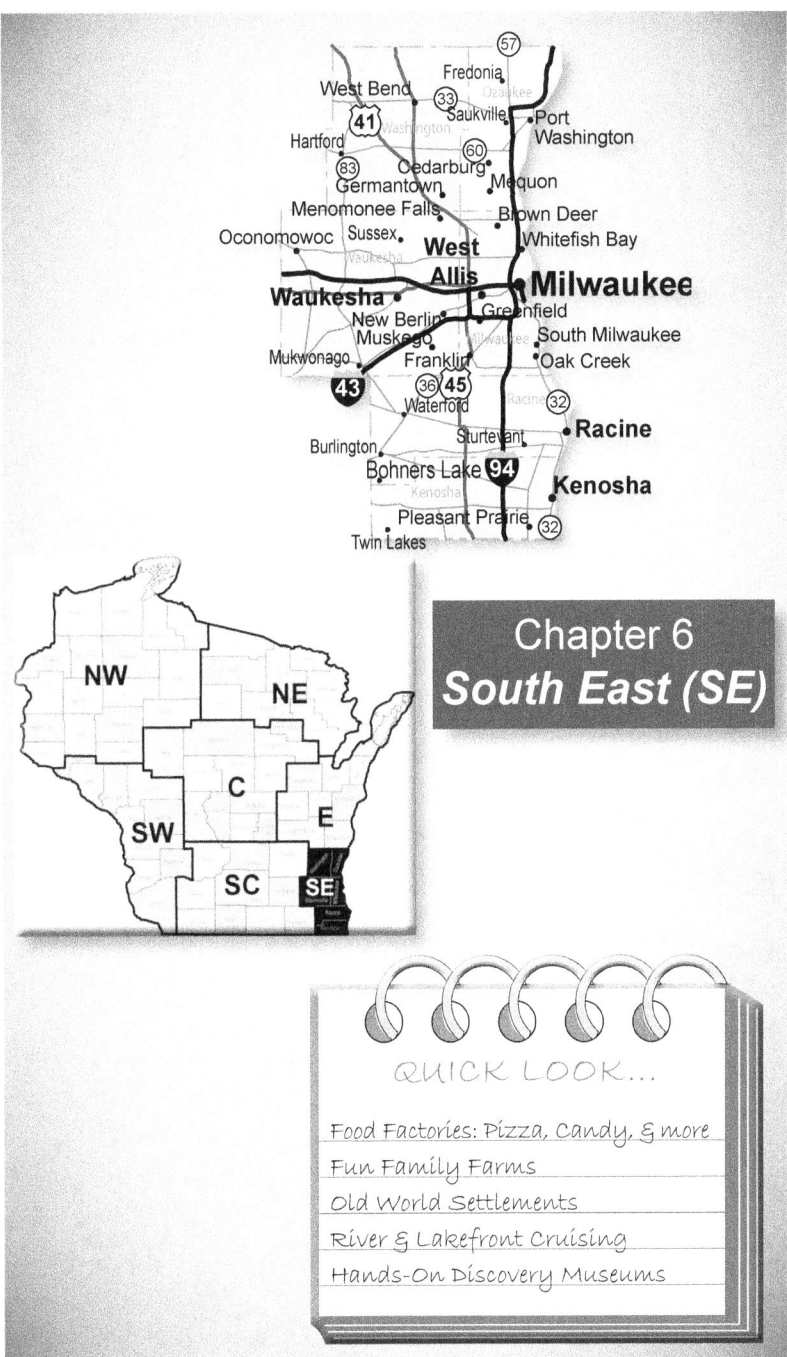

Chapter 6
South East (SE)

QUICK LOOK...

Food Factories: Pizza, Candy, & more

Fun Family Farms

Old World Settlements

River & Lakefront Cruising

Hands-On Discovery Museums

Belgium
- Harrington Beach State Park

Burlington
- Chocolate Fest
- Hall Of Logic Puzzles Museum
- Spinning Top & Yo-Yo Museum

Burlington (Kansasville)
- Richard Bong State Recreation Area

Cedarburg
- Cedar Creek Settlement
- Winter Festival

Delafield
- Hawks Inn Living Museum
- Lapham Peak State Park

Eagle
- Old World Wisconsin

East Troy
- East Troy Electric Railroad Museum

Elkhorn
- Alpine Valley Ski Resort
- Applefest

Franklin
- Wehr Nature Center

Grafton
- The Family Farm

Greendale
- Reiman Publications Visitor Center & Country Store

Hartford
- Pike Lake State Park
- Wisconsin Automotive Museum

Kenosha
- Bristol Renaissance Faire
- Civil War Museum

- Dinosaur Discovery Museum
- Frank's Diner
- Jack's Café At Andreas
- Jerry Smith Produce & Country Store Pumpkin Patch
- Kenosha History Center & Southport Light
- Kenosha Public Museum
- Kenosha Streetcars
- Pike River Rendezvous

Milwaukee
- African World Festival
- Betty Brinn Children's Museum
- Discovery World At Pier Wisconsin
- German Fest
- Great Circus Parade
- Harley-Davidson Museum
- Holiday Folk Fair
- Indian Summer Pow Wows
- Lake Express High Speed Ferry
- Miller Park
- Milwaukee Air & Water Show
- Milwaukee Art Museum
- Milwaukee Boat Line
- Milwaukee County Historical Society Museum
- Milwaukee County Zoo
- Milwaukee Irish Fest
- Milwaukee Public Museum
- Milwaukee River Cruise Line
- Milwaukee Sports
- Mitchell Park Conservatory (The Domes)
- North Point Lighthouse
- Palermo's Pizza Tours
- Polish Fest
- Schlitz Audubon Nature Center
- Summerfest
- Wisconsin State Fair

Milwaukee (West Allis)
- Milwaukee Mile Race Track

Newburg
- Riveredge Nature Center

Pleasant Prairie
- Jelly Belly Factory Warehouse Tour

Port Washington
- Port Washington Lighthouse & Lightstation Museum
- World's Largest One-Day Outdoor Fish Fry

Racine
- Kewpee Hamburgers
- Kringle Bakeries
- North Beach
- Racine Heritage Museum
- Racine Zoo
- Root River Steelhead Facility
- SC Johnson Museum
- Wind Point Lighthouse

Racine (Sturdevant)
- Apple Holler

Richfield
- Cabela's

St. Francis
- Quality Candy & Buddy Squirrel Candy & Nut Tour

Waterford
- Bear Den Game Farm & Petting Zoo
- Green Meadows Farm

Waukesha
- Country Springs Water Park Hotel
- Waukesha County Materials Recycling Facility
- Waukesha Janboree

West Bend
- Meadowbrook Pumpkin Farm
- Museum Of Wisconsin Art

Williams Bay
- Yerkes Observatory

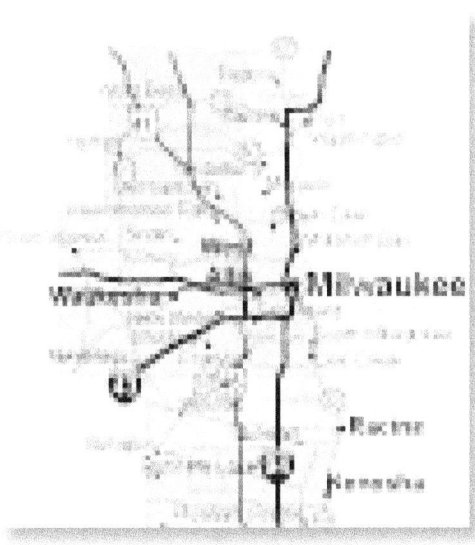

Sites and attractions are listed in order by City, Zip Code, and Name. Symbols indicated represent:

Restaurants   Lodging

HARRINGTON BEACH STATE PARK

531 County Highway D (I-43 exit 107 east) **Belgium** 53004

- ☐ Phone: (262) 285-3015
- ☐ **http://dnr.wi.gov/topic/parks/name/harrington/**
- ☐ Admission: A vehicle admission sticker is required. Daily $8.00-$11.00. Annual passes available.

On hot summer days the prime attraction of Harrington Beach State Park is its mile of Lake Michigan shore. The day-use 637-acre state park offering fishing, picnic areas, nature and cross-country ski trails. The park also offers swimming, scuba diving, surf fishing, hiking, nature programs and trails, the Wisconsin Explorer program, and bicycling. Spring, summer, or fall a walk around Quarry Lake on the hiking trail that rings it is sure to be enjoyable. Winters, this park features candlelight skiing and ice-skating. Open daily 6:00am-11:00pm with no overnight camping.

HALL OF LOGIC PUZZLES MUSEUM

533 Milwaukee Avenue, downtown **Burlington** 53105

- ☐ Phone: (262) 763-3946 **www.logicpuzzlemuseum.org**
- ☐ Hours: Please call or see website. Vary by season. Mostly Tuesday, Wednesday, & Saturdays. Spinning Top & yo-yo museum is next door.
- ☐ Admission: $12.00 General. Note: The museum is not appropriate for anyone under age 5 (young children or babies). Puzzles and puzzle pieces are too small for young ones, and pieces not suitable for baby or toddler play.

A puzzling, hands-on event with 100 different objects to figure out what they are! Gizmos, gadgets, antique tools, odd toys, parts & pieces. What are these things? Try to figure them out.

SPINNING TOP & YO-YO MUSEUM

533 Milwaukee Avenue, historic downtown (Hwy 36) **Burlington** 53105

- Phone: (262) 763-3946 **https://www.facebook.com/profile. php?id=100063753902097**
- Tours: 2.5 hour program for which tickets ($15.00/person) and reservations are required. The museum is for ages 4-104, not younger though.
- Note: Year Round: A free mini-exhibit of museum quality antiques & collectibles in the gift shop, available to buy.

Yo-yos galore. See 2000 tops, yo-yos, & gyroscopes on exhibit, along with videos, and try out 35 hands-on top games and experiments. The favorite part is the live presentation by the celebrity, The Top Lady, Judith Schulz. Spin top toys, see unusual spinner tops and actually try a number of different tops yourself. Afterwards visit the gift shop with hundreds of spinning things, both modern and antique.

RICHARD BONG STATE RECREATION AREA

26313 Burlington Road **Burlington (Kansasville)** 53139

- Phone: (262) 878-5607
  http://dnr.wi.gov/topic/parks/name/richardbong/
- Admission: A vehicle admission sticker is required. Daily $8.00-$11.00. Annual passes available.

Once designated to be a jet fighter base, Richard Bong State Recreation Area is fittingly named after Major Richard I. Bong, a Poplar, Wisconsin, native who was America's leading air ace during World War II. Richard Bong State Recreation Area offers a great variety of recreational opportunities including boating, fishing, swimming, horseback riding, and hiking.

Appropriate to its name, Richard Bong SRA offers an area where visitors may fly model airplanes, rockets, hang gliders, and hot air balloons. In spring 2008, Bong added another opportunity: for those with disabilities to experience the thrill of camping. A wheelchair accessible cabin for campers with disabilities is now offered.

CEDAR CREEK SETTLEMENT

N70 W 6340 Bridge Road (corner of Bridge Rd. and Washington Ave)
Cedarburg 53012

- Phone: (262) 377-4763 or (866) 377-4788 **www.cedarcreeksettlement.com**
- Hours: Monday-Saturday 10:00am-5:00pm, Sunday 11:00am-5:00pm. Extended summer hours.
- Note: The Cedarburg Visitor Center is located in the General Store. Every December, the Settlement celebrates Festive Friday Eves and Santa's workshop.

Browse through 30 shops, eateries and a winery in this restored 1864 woolen mill on the banks of Cedar Creek. Two buildings in town that really stand out for children are:

- GENERAL STORE - This 1860s era frame building has on display a collection of antique packaging and advertisements. Vintage grocery tins sit on a shelf above apothecary items and dry goods. Kids gravitate to the candy counter and share a chuckle over the outlandish claims on bottles of hair cream and health remedies. Open weekdays, half day Saturday and closed on Sunday.

- WOOLEN MILL TEXTILE MUSEUM - This one-of-kind shop specializes in wool, down, feathers and polyester cleaning and processing. Visit this working textile museum with custom wool carding on original 1860 machinery. Open Saturday from 9:00am-1:00pm.

STRAWBERRY FESTIVAL

Cedarburg - *Cedar Creek Settlement. Delicacies range from strawberry shortcake, strawberry pie, strawberry slush, chocolate-covered strawberries and even strawberry brats. There are lots of bands throughout the Historic District all weekend long. Kids have fun in the park with special activities, entertainment, and the Duck Races. Strawberry Contests take place at Cedar Creek Settlement. Ozaukee County Pioneer Village Open House (www.co.ozaukee.wi.us/ochs). More than 100,000 happy festival-goers attended last year. (fourth weekend in June)*

WINTER FESTIVAL

Cedarburg - *Mill Pond & Cedar Creek Park. Bed races on the millpond, barrel racing, dog pulling contest, snow parade, pancake breakfast, along with snow-and ice-sculpting competitions and indoor entertainment. Daily brat cookout and kids make n take projects. www.cedarburgfestivals.org. (second weekend in February)*

HAWKS INN HISTORICAL MUSEUM
426 Wells Street **Delafield** 53018

☐ Phone: (262) 646-4794 **www.hawksinn.org**
☐ Tours: Saturday 1:00-4:00pm. Guided every 30 minutes.

Rich with historic sites, visitors can tour Hawks Inn, a colorful frontier stagecoach stop. Built two years before Wisconsin became a state, Hawks Inn welcomed farmers in search of a homestead, trappers, traders, territorial politicians, and miners in search of a strike in the lead mines of western Wisconsin. Learn how many slept to one bed and what sort of foods were prepared for guests. Because this inn has been so crisply restored with its white walls and simple decor, kids won't feel squeamish about touring an "old" building.

LAPHAM PEAK STATE PARK
W329N846 County Road C (within Kettle Moraine State Forest)
Delafield 53018

☐ Phone: (262) 646-3025 **http://dnr.wi.gov/topic/parks/name/lapham/**
☐ Hours: Open 6:00am-11:00pm with no overnight camping.
☐ Admission: A vehicle admission sticker is required. Daily $8.00-$11.00. Annual passes available.

Lapham Peak State Park offers year-round recreation and a breathtaking view from atop their observation tower. Climb a 45-foot observation tower atop the highest point in Waukesha Country. The park's glaciated topography provides excellent hiking, backpacking and cross- country skiing on lighted trails, Features Handicap- accessible picnic area and campsites, seasonal naturalist programs, lighted trails, enclosed shelters, 14.5 miles of hiking trails, 5 miles of off-road bicycle trails (State Trail Pass required), 12.6 miles of cross- country ski trails (State Trail Pass required). A portion of the Ice Age National Scenic Trail runs through here.

OLD WORLD WISCONSIN

S103 W37890 Hwy 67 (main entrance is approximately one mile north of the postal address on Hwy 67) **Eagle** 53119

- ☐   Phone: (262) 594-6300 **http://oldworldwisconsin.wisconsinhistory.org/**
- ☐   Hours: Season is from May-September and hours vary by season. Wednesday-Sunday 10:00am-4:00pm (mid-June - late August). Weekends only (May and September).
- ☐   Admission: $20.00 adult, $18.00 senior (65+), $13.00 child (5-12). Fees include an all-day tram transportation pass.
- ☐   Note: Clausing Barn Restaurant-Choose from brats and burgers to veggie wraps and panini sandwiches. And don't forget dessert! Homemade strudels, breads, cookies and sweet treats are baked fresh every day, without preservatives, just like in the 1800s. Vintage Baseball Games.

Old World Wisconsin is a 600-acre "living history museum" that showcases 67 historical buildings in five ethnically themed villages. Walk the trails and roads among 19th and early 20th century buildings and see how immigrant settlers lived. Your admission includes tram transport from one village to the next. Enjoy viewing more than 100 historic breed animals on the beautiful Kettle Moraine landscape. Within the historic structures you will see more than 80 percent of the 50,000 artifact collection on display and some replicas used to demonstrate their use. Some buildings, you peer through the windows, others, costumed guides invite you in. In the Farmers' Club Hall, families can play historic board games, toys, stilts, or hoops and sticks. Children enjoy the animals and interactive activities.

- •   CROSSROADS VILLAGE - Experience firsthand how life in small towns began to change as the railroads challenged craft workers and local businesses to compete with new goods and services. Visitors may help craftsmen like the shoemaker and blacksmith ply their trades while they explain how the "new" economy affected their lives. Wash clothes at the Hafford House, churn real butter, or be part of the congregation at St. Peter's Church. You can also visit the general store.

- •   GERMAN AREA - Life for most children in 19th century Germany took place on farms. It was all about feeding a family, caring for animals and making the farm a home. By weaving, baking and visiting the oxen, kids get a touch of this life.

- •   NORWEGIAN AREA - Learn how hard-working immigrants transformed primitive homesteads into working farms. Card wool, learn how Norwegian children attended a one-room school house to learn ABCs but also how to be an American.

- FINNISH AREA - Weaving and carpentry are the focus here.

- AFRICAN AMERICAN AREA - From the 1860s through the 1880s, Pleasant Ridge was settled by escaped or emancipated African American slaves, immigrant Europeans, and European Americans. Children will have a chance to imagine being an escaped slave, do rubbings in the recreated cemeteries, take home a family tree activity and visit the church to learn more about the Pleasant Ridge community.

Most importantly, the multi-ethnic style of this village helps kids visually compare and contrast different cultures and how they used their regional skills to thrive and adapt in America - the New World.

AUTUMN ON THE FARMS

Eagle - *Old World Wisconsin. From the sounds of draft horses helping harvest autumn crops to the smells of old world cooking, visitors to Old World Wisconsin are instantly transported to the 19th century as costumed interpreters give them a first hand look at what it was like to live and work during the harvest season in early America. The four-day event is filled with demonstrations of farm chores, tradesmen and family life. (second and third weekends in October)*

SPIRIT OF CHRISTMAS PAST

Eagle - *Old World Wisconsin. Stroll the 1870s Crossroads Village and discover the charms of many holiday traditions. Walk house to house, shop to shop, as you sample the treats, join in the festivities, and see how different cultures contributed to the rituals we enjoy today. (first weekend in December)*

EAST TROY ELECTRIC RAILROAD MUSEUM

2002 Church Street (I-43 exit at Hwy 20) **East Troy** 53120

- Phone: (262) 642-3263 **www.easttroyrr.org**
- Hours: Vary by season. Weekends (May), Wednesday-Sunday (June-August), Weekends (September-October). Trains depart late morning through afternoon. Seasonal trains early December weekends. Call or visit website.
- Admission: Fares: $15.00 adult, $12.50 senior (65+), $9.50 Youth (3-14).
- Tours: The actual running time is 20 minutes in each direction, with a 25 minute layover at either end, for a total of a little over an hour.

Experience a relaxing train ride through the Wisconsin countryside aboard one of their historic electric railcars. Learn the history of this 103 year old rail line in the depot museum. The railroad features a 11-mile vintage train ride, a museum, gift shop, coffee shop, as well as visits to an old-fashioned ice cream parlor and a farm featuring a deli, bakery and farm produce. Most every holiday, they offer special rides with characters and seasonal treats or discounts.

ALPINE VALLEY SKI RESORT

W2501 County Road D **Elkhorn** 53121

☐   Phone: (262) 642-7374 or (800) 227-9395
www.alpinevalleyresort.com

Alpine Valley Resort is one of the largest ski resorts in Southeastern Wisconsin. The only resort In the Midwest with two high speed quads and four wonder carpets. They have snowboard and ski packages - some with overnight accommodations.

APPLEFEST

W6384 Sugar Creek Road Apple Barn Orchard (off Hwy 11 or 12) **Elkhorn**

☐   Phone: (262) 728-3266 **www.applebarnorchardandwinery.com/**
☐   Tours: Group tours are offered for $6.00/person. One hour tour of family farm including a train (modified John Deere Tractor) ride into orchard to pick apples. Also includes a short video of the operation of a fruit orchard, a healthy snack of apple slices, cider and cider donuts.

This apple orchard has been in the same family since the mid-1800s and grows nearly two dozen varieties of the fruit.
•   GRANDPARENTS DAY (early September)
•   HAPPY BIRTHDAY, JOHNNY DAY (late September)
•   APPLE FEST WEEKEND (October)
•   PUMPKIN DAZE (October)

Already picked apples available in the Apple Barn, Caramel Apples, Wisconsin Cheeses, Caramel Apple Delight, Fresh Baked Breads & Cookies, Cider Donuts, Arts & Crafts, Inflatable Jump/Slide for Children - fee charged, Children's Games, Face Painting, Free rides through the Orchard, Pumpkin Patch Opens for picking the perfect pumpkin, Antique Fire Engine for the kids to play on. Family entertainment on Saturday and lunch available weekends.

WEHR NATURE CENTER

9701 W. College Avenue (Whitnall Park) **Franklin** 53132

- Phone: (414) 425-8550
  https://county.milwaukee.gov/EN/Parks/Explore/Wehr-Nature-Center
- Hours: 8:00am-4:30pm.
- Admission: FREE, except for some programs and special events. $5.00 parking fee.

200-acres with 6.5 miles of hiking trails through five distinct habitats including a 20-acre lake, prairie, wetlands and woodlands. Nature center with restrooms, binoculars for rent and a nature store.

THE FAMILY FARM

328 Port Washington Road (County W) (I-43 exit 89 west. Turn north on County W) **Grafton** 53024

- Phone: (262) 377-6161 **www.familyfarmllc.net**
- Hours: Wednesday-Saturday 9:00am-4:00pm, Sunday 11:00am-4:00pm (mid-May thru September). Closed Memorial Day, July 4 and Labor Day. Open daily except Mondays in October.
- Admission: $6.25 adult, $5.25 senior (62+), $3.75 child (2-12). Wagon rides (when available) are $1.00 extra. Animal Feed is $0.75.
- Note: Café in main building. Bed n Breakfast on property. October is Fall.O.Ween Fun with PYO pumpkin patch hayrides. Short film on farm history plays in the Admission Barn.

Bring the family for fun at the farm. Discover turn-of-the-century 30 acre farm with lots of sights, sounds and smells of rural farming. Teachers enhance classroom learning, seniors reminisce and children delight in seeing real farm animals. Enjoy this self-guided, educational and recreational excursion:

- Farm Zoo and Nursery - pet and feed traditional farmyard animals, from 2 oz. chicks to Belgian Draft horses weighing over one ton each! See how each barnyard family lives and takes care of its' young.
- Wagon Rides - provide visitors with a 15 minute pastoral ride through the woods, prairie and pumpkin fields.
- Farm Buildings - Visit the Silo - you see them from afar, now stand inside and see how small you are! The Corncrib, Milk House, Granary and the Pig'n'Chicken Shed each have a unique use on the farm.
- Mural Tour with Antique Tools & Implements - pick up the Tour Text and learn how to start your own farm. Colorful artwork, interesting and odd tools are all part of the fun.

- Nature Walk - a 3/4 mile excursion with three stimulating environments. Discover woodland underbrush and fungi; prairie plants, colorful caterpillars and insects; wetland grasses, trees and birds...the Farm is in the migratory flight path along Lake Michigan's coast.

- Hay Romp - no one too young or too old for the romp of all times. Huge round bales and fluffy hay provide last century's answer to the trampoline.

GREENDALE VISITOR CENTER

5676 Broad Street **Greendale** 53129

☐ Phone: (414) 423-3080 **www.facebook.com/greendalevisitorcenter/**
☐ Hours: Monday-Saturday 10:00am-5:00pm, Saturday until 4pm.

Begin your tour watching a 14-minute film of the history of the company shown every half hour (on the half hour) in the Theater. Next, you can actually see one of the *Taste of Home* Test Kitchens. This is a working test kitchen, and the Home Economists inside are testing recipes for upcoming issues of magazines as well as various cookbooks. Occasionally, the Test Kitchen has some "extras" for visitors to sample! Samples of the "Cookie of all Cookies" are available at most times for a small contribution.8"Slightly imperfect" and discontinued items from their catalog are offered at closeout prices. Wouldn't you love the job of being a "taste tester" around here? (group tours are $20.00/person)

PIKE LAKE STATE PARK

3544 Kettle Moraine Road **Hartford** 53027

☐ Phone: (262) 670-3400 **http://dnr.wi.gov/topic/parks/name/pikelake/**
☐ Admission: A vehicle admission sticker is required. Daily $8.00-$11.00. Annual passes available.

Within Kettle Moraine State Forest is a 678-acre park highlighted by Powder Hill, a 1,350-foot glacial kame, with panoramic views. Features 32 campsites, showers, a dumping station, handicap- accessible picnic area and campsites, seasonal naturalist programs, shoreline with marked beach area, fishing, 0.8 miles of nature trails, 7.1 miles of hiking trails, 1.5 miles of snowmobile trails, 6.4 miles of cross- country ski trails. Open 6:00am-11:00pm with overnight camping.

DID YOU KNOW? Geologically, a kame is a cone-shaped hill formed by debris washing down melt-holes in the last great Wisconsin glacier.

WISCONSIN AUTOMOTIVE MUSEUM
147 North Rural Street Hartford 53027

- ☐ Phone: (262) 673-7999 **www.wisconsinautomuseum.com**
- ☐ Hours: Wednesday-Saturday 10:00am-5:00pm.
- ☐ Admission: $12.00 adult, $10.00 senior (62+), $6.00 youth (6-16).

Wisconsin's largest auto museum, featuring a display of classic, vintage automobiles and artifacts! Included is the Hartford manufactured "Kissel" (1906—1931). Other exhibits are dedicated to the Nash and Hudson Esses Terraplane, in addition to over 90 other rare vehicles, such as Reos, Pierce-Arrows, Pontiacs, Studebakers, Chevies and Ford.

CIVIL WAR MUSEUM
5400 1st Ave Kenosha 53140

- ☐ Phone: (262) 653-4141 **https://museums.kenosha.org/civil-war-museum**
- ☐ Hours: Monday-Saturday, 10:00am-5:00pm, Sunday, Noon-5:00pm (year-round).
- ☐ Admission: $9.00 General (16+). Youth ages 15 and under, accompanied by an adult - FREE. Discounts for area residents.

This Civil War Museum's state-of-the-art exhibit technology examines the connections between the home front and the battlefront during the nation's bloodiest conflict. No other museum in the country tells the story of this crucial period in our nation's history as it was experienced by the people of the upper middle west states. You can sit along side "people" on a train and listen to their stories. You might sit right next to a soldier or a former slave. There is a riverboat setting where you can experience the same technology. Across the hall, veterans are posed around a campfire and stories of men off to war, all American wars, is touching. And to keep with that theme, the museum has a library where adults can research their relatives who fought in the war while there are puzzles and games to keep grade school children occupied. You can tell the folks that designed this space had kids and modern technology in mind.

DINOSAUR DISCOVERY MUSEUM

5608 10th Avenue **Kenosha** 53140

- ☐ Phone: (262) 653-4450 **https://museums.kenosha.org/dinosaur-discovery-museum**
- ☐ Hours: Tuesday-Sunday, Noon-5:00pm (year-round). Open Mondays Noon-5:00pm (March-August).
- ☐ Admission: FREE. $5.00 per person donation suggested.
- ☐ Educators: Simulated Dino Digs on weekends. Print the I Spy activity sheet and play the game on your self-guided tour.

Discover the link between meat-eating dinosaurs and birds. The museum's galleries feature dramatic life-size dinosaur replica casts, bones and fossils, interactive exhibits, family programs, and a real working on-site paleontology lab. Learn what dinosaurs were, how we know they existed, what they ate, and how big or small they were. Check out the new soundscape of environmental and animal sounds added to the exhibit gallery. Step back into the Mesozoic era with outdoors sounds in different terrains and weather conditions during the Age of Dinosaurs. Touch real fossils, see replica dinosaur teeth and measure the length of dinosaurs. Discover how paleontologists work together to find and study dinosaur fossil bones. Learn about their tools and methods of discovery in a real dino lab located on the museum's lower level. Before you leave, be sure to meet the newest theropod - Carnotaurus or "flesh eating bull," - 25 feet long and 6.5 feet tall at the hips.

FRANK'S DINER

Kenosha - 508 58th Street 53140. Phone: (262) 857-2663. In 1926, six horses pulled Franks Diner to the downtown spot where it stands today. The structure was built in New Jersey and shipped to Kenosha on a railroad flat car. The unusual lunch car diner is celebrating more than 80 years in business in its original 58th Street location. Franks Diner is a local favorite and the oldest continuously operating lunch car diner in the U.S. Many celebrities, including Duke Ellington, Liberace and the Lawrence Welk orchestra, have visited Franks Diner. Recently, the diner was featured on the Food Network series "Diners, Drive-Ins and Dives." The staff offers friendly smiles, sassy service. Dig into the homemade bread, gigantic pancakes, juicy burgers and the renowned best-seller — "Franks Garbage Plate." Serving breakfast and lunch daily. Price range: $5.00-$12.00. **www.franksdinerkenosha.com/**

KENOSHA HISTORY CENTER & SOUTHPORT LIGHT

220 51st Place Kenosha 53140

- Phone: (262) 654-5770 **www.kenoshahistorycenter.org**
- Hours: History Center - Tuesday-Friday 10:00am-4:30pm, Saturday 10:00am-4:00pm, Sunday Noon-4:00pm.
- Admission: Light: $10.00 adult, $5.00 child (8-12). $2.00 donation for center.
- Lighthouse Tours: Saturdays 10:00am to 4:00pm and Sundays Noon to 4:00pm (May-October). Weather pending.

SOUTHPORT LIGHT: Kenosha's newest museum, the Southport Light Station Museum, consists of the 1866 Southport lighthouse and the 1867 Lighthouse Keeper's residence. 55 feet tall, this lighthouse was constructed in 1866 and served as a navigation aid until 1906 at which time the light was extinguished. Following a transfer in the mid-1950s to the City of Kenosha the light was again relit in 1994, although it no longer serves in an official capacity. View the surrounding area from 55 feet up in the air.

The lighthouse tower, former lightkeeper's residence and surrounding grounds represent the fourth gallery space of the KENOSHA HISTORY CENTER. The History center (down the hill) has rooms with different themes. The museum features the Yesteryear Gallery, the Rambler Legacy Gallery with changing Kenosha automobile exhibits, the adjacent Southport Light Station, and a gift shop with lighthouse and other mementos. In 1902, Thomas Jeffery's first automobile, the Rambler, was sold at the auto show in Chicago. The Model C car, the nation's second mass-produced car, was manufactured at his factory in Kenosha. His Rambler was the first to have removable and interchangeable wheels, and the first to have an optional spare tire. The Kenosha History Center celebrates Jeffery's original invention in the first exhibit space.

KENOSHA PUBLIC MUSEUM

5500 First Avenue **Kenosha** 53140

☐ Phone: (262) 653-4140 **www.kenoshapublicmuseum.org**
☐ Hours: Monday -Saturday 10:00am-5:00pm, Sunday Noon-5:00pm.
☐ Admission: FREE. $5.00 suggested donation.

The Kenosha Public Museum is a natural sciences and fine and decorative arts museum. Visitors experience the change in climate, the development of a variety of ecosystems, the evolution of plants and animals, and the life of Native Americans as it happened in this area over thousands of years. Highlights include going from a coral reef to the Ice Age, melting of the glaciers, the mammoths and then the story of Native Americans. And those mammoths - found right here in Kenosha County! The Schaefer mammoth, excavated by the Museum, documents the earliest interaction of mammoth and man east of the Mississippi River. The actual Schaefer mammoth bones are set in a special floor display exactly as found on the Schaefer farm in Paris, Wisconsin. The Hebior mammoth is the largest, most complete mammoth excavated in North America. Other exhibits include world cultures, zoology, geology, fossils, and arts. The Field Station is a room to apply what you saw in the galleries to things you can touch (explore drawers) and create.

KENOSHA STREETCAR DAY

724 54th Street, downtown (Kenosha Transit Center) **Kenosha** 53140

☐ Phone: (262) 653-4287 **https://www.kenoshastreetcarsociety.org/ streetcar-day.** Admission. Mid September weekend.
☐ Note: Trolley Dogs, a block from the electric streetcar line, is known for its Chicago-style dogs and its signature "Trolley Dog" - a Hot Dog Its own trolley circulates above the tables.

Located on Lake Michigan just north of the Illinois border, Kenosha's crown jewel is its lakefront development, HARBORPARK. This parkland along the waterfront blends beautifully with the adjacent historic downtown featuring quaint shops, galleries, an outdoor market, and eateries – all linked by a vintage electric streetcar system. Five beautifully restored electric streetcars travel a two-mile loop, providing a scenic tour of the Lake Michigan shoreline, HarborPark, downtown and the METRA train station. Stops include the city's lakefront museum campus. Kids love to wave out the window, while many grandparents fondly recall life when they rode as children.

BRISTOL RENAISSANCE FAIRE

Kenosha - (I-94 at Russell Rd on IL/WI border). A magical 16th century village is re-created to celebrate the food, games and crafts of Elizabethan England. Hundreds of costumed performers offer continuous entertainment on 16 open-air stages and in the village streets. Highlights include a joust on horseback, Queen Elizabeth I and her glittering court, Robin Hood, a festive kids' kingdom and craft demonstrations. Admission. ***www.renfair.com.*** *(Open Saturday's, Sunday's and Labor Day, mid-July thru first weekend in September)*

JERRY SMITH PRODUCE & COUNTRY STORE PUMPKIN PATCH

Kenosha - 7150 18th Street (Highway L). ***www.smithpumpkinfarm.com*** *Phone: (262) 859-2645. Each fall, the Pumpkin Farm has a display of pumpkin-head characters with hand-painted pumpkins. Take a hay ride out to the patch, explore the Western Village or kid's playground, and challenge yourself to the 8-acre corn maze. Weekends they serve brats and hot dogs and pony rides. Smith Produce also has carriage rides and a petting zoo.*

MILWAUKEE SPORTS
Milwaukee

MILWAUKEE BREWERS BASEBALL - www.brewers.mlb.com. A Major League Baseball team, Milwaukee Brewers. The team was established in 1969 and currently is a member of Central Division of the National League. In 1982, the team won its first AL Pennant. The team plays their home games at American Family Field, a baseball stadium located in Milwaukee, Wisconsin. (see separate listing)

MILWAUKEE ADMIRALS HOCKEY - **www.milwaukeeadmirals.com**. The team was established in 1970 and is a member of the West Division of the Western Conference in the American Hockey League. The team plays their home games at Panther Arena. Nashville Predators affliate.

MILWAUKEE WAVE SOCCER - www.milwaukeewave.com. Professional indoor soccer.

MILWAUKEE BUCKS BASKETBALL - **www.nba.com/bucks/**. A pro basketball team. The team plays their home games at Fiserv Forum.

HARLEY-DAVIDSON MUSEUM

400 Canal Street **Milwaukee** 53201

- ☐ Phone: (877) HDMUSEUM
  https://www.harley-davidson.com/us/en/museum.html
- ☐ Hours: Daily 10:00am-5:00pm.
- ☐ Admission: $22.00 adult, $18.00 seniors (65+), military, $8.00 child (ages 5-17).
- ☐ Note: Sunday is Family Day w/ storytelling, temporary tattoos and a hands-on activity. Motor Bar & Restaurant or Café Racer has kids meals available.
- ☐ Educators: easy to follow pdf physics and history downloads **www.harley-davidson.com/content/h-d/en_US/home/museum/visit/field-trips.html**.

The wide-ranging collection of motorcycles and historic artifacts help students understand the rich history that has made Harley-Davidson what it is today. Visitors who have never ridden a bike before – including children – can sit in the saddle of a number of legendary bikes and enjoy a video simulation of the freedom and camaraderie felt while riding. H-D's motto "It's all about the ride and the destination." Faves for kids include:

- Hill Climber - Drive a racer bike up the track curve. Tank Wall – Will you be the next custom paint designer? Imagination Station - get decked out in gear and rev up the engine. Games and puzzles area.

- Tool Box - The Tool Box is an interactive, hands-on activity. Here you'll engage the senses and get a better understanding of Harley-Davidson by touching objects, trying-on clothing and interacting with staff in fun and creative ways.

BETTY BRINN CHILDREN'S MUSEUM

929 East Wisconsin Avenue **Milwaukee** 53202

- ☐ Phone: (414) 390-5437 **www.bbcmkids.org**
- ☐ Hours: Wednesday-Monday 9:00am-4:30pm.
- ☐ Admission: $12.00 General (age 1+), $11.00 senior (age 55+).
- ☐ Nearby: Happy Days are here again! The King of Cool, Arthur "The Fonz" Fonzerelli, now resides on the eastern bank of the Milwaukee River along the city's RiverWalk in the form of a bronze statue. Complete with leather jacket and signature double thumbs-up, this life-sized likeness of the pop culture icon provides a perfect photo opportunity.

Milwaukee's only museum designed specifically for kids ages 10 and under. Kids learn about everyday life in imaginative ways, from climbing in a giant train set to role-playing jobs. Besides the theater and dance area, kids can actually play pretend grocery store clerk, a news anchor, a cameraman or a producer, too. There's also a play auto shop and bank plus a post office with a postal sorting area that uses conveyor belts. One of the most unique features: connecting phone lines between the play city buildings so kids can call each other. The Let's Play Railway is a larger-than-life size replica of BRIO's famous wooden toy train cars with items you can move, crank, turn or ring. Infants and toddlers have their own space in Pocket Park with soft play toys.

DISCOVERY WORLD AT PIER WISCONSIN

500 N Harbor Drive (off of Lincoln Memorial Drive on Milwaukee's Lakefront between the Milwaukee Art Museum and Summerfest Grounds) **Milwaukee 53202**

- ☐ Phone: (414) 765-9966 **www.discoveryworld.org**
- ☐ Hours: Wednesday-Sunday 9:00am-4:00pm.
- ☐ Admission: $22.00 adult, $18.00 senior (60+) and child (3-17). $16.00 college student. Parking fee extra.
- ☐ Tours: Deck tours ($5 per person) and public sails ($30-$45.00 on the S/V Denis Sullivan require advance reservations.
- ☐ Note: Café. Total immersion virtual reality experiences. Interactive flight and driving simulators in some of the techno areas. Films shown daily in both theaters on a continuous schedule.

Discovery World on Milwaukee's lakefront lets visitors explore the surface vessels that once ruled the Great Lakes, the creatures that live in these waters, and the technology to study them. Hands-on exploration is a must.

Start with a visit to the S/V Denis Sullivan and her dry-dock companion, the Challenge. During the summer, the Sullivan—the world's only re-creation of a three-masted 19th-century Great Lakes schooner—is berthed here, and visitors can climb aboard for scheduled deck tours and public sails (extra charge). In winter, the Sullivan heads south to Florida, but her sister ship, the Challenge, stays behind. This 1852 clipper schooner replica permanently sails on the second floor of the Aquatarium, and her deck offers the chance to try your hand at all kinds of sailing skills, from grappling with a windlass to turning the quarterdeck's wheel.

For a look at the living exhibits, head to the Aquatarium. The 40-by-40-foot scale model of the Great Lakes on the main level gives you a chance to play nature by controlling the weather and seeing its effects on the Great Lakes. In the Great Lakes giant Map area, you can actually make it rain. The touch tanks prominently feature stingrays that have been de-armed and are actually very friendly and like to be "petted." We like that they had handfuls of freshwater creatures to touch, too.

The Technology Wing features man-made innovations, many of them Milwaukee born. Play tic-tac-toe with a robot or visit with Mr. Bradley in the Dream Machine. Mr. B will invite you to try your hand at making a few free take-home trinkets using Rockwell machinery, from a replica of the Sullivan to a set of Allen-Bradley coasters. Like Rock n Roll? The "inventor" of this sound, Les Paul, a Wisconsin native, has a journey space here in the House of Sound. There's science in guitars?

Finally, climb the Double Helix staircase to the TechnoJungle on the second floor - an area full of science experiments. Our favorite - resting on a bed of nails - and not getting hurt! And, because this place is so focused on technology, they've created HIVE - human interactive virtual education - it's wild. Take a 3-D journey into virtual environments that respond to your actions - explore outer space without leaving the ground or the depths of the sea without getting wet, when you enter the HIVE.

Honestly, we don't think there's a better engaging offering of technology, history (ships) and a fun study of the Great Lakes in the country!

MILWAUKEE ART MUSEUM

700 N. Art Museum Drive **Milwaukee** 53202

- Phone (414) 224-3200 **http://mam.org**
- Hours: Tuesday-Sunday 10:00am-5:00pm. Until 8:00pm on Thursday.
- Admission: $22.00 adult, $17.00 senior (65+), student. Free to children 12 and under.
- Note: Café Calatrava serves children's dishes.

This is one art museum that grabs the kids from the outside, in. The unique architecture of the main building's annex looks like a delicate white bird about to take flight over Lake Michigan. Inside, the museum exhibits classics and modern art but families most like that it includes the Kohl's Art Generation

Gallery and Studio where kids participate in exciting and creative projects—all while seeing some of their best work showcased exclusively at the Museum. Storytime in the Galleries, Weekend Family Programs and assorted themed "festivals" are the best ways to engage the kids. Make your visit interactive. Challenge kids to find the oldest, biggest, smallest, heaviest, or weirdest objects in the Museum. Imagine time traveling as you pass through galleries, which are arranged in chronological order. Encourage kids to make up stories about the pictures they see: what are the people saying, thinking, or doing? (Find more activity ideas in the ArtPacks).

MILWAUKEE BOAT LINE

101 W Michigan St (dock located on the RiverWalk, near the Grand Avenue Mall, where Downtown meets the Historic Third Ward) **Milwaukee** 53203

- Phone: (414) 294-9450 **www.mkeboat.com**
- Hours: Sightseeing - Daily Noon & 4:00pm (summer). Weekends Noon & 4:00pm (May & September). Many additional theme cruises are available at various times and hours are extended on most holiday weekends. Call or see website for m28t current schedule.
- Admission: $17.99 adult, $14.49 child (4-12).
- Tours: Sightseeing - 90 minutes with fun narration by the captain. Historical tours are also available for a slight increase in fee.

These sightseeing cruises highlight some of the best sights along the river with a good view of shipping docks and the lighthouse. Travel out of the harbor and out into Lake Michigan, the Menomonee and the Kinnickinnic Rivers. The captain gives the narration on the sightseeing cruises, Historic Society docents on the Historical cruises.

MILWAUKEE COUNTY HISTORICAL SOCIETY MUSEUM

910 N. Old World Third Street **Milwaukee** 53203

- Phone: (414) 273-8288 **www.milwaukeehistory.net**
- Hours: Monday, Wednesday-Saturday 9:30am-5:00pm
- Admission: $8.00 adult, $6.00 senior (62+), military, student (13-18). Children Free.
- Educators: their online Historic Timeline is popular page on their website. It has all the stuff a student could want to write an historical essay about Milwaukee. **https://milwaukeehistory.net/education/milwaukee-timeline/**

This is located in a landmark building with two floors of historical exhibits that explore Milwaukee County's past and the achievements of its people and the community's ties to the state and nation. Experience Milwaukee during the late 19th century through the mid-20th century. The museum features a panoramic painting of Milwaukee, firefighting equipment, period replicas of a pharmacy and a bank, and Children's world - an exhibit that includes vintage toys, clothes and school materials. The museum is undergoing extensive renovations so check website updates before you go.

MILWAUKEE RIVER CRUISE LINE

205 W Highland Avenue **Milwaukee** 53203

- ☐ Phone: (414) 276-7447 **www.edelweissboats.com**
- ☐ Hours: Sightseeing - Friday & Sunday 3:00pm, Saturday 1:00pm (May-October). Many additional theme cruises are available at various times. Call or see website for most current schedule.
- ☐ Admission: Sightseeing - $29.25 adult, $14.63 child.
- ☐ Tours: Sightseeing - 75 minutes with narration that is based on John Gurda's "Making of Milwaukee" series.

This is the only tour that includes a tour of downtown Milwaukee, the lakefront and its history. Expect to learn of Milwaukee's Brewing History, German heritage, manufacturing contributions, famous locals and its current "Renaissance."

Kids Caribbean Pirates Cruises: Join Captain Jack and crew to help defend the vessel from unruly pirates with water canons and balloons. Dress up! The boats are comfortable and clean and the staff is noted for being very friendly.

LAKE EXPRESS HIGH SPEED FERRY

2330 S. Lincoln Memorial Drive **Milwaukee** 53207

- ☐ Phone: (866) 914-1010 **www.lake-express.com**
- ☐ Hours: 3 round-trips daily in summer; 2 in spring and fall. Call or visit Web site for departures (May-October).
- ☐ Admission: Varying fares based on options chosen. Ranges from $187.00+ RT adult (18+) with children 5-17 about $92.00 round trip. Promotions vary. Additional charge for vehicles and upgraded accommodations.

The Milwaukee-based ferry began service in 2004 and accommodates 250 passengers. It also carries up to 46 vehicles and 12 motorcycles. The ferry makes multiple daily trips across Lake Michigan between its Muskegon and Milwaukee terminals. Each voyage takes about 2 1/2 hours. Lake Express offers light breakfasts, salads, warm sandwiches and snacks throughout the passage. Spend some of the time sitting in their spacious passenger cabin, watch a movie or take a few strolls about the vessel during the crossing. This vessel is ultra-modern but lacks a lot of entertainment options. Bring games to play on board.

PALERMO'S PIZZA TOURS

3301 W. Canal Street **Milwaukee** 53208

  ☐   Phone: Tours - (414) 455-0383 **www.palermospizza.com**
  ☐   Admisson: $4.00-$8.00/person for a tour. Children under 2 are FREE. Other tour packages are available.
  ☐   Tours: Many Fridays at 1:30pm. Call ahead to reserve your space. Occassional Monday-Thursday tours offered each summer.

Milwaukee's only pizza factory tour. The company -- started by Gaspare "Jack" Falluca and still run by the family -- entered the frozen food market in 1978 after having run the East Side Palermo Villa pizzeria since 1969. Tours of the Villa Palermo facility are available during which you'll learn about how pizzas are made, their company's history and other fun facts about pizza. Watch the staff work on a production line preparing the dough, a machine flattens it just right, then more employees squirt sauce and spread cheese and other toppings before the pizzas are sent to the flash-freezers. Tours also get to see the testing lab where new and long-standing products get baked and tested for consistency, flavor and more. (wouldn't you like to be a taste tester?) Tours take approximately 1 hour to complete and include a 20-minute video of their company history; a walking tour of the plant and a slice of fresh pan pizza in the Pizzeria & Café.

NORTH POINT LIGHTHOUSE

2650 North Wahl Avenue, Lake Park **Milwaukee** 53211

- ☐ Phone: (414) 332-6754 **www.northpointlighthouse.org**
- ☐ Hours: Saturday & Sunday 1:00pm-4:00pm.
- ☐ Admission: $8.00 adult (12+), $5.00 senior (65+) and child (5-11).

With completion of the restoration of the Keepers Quarters in the fall of 2007, this historic site is open to the public for tours and visits. Located in Lake Park, one of Milwaukee's first public parks, the North Point Light Station is one of the oldest structures built and still standing in the now-urban area. Constructed in 1855, a new iron lighthouse 30 feet high was built 100 feet inland (west) in 1888, when it threatened to slide down the bluff and into Lake Michigan. A Queen Anne style house was built in 1888 as a keeper's quarters and still stands today. The tours enable visitors to climb to the top of the 74-foot tower for spectacular views of the lakefront, park and city.

AMERICAN FAMILY FIELD

1 Brewers Way **Milwaukee** 53214

- ☐ Phone: (800) 933-7890 **https://www.mlb.com/brewers/ballpark/tours**
- ☐ Tours: public walk up tours run from April - September. Prices: $10.00-$15.00. View their website page: http://m.mlb.com/brewers/tickets/tours/ for days and times. Most tours are late morning, early afternoon. Tours cover over slightly over 1/2 mile and last approximately 70 minutes. Wear comfortable shoes!

Recently named the second best ballpark in the league in fan voting, Miller Park has something for everyone. Visit the Fan Zone, home of Autograph Alley, an exhibit featuring baseballs autographed by baseball legends and the Kids Zone, a special interactive playground for the younger fans. Eating - the staple here is wonderful sausages, brats and hot dogs.

TOURS: Milwaukee has been home to the home run legend Hank Aaron, Mr. Baseball Bob Uecker, and Hall of Famers Robin Yount, Paul Molitor, and Rollie Fingers. Tours include the dugout, visitors clubhouse, press box, luxury suites, and even Bob Uecker's broadcast booth. Here, without the display of Brewers blue and gold, Packers or Badgers colors, you'll probably stand out like a sore thumb. (hint: the gift shop is usually open for shopping)

MITCHELL PARK CONSERVATORY (THE DOMES)
524 S. Layton Blvd. **Milwaukee** 53215

- Phone: (414) 649-9830
  https://county.milwaukee.gov/EN/Parks/Explore/The-Domes
- Hours: Wednesday-Monday 9:00am-5:00pm. Weekends 9:00am-4:00pm.
- Admission: $9.00 adult, $6.00 student (3-12).

The only structure of its kind on earth, the Conservatory houses a world-wide variety of plant collections in the tropical rainforest, an arid desert and seasonal domes…all in one place. Come to the deserts of Africa, Madagascar, South America and North America in the Arid Dome. You'll be most familiar with the cacti but look for some oddities. Stroll the jungle-like trails of the Tropical Dome and see a rich diversity of plants from the rainforests of five continents. Showy flowers, fruits, nuts, spices and a multitude of orchids. Be sure to look for the colorful birds that call the Tropical Dome their home. They have a lighting display in the evening and their seasonal domes really catch the mood of the season or holiday. A good way to spend a rainy day.

SCHLITZ AUDUBON NATURE CENTER
1111 East Brown Deer Road **Milwaukee** 53217

- Phone: (414) 352-2880 **www.schlitzauduboncenter.com**
- Hours: Daily 8:30am-5:00pm.
- Admission: $10.00 adult, $7.00 child (3-17).

A 185-acre stretch of untouched land along the shore of Lake Michigan, 15 minutes from downtown Milwaukee. Hike trails, walk along the beach, and enjoy the spectacular view from the 60' observation tower. Five ponds, ravines, woodlands and prairies provide habitat for hawks, ducks, owls, warblers, finches and falcons. Attend programs, nature exhibits, meet resident raptors (eagles, owls, and more!), or go snowshoeing or cross-country skiing.

MILWAUKEE COUNTY ZOO

10001 West Blue Mound Road **Milwaukee** 53226

- ☐ Phone: (414) 256-5412 **www.milwaukeezoo.org**
- ☐ Hours: Daily 9:30am-4:30pm.
- ☐ Admission: $16.75 adult, $15.75 senior (60+), $13.75 junior (3-12). Reduced winter pricing. Parking $15.00. Discounts available for Milwaukee residents.

This museum's catch? With each exhibit separated only by hidden moats - predators and their prey seem to live side by side in natural environments. The Small Mammals building features both day and night animals. With the flip of a switch, day can turn into night, allowing red fluorescent lights to illuminate nocturnal animal spaces. The Zoo is home to 21 bonobo apes, which is the largest captive group of this species in the world. You'll notice they have a lot of monkey areas. Other favorites are the polar bears, kangaroos and the Family Farm animal encounter area. Springtime there are always new babies to name. The zoo is filled with special attractions and activities to keep the children excited the whole day including camel and pony rides and interactive exhibits. Visitors can also enjoy a leisurely ride aboard the Safari Train or on the Zoomobile.

MILWAUKEE PUBLIC MUSEUM

800 West Wells Street **Milwaukee** 53233

- ☐ Phone: (414) 278-2728 or **www.mpm.edu**
- ☐ Hours: Wednesday-Monday 10:00am-5:00pm.
- ☐ Admission: $24.00 adult, $20.00 senior (65+) & $18.00 youth (4-13). Discount admission to Milwaukee County Residents. Additional charge for IMAX and Planetarium with combo rates available.
- ☐ Note: Also on location Humphrey IMAX Dome Theater & Daniel M. Soref Planetarium. Café.

Explore faraway places like Africa, Europe, the Arctic, and South and Middle America. Exhibits range from a Costa Rican rain forest to life-size dinosaurs. Take a giant leap back to the land of dinosaurs. Gaze at ancient Mediterranean civilizations and see real mummies. Surround yourself with the sounds and feel of a tropical rainforest. Walk the turn-of-the-century Streets of Old Milwaukee. Watch a butterfly wiggle out if its chrysalis and feel the tickle of hundreds of live butterflies in the Puelicher Butterfly Wing, a two-story, glass-enclosed butterfly garden.

Visit the new exhibit-Exploring Life on Earth - and discover your place in the web of life on Earth. Through life-sized dioramas, multimedia stations, hands-on laboratories and animatronics, experience the incredible story of life on Earth and how it has changed over time.

POLISH FEST

Milwaukee - *Summerfest Grounds. Celebrate the annual Polish Fest. This festival recognizes the culture of Poland with Polka music, folk dancing, cultural village, exhibits, folk art demonstrations, fireworks, marketplace, children's stage, delicious food and more. Admission.* **www.polishfest.org**. *(third weekend in June)*

SUMMERFEST

Milwaukee - *Downtown Milwaukee Shoreline. America's party on Lake Michigan, Summerfest fills 12 stages with more than 800 national, regional and local acts in just 11 days. The "World's Largest Music Festival" draws nearly a million music lovers to revel in alternative, pop, hip-hop, classic rock, jazz, country, blues, Cajun/ zydeco, alternative, soul and comedy. Target Kids Activity Tents, kids entertainers and a Playzone are the area kids gravitate to. While there, nearly 50 area restaurants provide a food to purchase. Admission.* **www.summerfest.com**. *(last two weekends in June thru July 4th week)*

GERMAN FEST

Milwaukee - *Shores of Lake Michigan. "Gemütlichkeit," loosely translated from German as good cheer and comfort, surrounds visitors to the nation's largest four-day German festival of its kind. Fest goers of all nationalities immerse themselves in German culture with tuba-playing contests, polka extravaganzas, authentic German food, fireworks, and drink. An extensive cultural area includes artisans and computerized genealogy assistance for those interested in tracing their family roots.* **www.germanfest.com**. *(last full weekend in July)*

BIG TOP CIRCUS PARADE

Milwaukee (Baraboo) - *Downtown. This spectacular parade, which at one time was the third largest parade in the country, behind only the Tournament of Roses parade and the Macy's Thanksgiving Day parade will be held again in the Milwaukee area. The parade features more than 100 units, including 52 historic circus wagons pulled by horses of all major breeds. Around 300 horses pull colorful wagons and carriages, accompanied by 14 top bandwagon bands, 10 marching bands and several specialty musical units.* **http://bigtopparade.com/** *(early Saturday in June)*

MILWAUKEE AIR & WATER SHOW

Milwaukee - *Bradford Beach on shores of Lake Michigan. The Milwaukee Air & Water Show takes place at Bradford Beach on the shores of Lake Michigan. This FREE show will treat the Greater Milwaukee area to the highflying action of the USAF Thunderbirds and the US Army Golden Knights as well as other military and civilian aircraft. Water acts also will thrill the crowds as they gather with friends and family near show center, Bradford Beach.* **www.milwaukeeairshow.com**. *(mid July weekend)*

MILWAUKEE IRISH FEST

Milwaukee - *Maier Festival Park. Visit Milwaukee Irish Fest, the world's largest celebration of Irish music and culture, showcasing more than 100 entertainment acts annually at the four-day, 16-stage event at the Henry W. Maier Festival Park on Lake Michigan. Passionately committed to igniting a love of Irish culture in all people, Irish Fest teaches Ireland's music, dance, drama, sports, culture, children's activities and genealogy at the festival.* **www.irishfest.com**. *(mid month long weekend in August)*

WISCONSIN STATE FAIR

Milwaukee - *Wisconsin State Fair Grounds. Wisconsin State Fair attracts nearly 1 million visitors annually. Visitors can enjoy diverse entertainment, demonstrations and family programming on 30 free stages, plus national acts on The Main Stage. Fairgoers enjoy more than 350,000 mouthwatering and delicious cream puffs during the 11-day fair where bakers create dozens of cream puffs each minute. More than 200 food concessions, over 700 commercial exhibitors, a spectacular Midway and Kiddie Kingdom filled with rides and games, and more than 10,000 animals in the Ag Village. A small museum section is available for viewing from the INTERNATIONAL CLOWN HALL OF FAME.* **www.wistatefair.com**. *(eleven days early to mid-August)*

INDIAN SUMMER POW WOWS

Milwaukee - *Wisconsin State Fair Park (winter) or Milwaukee's Lakefront . A Traditional Pow Wow open to the public. Native Dance, Marketplace, Food. Setting the rhythm for each dance is a powerful drumbeat, which remains at the heart of modern American Indian culture. Two types of drums are used at most Pow Wows: the traditional drum, made by stretching hides over a cylindrical frame and lacing them together with rawhide, and a regular modern bass drum. Both types are greatly respected by all tribes. Admission. (first weekend in March - winter pow wow)* **www.indiansummer.org**. *(mid-September weekend)*

HOLIDAY FOLK FAIR

Milwaukee - *Wisconsin State Fair Park. Phone: (800) 324-7468.* **www.folkfair.org***.
For three days, explore the customs and traditions of the world's diverse cultures as
you sample many different ethnic cuisines, enjoy live music and dance, and purchase
beautifully handcrafted goods. Experience the sights, sounds and tastes of the world
right in your own backyard. On Education Day (Friday) students will have the
opportunity to personally experience global connections through ethnic displays,
workshops, mini-language classes, demonstrations, music and dance performances,
foods and a marketplace. Admission. (weekend before Thanksgiving in November)*

MILWAUKEE MILE RACE TRACK

7722 W Greenfield Avenue (Wisconsin State Fair Grounds)
Milwaukee (West Allis) 53214

☐ Phone: (414) 453-5761 **http://wistatefair.com/wsfp/milwaukee-mile-
speedway-and-peck-media-center/**
☐ Hours & Admission: Various races and admission throughout the season.

Experience world-class racing of all styles at the oldest active motor speedway
in the world. Early motor races date back to 1903 when it was a horse track
with a dirt surface. See Indy 500-style racing the Sunday following the Indy
500 and other racing series at the storied one-mile oval.

RIVEREDGE NATURE CENTER

4458 Hawthorne Drive **Newburg 53060**

☐ Phone: (262) 375-2715 **www.riveredgenaturecenter.org**
☐ Hours: Visitor Center - Monday-Friday 8:30am-4:30pm, Saturday 9:00am-
5:00pm.
☐ Admission: Trail Fee $5.00 adult, $2.00 child (4-13), $15.00 family.
☐ Note: Maple Syrup Pancake Breakfast each March.

One of the first and one of the largest nature centers in Southeastern
Wisconsin, Riveredge offers hands-on environmental education, through a
variety of special events, weekend programs and summer camps. 10 miles
of hiking trails, six miles of X-C ski trails and a visitor center offer activities
throughout the year - along the banks of the Milwaukee River. Snowshoers
have a special snowshoeing area in the Mayhew Woods

MAPLE SYRUP MAGIC OPEN HOUSE

Newburg - Riveredge Nature Center. Riveredge's Open House will take you back to the origins of maple syrup making. Witness the collection and distillation of sap, stir the syrup cooking over an open fire, and see how our pioneers lived. Guests will learn how to identify and properly tap a maple tree. Children can explore signs of animal survival in the woods as well as arts and crafts projects. Children are invited to solve an animal treasure hunt. Complete your forest exploration at the Sugar Shack for wonderful Riveredge pancakes made from organic flours. FREE for most Open House events. (third Saturday in March)

PORT WASHINGTON LIGHTHOUSE & LIGHTSTATION MUSEUM

311 Johnson Street **Port Washington** 53074

- ☐ **https://www.pwhistory.org/1860-light-station**
- ☐ Hours: Saturday 11:00am-4:00pm, Friday and Sunday Noon-4:00pm (May - mid September).
- ☐ Admission: $5.00 adult, $2.00 child (6-17).

Take a guided tour of the restored 1860 light station and museum. Kids especially like the hands on wooden Pilot House with artifacts from S.S. Christopher Columbus, Tug Admiral, S.S. Cedarville. Children can play steamboat Captain! Outside, ask the guide why there are no trees, bushes or plants on the side of the light facing the lake.

WORLD'S LARGEST ONE-DAY OUTDOOR FISH FRY

Port Washington - Lakefront. Port Washington's lakefront is the site of this family-oriented event billed as "The World's Largest One-Day Outdoor Fish Fry." The day includes a parade, live entertainment on the five stages, affordable family entertainment, a kidzone, arts and crafts, a classic car show and fireworks. **https://statetrunktour.com/event/port-washington-fish-day/** *(third Saturday in July)*

WIND POINT LIGHTHOUSE

4725 Lighthouse Drive **Racine** 53400

- ☐ Phone: (262) 639-3777   **www.windpointlighthouse.org**
- ☐ Hours: The tower is open on the first Sundays (June-October). Due to high demand to see for miles at the top of the lighthouse, reservations are recommended.
- ☐ Admission: $12.00 adult (12+) $6.00 child (6-11) for lighthouse tour. Call

(262) 639-2026 for reservations. No children under the age of 6.

Built in 1880, the Wind Point Lighthouse is the oldest and tallest in operation on Lake Michigan. Fully automated in 1964, the building now serves as a town hall, but the grounds are open to the public. The Wind Point Grounds are open as a park 365 days a year. Park hours are sunrise until 11:00pm. The Wind Point Lighthouse grounds are a wonderful spot for family picnics, leisurely walks on the Lake Michigan Shore and fantastic bird watching.

NORTH BEACH

1501 Michigan Blvd. **Racine** 53402

☐   **https://www.cityofracine.org/NorthBeach/**

This 50-acre sandy paradise has soft, fluffy sand groomed daily in the summer. It reminds many of a West Coast beach in California. The North Beach Oasis, North Beach's concessions stand, serves sandwiches, ice cream, water, soda, and on weekends from Memorial Day through Labor Day, live music entertains beach-goers. A community of volunteers has also built "Kid's Cove", an ever entertaining children's playground. This nautical themed playground is fun for the young and the old. Also at North Beach a newly paved bike path runs along the length of the beach, north to the Racine Zoo and south to Downtown. Bring your bikes, roller blades or walking shoes for a beautifully scenic experience.

RACINE ZOO

2131 North Main Street **Racine** 53402

☐   Phone: (262) 636-9189 **www.racinezoo.org**
☐   Hours: Daily 10:00am-4:00pm, extended hours in spring/summer.
☐   Admission: $11.00 adult, $10.00 senior (62+), $9.00 (3-15). Racine County residents receive $1 off admission. Reduced general admission in the fall/ winter seasons.

Nestled on the sandy shores of beautiful Lake Michigan, the walk is easy for kids and seniors, making the Racine Zoo a great way to enjoy the outdoors with the entire family. The collection features Amur tigers, Transvaal lions, Andean Bears, Masai giraffes, eastern black rhinoceros, the beloved orangutans, Max and Jenny, red kangaroos, common wallaroos and many more mammals, birds, reptiles, amphibians as fish. They have a newer aquarium and aviary.

Afterwards, head down by the lake and see all the boats, pick up some Kringle, and take a stroll down Main street with its great shops and restaurants. Although it's a smaller zoo, it's also a smaller admission and easy to navigate with young ones.

KEWPEE HAMBURGERS

Racine - *520 Wisconsin Avenue (I-94 to Hwy 20 exit into downtown) 53403. Phone: (262) 634-9601 www.facebook.com/pg/Kewpee-Lunch-226801137258/. Hours: Monday-Friday 7:00am-6:00pm, Saturday 7:00am-5:00pm, Closed Sunday. The Kewpee is famous throughout the midwest as one of the oldest hamburger restaurants. Restaurant critics often vote the Kewpee as one of the 20 best hamburgers in Wisconsin. But the only critics they care about are the 700-1000 customers that walk in the door each day. The biggest burger you can order (double cheeseburger) is only $4.20 and you can still get a cheese sandwich (plain or grilled) for just under $2.00! Because Racine is the birthplace of malted milk, their hand-dipped malts are popular with locals. Our kids liked their little ditty: "Hamburg with pickle on top...Makes your heart go flippity-flop."*

RACINE HERITAGE MUSEUM

701 Main Street **Racine** 53403

- Phone: (262) 636-3926 **www.racineheritagemuseum.org**
- Hours: Tuesday-Friday 10:00am-5:00pm, Saturday 10:00am-3:00pm, Sunday Noon-4:00pm.
- Admission: FREE.

The Racine Heritage Museum offers three floors of entertaining and interactive exhibits celebrating the rich heritage of our unique community. Discover the tales of Racine's people, innovations and products including the stories behind Hamilton Beach, SC Johnson, Modine, Twin Disc, Case and Horlick's Malted Milk. Additionally, uncover Racine County's brilliant history as a shipbuilding center and port, our area's role in the Underground Railroad and exhibits honoring fallen astronaut Laura Salton Clark. They even have a real mummy called "Malty."

ROOT RIVER STEELHEAD FACILITY

Lincoln Park **Racine** 53403

- ☐ **http://dnr.wi.gov/topic/fishing/lakemichigan/rootriver.html**
- ☐ Hours: Daily 8:00am-4:00pm.

Steelhead and salmon egg-gathering station with fish ladder and observation window. Self-guided tours via interpretive signage. You may wonder how fish go against the flow, climb a fish ladder and then rest in the holding pond - and like it? From the two large viewing windows at ground level, you can watch fish as they swim up the last series of steps and enter the holding pond to find out the answer.

SC JOHNSON MUSEUM

14th and Franklin Street **Racine** 53403

- ☐ Phone: (262) 260-2154 **www.scjohnson.com/en/company/visiting.aspx**
- ☐ Admission: FREE.
- ☐ Tour: Thursday, Friday, Saturday, Sunday (March thru December) - Begins at SC Johnson - Golden Rondelle Theater, 1525 Howe Street, Racine, WI 53403. Reservations required. The tours are 1.5 hours long so you may want to tag along and then drop out if the kids get bored.

The tours highlight the outstanding architectural features of the Wright-designed building and Fortaleza Hall and give a broad overview of SC Johnson's history. The complex of Administration buildings displays the adventure of finding exotic materials and new formulations. Kids will be most engaged by the Carnauba plane - the replica twin-engine amphibious aircraft used by Sam Johnson and his sons for trips into tropical gardens to find new wax materials. Other plant and material art landscape the building - a vertical garden wall with living plants, a mosaic map of different types of wood, a reflecting pool, a computer-operated soundscape of Brazil and finally a Legacy gallery where you hear stories about creation of old and new products used by most American homes. And thousands of people have delighted in the spectacular "bird-cage" elevators.

KRINGLE BAKERIES

Racine *Kringle* - the oval-shaped, authentic Danish pastry produced predominately in Racine County. Thirty-two layers of flaky dough - and filling choices from fruits to nuts. Racine is now known as the Kringle Capital of America. Here's some places in town where you can be tempted:

- **BENDTSEN'S BAKERY** - **www.bendtsensbakery.com** or (262) 633-0365. (3200 Washington Avenue (corner of Hwy. 20 & Grove Avenue)

- **LARSEN BAKERY** - **www.larsenskringle.com** or (262) 633-4298. 3311 Washington Avenue.

- **O & H DANISH BAKERY** - **www.ohdanishbakery.com** or (800) 709-4009. 1841 Douglas Ave.

- **LEHMANN'S BAKERY** - https://lehmannsbakery.com/

APPLE HOLLER

5006 South Sylvania Ave. (I-94 exit 337. Turn right onto S Sylvania Ave)
Racine (Sturdevant) 53177

- ☐   Phone: (800) 238-3629 **www.appleholler.com**
- ☐   Hours: Daily 9:00am-5:00pm. Extended seasonal and weekend hours.
- ☐   Note: August thru October, they have apple & pumpkin picking hours from the patch or their 74 acre apple orchard with more than 15,000 select dwarf apple trees in thirty varieties. And guess what? You don't need a ladder to pick them!

Enjoy a friendly country restaurant which serves up hearty home-style meals for breakfast, lunch and dinner.

Their specialty is Applewood Smoked Meats which includes Prime Rib, Ham, Chicken, Chops, Bacon and Turkey. At the Red Barn Theater, you can enjoy a professional musical comedy review with your lunch or dinner. Enjoy delicious homemade cornbread, apple butter and choice of one side dish. Their apple pies are filled with a whopping 5 lbs. of apples straight from the orchard! Don't forget about the apple cider donuts, apple dumplings and apple cinnamon nut bread. Their breakfast buffets are plentiful and run about $12.00 for adults, half price for kids. If you're trying to wear off the extra calories, you can go out and walk the property and visit with the barn animals or ride on a pony (seasonal) or pet a miniature donkey.

BUDDY SQUIRREL CANDY & NUT FACTORY STORE

1801 E. Bolivar Avenue **St. Francis** 53235

- ☐ Phone: (414) 483-4500 or (800) 972 2658 **https://buddysquirrel.com/**
- ☐ Hours: Store Hours: Monday 11:00am-3:00pm, Tuesday-Thursday 9:00am-5:00pm. Friday 9:00am-3:00pm.
- ☐ Tours: Weekdays to groups of 10 or more. Call their factory number.

Look into their kitchens including stations where they make their own centers from scratch, including butter almond toffee, nougats, caramels and meltaways. And, keeping with the Wisconsin traditions, drenched in pure Swiss style milk and dark chocolate. It's pretty amazing to see the "centers" lined up to go under the chocolate "waterfall." Did you know they brush the candy to enhance the shine of their chocolates? Buddy Squirrel is Wisconsin's largest retail nut and popcorn operation. You get to see those giant poppers and the roasting rooms are hot, but smell so good.

BEAR DEN GAME FARM & PETTING ZOO

6831 Big Bend Road (Hwy. 164) **Waterford** 53185

- ☐ Phone: (262) 895-6430 **www.beardenzoo.com**
- ☐ Hours: Weekends 11:00am-3pm (mid-May-October). Tuesday, Wednesday, Friday 11:00am-3:00pm (June -August).
- ☐ Admission: $12.00 adult, $10.00 child (2-11). CASH ONLY. Seasonal activities available at extra cost. Admission includes a hayride through the woods. Feed bags extra $2.00-$5.00. Pumpkins $3.00.

This zoo features exotic, woodland & farm animals, plus a petting zoo and pony rides. Bears, mountain lions, meaty siberian tigers, llamas and porcupine. Some tell us they have gotten to pet the porcupine - with instruction, of course.

DID YOU KNOW? A full grown porcupine has up to 30,000 quills.

GREEN MEADOWS FARM

33603 High Drive (Hwy. 20 - 3 miles west of Waterford) **Waterford (East Troy)** 53120

- ☐ Phone: (262) 254-1134 **www.greenmeadowsfarmwi.com**
- ☐ Hours: Tuesday-Sunday 10:00am -4:00pm (May - August). Fall hours vary greatly. See website. Last admission at 2:00pm.
- ☐ Admission: $15.75 general (age 2+).

Farm animals, children's petting zoo, hayrides, pony rides. Kids can milk their friendly cow, jump in straw, play with the kitties, bunnies and baby chicks, brush the potbelly pigs!, pick your own pumpkin (fall) or just play or picnic the day away. A corn maze is available in the fall.

INGLESIDE HOTEL & SPRINGS WATER PARK

2810 Golf Road (I-94, 20 minutes west of Milwaukee) **Waukesha** 53187

- ☐ Phone: (262) 547-0201 **https://www.theinglesidehotel.com/**
- ☐ Hours: Waterpark hours vary by season and day of the week. Generally, the park opens by 10:00am and closes around 9:00pm. Be sure to check their website before making plans.
- ☐ Admission: Day Pass pricing is $25.00-$30.00 weekdays and $40.00-$50.00 on Friday-Sunday.
- ☐ Note: Casual restaurants and waterpark snack bar on property.

With a three person boat ride, lazy river, zero-depth entry play area, water basketball and Geyser Games Arcade, a visit to The Springs Water Park is the perfect year round reward for kids of all ages. Parents like the indoor/outdoor whirlpool, too.

Hotel - All rooms include a complimentary continental breakfast every morning and a copy of USA Today is available at Continental Breakfast Monday through Friday. Workout opportunities include an indoor swimming pool with atrium, hotel fitness center with whirlpool and a walking or jogging trail. Recreation fun includes basketball, horseshoes or nearby golf. Deluxe rooms and suites are available. Packages to stay and play start at $139.99 and include room, water park passes, a pizza meal and arcade tokens.

WAUKESHA JANBOREE

Waukesha - With winter temperatures and an average of 45 inches of annual snowfall in Wisconsin, it comes as no surprise that the art of snow sculpting is so popular. The annual event features professionally-carved snow sculptures on display throughout downtown Waukesha. **www.janboree.org** *(late January weekend)*

MUSEUM OF WISCONSIN ART

205 VeteransAvenue **West Bend** 53095

- ☐ Phone: (262) 334-9638 **www.wisconsinart.org**
- ☐ Hours: Wednesday-Sunday 9:30am-4:00pm.
- ☐ Admission: One adult $15, two adults $25, family $50.
- ☐ FREEBIES: They have scavenger hunts designed to sharpen the kids' observation and create thinking skills as they explore the museum's collection. Once complete, kids can win prizes.

In West Bend, The Museum of Wisconsin Art displays the exquisite paintings of German/American master Carl Von Marr. More than twenty works of contemporary art can be enjoyed on a outside stroll along the intriguing West Bend Sculpture Walk. The city's winding Riverwalk provides gorgeous views of the Milwaukee River. MOWA welcomes families of all ages to this new, interactive, fun program series. Drop in for special art making projects, gallery tours, exploration games, performances and surprises.

DID YOU KNOW? West Bend is also known as the "Geocaching Capital of the Midwest," offering more than 450 caches within a 7-mile radius.

MEADOWBROOK PUMPKIN FARM

West Bend - 2970 Mile View Road. **www.meadowbrookfun.com**. *Phone: (262) 338-3649. Meadowbrook Market and Pumpkin Farm is a family Farm since 1960's that raises many varieties of pumpkins. They have an animal park and petting area, wagon rides in October and have both pick your own Pumpkins as well as 17 varieties already picked. Entertainment... The Creepy and haunted Cornfields... By Day it is filled with extensive creepy and scary well done scenes, many with sound and action. 40 minutes of adventurous excitement for you and your kids...Evenings, it's gets too scary for young kids. ($24.95) There is no admission to visit the Farm. Activities require fees per event. Prices range from $2.00 to $12.00 w/ combo packages available. (Farm open August through December but Pumpkin activities are mostly in October).*

YERKES OBSERVATORY

373 West Geneva Street **Williams Bay** 53191

- Phone: (262) 245-5555 h **https://yerkesobservatory.org/**
- Admission: FREE, but suggest a $5.00 per person donation. This is the property grounds only. Special events are by reservation only and range from $5.00-$30.00 per person.
- Tours: Note that the dome interior is unheated, and during late fall and winter temperatures inside are as chilly as outdoors. Please dress appropriately.

You don't usually get to see a big scope like this one up close and personal - this is the world's largest lens-type telescope. The volunteers and astronomists are eager to answer questions and explain what to look for. Young children won't last long here, though. Use it for the 3rd graders on up who have some earth science knowledge.

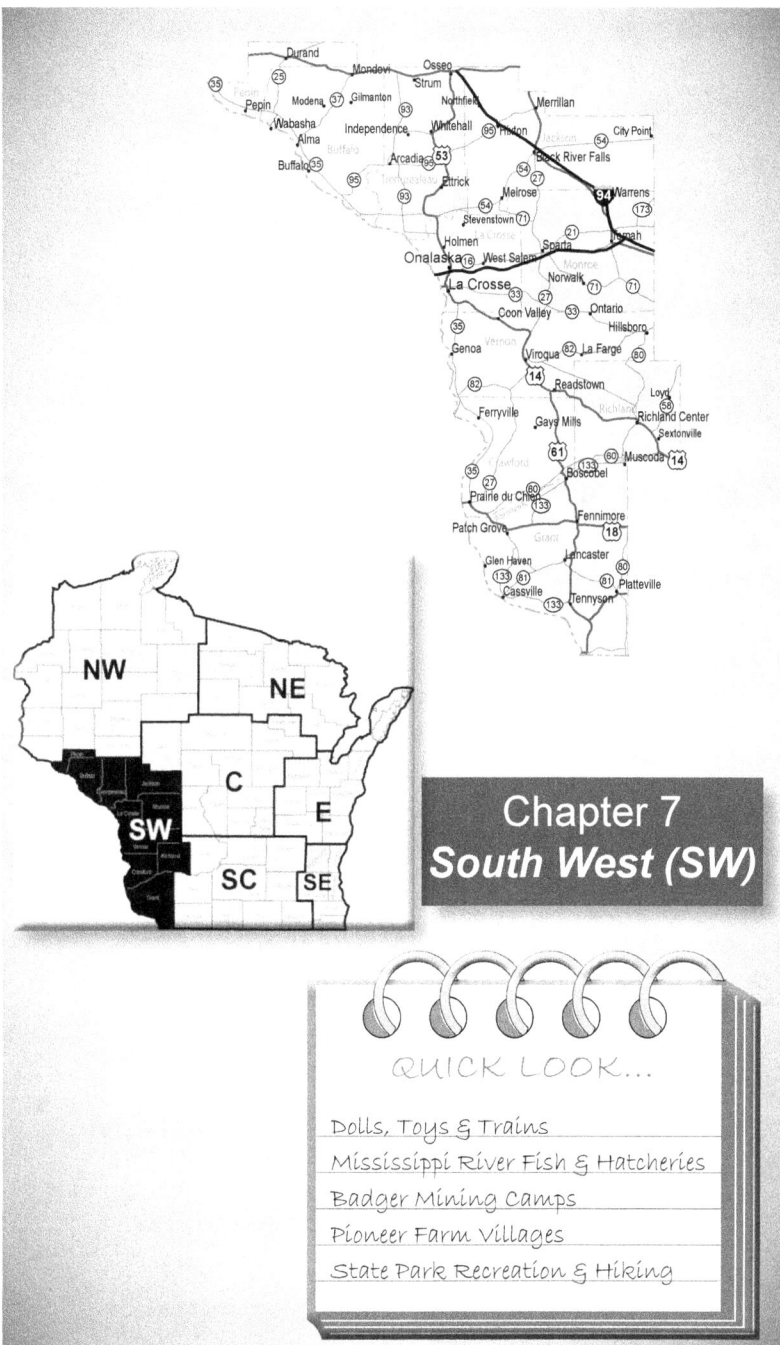

Chapter 7
South West (SW)

QUICK LOOK...

Dolls, Toys & Trains

Mississippi River Fish & Hatcheries

Badger Mining Camps

Pioneer Farm Villages

State Park Recreation & Hiking

Blanchardville
- Yellowstone Lake State Park

Blue River
- Eagle Cave Natural Park

Cassville
- Cassville Car Ferry
- Nelson Dewey State Park
- Stonefield Village

Coon Valley
- Norskedalen Nature & Heritage Center

Dubuque, IA
- Fenelon Place Elevator Company
- National Mississippi River Museum & Aquarium

Durand
- Eau Galle Cheese Factory

Fennimore
- Fennimore Doll And Toy Museum
- Fennimore Railroad Historical Society Museum

Fountain City
- Elmer's Auto And Toy Museum

Gays Mills
- Gays Mills Apple Festival

Genoa
- Genoa National FIsh Hatchery

La Crosse
- Children's Museum Of La Crosse
- La Crosse Queen
- Riverside Park
- Upper Mississippi Environmental Science Center

La Crosse (Onalaska)
- Upper Mississippi River National Wildlife & Fish Refuge

Mineral Point
- Pendarvis State Historic Site

Muscoda
- Meister Cheese Company

Ontario
- Wildcat Mountain State Park

Pepin
- Laura Ingalls Wilder Museum

Platteville
- The Mining Museum / Rollo Jamison Museum

Prairie Du Chien
- Droppin Of The Carp New Years Eve Carp Fest
- Fort Crawford Museum
- Prairie Villa Rendezvous

Prairie Du Chien (Bagley)
- Wyalusing State Park

Sparta
- Little Falls Railroad & Doll Museum

Tomah
- Little Red School House Museum

Trempealeau
- Perrot State Park

Warrens
- Warrens Cranberry Festival
- Wisconsin Cranberry Discovery Center

Wauzeka
- Kickapoo Indian Caverns

Westby
- Snowflake Ski Jump Tournament

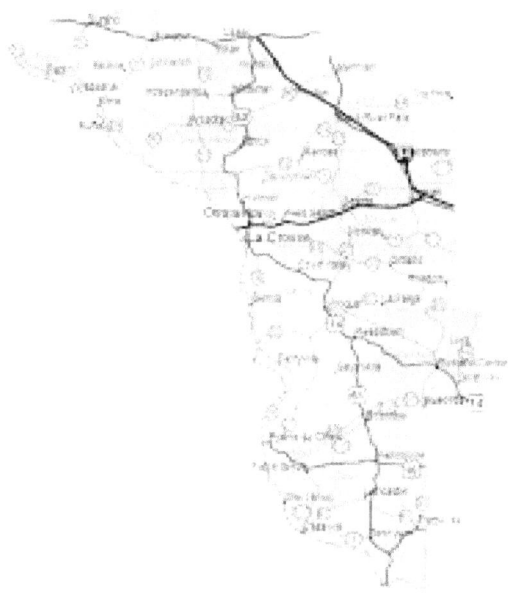

Travel Journal & Notes:

Sites and attractions are listed in order by City, Zip Code, and Name. Symbols indicated represent: 🍽 Restaurants 🛏 Lodging

YELLOWSTONE LAKE STATE PARK

8495 North Lake Road (Take Highway F for about 8 miles to Lake Road) **Blanchardville** 53516

☐ Phone: (608) 523-4427
   http://dnr.wi.gov/topic/parks/name/yellowstone/
☐ Admission: A vehicle admission sticker is required. Daily $8.00-$11.00. Annual passes available.

This 1,000-acre park, with an additional 455-acre lake offers visitors ample space to enjoy camping, swimming, fishing, boating, hiking, biking and picnicking. Bluff- top campsites are a popular feature. A concession stand and boat rentals are located at the east end of the lake and are available during summer. In winter the park is open to ice fishing, snowmobiling and cross-country skiing.

EAGLE CAVE NATURAL PARK

16320 Cavern Lane, Eagle Cave Road (off Hwy 60) **Blue River** 53518

☐ Phone: (608) 537-2988 **www.eaglecave.net**
☐ Tours: Guided one hour cave tours are available Thursday-Sunday from 10:00am-5:00pm (Memorial Day-Labor Day). $16.00 general (age 13+), $9.00 child (age 4-12).

Come and explore inside Wisconsin's largest onyx cave. The cave is a constant 52 degrees all year long, so bring a jacket or sweater to keep warm. Perfect for those hot summer days. Kids under 13 pay just 75c for the tour.

CASSVILLE CAR FERRY

Cassville 53806

☐ Phone: (608) 725-5180 **www.facebook.com/Cassville-Car-Ferry-222503077861763/**
☐ Hours: Daily (Memorial Day - Labor Day), 9:00am-9:00pm. Friday, Saturday, Sunday (May, September, October). Last trip from Cassville leaves at 8:20pm, last trip from Iowa leaves at 8:40pm.
☐ Admission: $5.00 walk-on passenger, $15.00 Car, Van, Pickup (includes passengers).

A car ferry across the Mississippi River into Iowa. The Cassville Car Ferry connects two National Scenic Byways; the Great River Road and the Iowa Great River Road. The ferry served the early settlement as far back as 1833 and it continues today, making the same trip back and forth across the mighty Mississippi. It is the oldest operating ferry service in the state of Wisconsin.

NELSON DEWEY STATE PARK

County Highway V V (across from Stonefield Village Historic Site)
Cassville 53806

- Phone: (608) 725-5374
- **http://dnr.wi.gov/topic/parks/name/nelsondewey/**
- Admission: A vehicle admission sticker is required. Daily $8.00-$11.00.

Take in a panoramic view of the Mississippi from a campsite atop the river bluffs. Nearby you can tour the home of Wisconsin's first governor or relive history at Stonefield Village. Features 43 campsites, 16 electric sites, showers, a dumping station, handicap- accessible picnic area and campsites, vistas, canoeing nearby, boating nearby, fishing nearby, 0.2 miles of nature trails, 1.6 miles of hiking trails. The wooded river bluffs of Nelson Dewey State Park are a great place to watch a resident population of bald eagles soar above the river valley. Their hiking trails are all very short - some with a view of the Mississippi, others pass near Indian mounds or through prairie. Open daily 6:00am-11:00pm with overnight camping.

STONEFIELD VILLAGE

12195 Hwy VV (one mile north of Cassville, off WI-133 on CR-VV)
Cassville 53806

- Phone: (608) 725-5210 **http://stonefield.wisconsinhistory.org/**
- Hours: Thursday-Sunday 10:00am-5:00pm (June 1-Oct 1).
- Admission: $13.50 adult, $11.50 senior (65+), $8.00 child (5-12).
- Note: The Stonefield Stores carries old-fashioned goods, crafts, children's toys (no batteries), candy and railroad-themed souvenirs. Snacks are sold in the Visitors Center and picnic facilities abound on the property.

This village is a replica of an 1900s Wisconsin rural town with an emphasis on agriculture and historic farm machinery. The turn of the 20th century marked the rise of dairy farming and the beginnings of modern farm tools such as tractors, reapers and threshing machines.

The attraction is home to the <u>WISCONSIN STATE AGRICULTURAL MUSEUM</u> featuring the changes in farm tractors and rare examples of McCormick patent models of the reaper. The museum's dioramas and exhibits tell the story from subsistence farming through the age of industrialization. The museum contains the most extensive collection of historic farm machinery in Wisconsin. It is completely self-guided.

The 1901 Farmstead offers a costumed interpreter leading tours through a recreated farmhouse. Seeing the small domestic farm animals in the barns and fields is a kid's favorite. Another docent lead tour explores the village's Farmers Store and Meat Market - an old-fashioned "Walmart" and the Nelson Dewey Home of an upper-class 19th century family. The rest of the village can be discovered on your own. Peek in over 30 shops, offices and services that were typical in a Wisconsin village…even the one-room schoolhouse.

CHILDREN'S DAYS

Cassville - *Stonefield Village. Hands-on for kids showing them how to cook on a wood-fired stove, bake bread and process honey. (mid-June)*

RAILROAD DAYS

Cassville - *Stonefield Village. Hop aboard the caboose at the Stonefield Depot. See model railroads and savor Mulligan Stew. (third weekend in August)*

NORSKEDALEN NATURE & HERITAGE CENTER

N455 O. Ophus Rd (3 miles north of Coon Valley) **Coon Valley** 54623

- ☐ Phone: (608) 452-3424 **www.norskedalen.org**
- ☐ Hours: Monday-Saturday 10:00am-5:00pm, Sunday 11:00am-5:00pm (May - October). Monday-Saturday 9:00am-4:00pm, Sunday 11:00am-4:00pm (November-April).
- ☐ Admission: $6.00 adult, $3.00 student, $15.00 family.
- ☐ Note: for the same admission price, you can come during one of their monthly special events (usually near holidays) to really get an engaged experience - including foods (everything from Norwegian stew to rommegrot (cream pudding).

The property is a historic open-air museum owned and operated by Norskedalen as a museum and cultural center for classes and events. It has eleven restored pioneer log buildings nestled in a picturesque valley with a creek and croplands surrounded by forested hills. The Bekkum Homestead seeks to re-create a typical local farm at the turn of the century. The homestead is comprised of a house, summer kitchen, springhouse, corncrib, granary, outhouse, chicken coop, machine shed, stable, barn, blacksmith's shop, and storage shed. Begin your visit at the Thrune Visitors Center by watching a short video about the site and looking over the heritage and nature rooms. Norwegian gifts and food items can be purchased in the gift shop.

FENELON PLACE ELEVATOR COMPANY

512 Fenelon Place **Dubuque, IA** 52001

- ☐ Phone: (563) 582-6496 **www.fenelonplaceelevator.com**
- ☐ Hours: Daily 8:00am-10:00pm (April - November).
- ☐ Admission: $2.00 to $4.00 per person (age 5+).

In 1882, Dubuque, IA was an hour and a half town - at noon everything shut down for an hour and a half when everyone went home to dinner. Frustrated to find a way to quickly get up and around the bluff, Fenelon petitioned to have a cable car built. One was built, modeled after those in the Alps. The cable system has been rebuilt many times since. The current elevator is described as the world's shortest, steepest scenic railway, elevating passengers 189 feet from Fourth Street to Fenelon Place. The top has a magnificent view of the Mississippi River and 3 states.

NATIONAL MISSISSIPPI RIVER MUSEUM & AQUARIUM

350 E. 3rd Street (follow signs off Rte 151 west, just over the bridge from WI) **Dubuque, IA** 52001

- ☐ Phone: (563) 557-9545 or (800) 226-3369 **www.rivermuseum.com**
- ☐ Hours: Daily 10:00am-5:00pm. Opens one hour earlier Summer and Fall seasons.
- ☐ Admission: $23.95 adult, $21.95 senior (65+), $17.95 youth (3-17). Movies extra $4.00.
- ☐ Note: Boat & Breakfast - stay overnight in bunks on a steam ship dredger. Have a hearty sailors' breakfast. Depot Café for lunch. Educators: click on the icon: EDUCATION & GROUPS for Lesson Plans (about two dozen) and complete conservation-themed curriculum.

Take an historic and natural journey on the Mighty Mississippi. Begin with the Mississippi Journey - a sight, sound and motion short film that grabs you into the river "scene".

Chart a course as you pass floor-to-ceiling glass panels framing gators, otters (so playful), ancient sturgeon and paddlefish. Walk on working riverboats, go into cargo holds in the Barge theatre, touch fish or "Noodle" a catfish (ewe!). Next, let their educators introduce you to freshwater mussels, snails, and crawfish in the touch tank. Kids can also roll on logs like lumberjacks, pilot a boat or crawl through a lead mine. Outside, tour the Logsdon towboat, see huge steamboat artifacts, and watch as a boat is launched into the Mississippi. The floating dock features houseboats, scientific vessels, and the traveling Audubon Ark. A recreated Indian village and nature boardwalk follows the outside historic trail. Finally, watch craftsmen carve a boat in the wood shop. A lot of money and time has produced an excellent site to feel the mighty Mississippi from on, and in, the water. Well worth the trip.

EAU GALLE CHEESE FACTORY

N6765 Hwy 25 (2 miles north of town) **Durand** 54736

- Phone: (715) 283-4211 http://**eaugallecheese.com**
- Hours: Monday - Saturday 9am - 5:30pm; Sunday til 5:00pm.

Eau Galle Cheese, family owned & operated since 1945, produces over 9 million lbs of cheese each year. Make sure to try the many samples available - especially their niche hard Italian cheese. There is a viewing area where you can look into the plant or you can watch, "The Art of Cheese-Making" video. In 2005, they completely automated their production line so this factory shines with a lot more motorized equipment moving up and down and spinning around.

FENNIMORE DOLL AND TOY MUSEUM

1135 6th Street (across the street from the Fennimore Railroad Museum) **Fennimore** 53809

- Phone: (608) 822-4100 **www.dollandtoymuseum.com**
- Hours: Thursday-Saturday 10:00am-4:00pm, Sunday 1:00-4:00pm (Summer). Weekends only (Sept-October)
- Admisson: Suggested donation 3.00 adult, $1.50 for student.

Come see what "Every Toy Has a Story to Tell" is all about. Enjoy reliving the past as you meander through this collection of dolls and puppets, tractors, circus memorabilia and pedal cars. Most every action figure and Barbie doll ever made is in this collection, donated by a local farm lady who collected them for 20 years.

FENNIMORE RAILROAD HISTORICAL SOCIETY MUSEUM

610 Lincoln Avene (across the street from the Fennimore Doll and Toy Museum)   **Fennimore** 53809

☐ Phone: (608) 822-6144 **www.fennimore.com/railmuseum**
☐ Hours: Thursday-Monday 10:00am-4:00pm. (Memorial weekend - Labor Day). Weekends only (September and October).
☐ Tours: Rides are available ($1.00 for a train ride) on the 15" miniature train system on weekends and scheduled holidays.

This museum building has been remodeled inside and out to resemble a depot of the turn-of-the-century. It is the home of the "Dinky" engine, depot and memorabilia of the narrow gauge (15" track) railroad that once traveled from Fennimore to Woodman. The Wilkinson Railroad consists of a depot, engine barn, water tower, gondola, 2 hopper cars, coach, two engines and a caboose. The diesel locomotive pulls the outdoor train, while the 4-4-0 steam engine is on display inside the museum. It is set up on a trestle using compressed air to show how moving parts of a steam engine operate. A steam boiler is set up to show how it is constructed. There are two sets of model trains with replica buildings featuring Fennimore in the early 1900s that will catch the kids' eyes. Miniature train rides are offered seasonally and on many weekends.

ELMER'S AUTO AND TOY MUSEUM

W903 Elmers Road **Fountain City** 54629

☐ Phone: (608) 687-7221 **www.elmersautoandtoymuseum.com**
☐ Hours: 9:00am-4:00pm, alternate weekends (mid-May - mid-October). Call or see website for current schedule.
☐ Admission: $10.00 adult, $8.00 senior (65+) $5.00 child (6-12).

Elmer never had many toys growing up as a boy so, when he could afford to, he began collecting toys for children and adults. This is one of the world's largest collections of pedal cars, antique and modern toys. Motorcycles, scooters, bikes, wagons and a large doll display are located in five buildings on a hill overlooking the Mississippi River. One building contains the little toys—such as toy cars, toy busses, toy trains, etc. You'll often hear parents and especially grandparents begin to share stories about an object they once owned…or wished they had. Part of the collection is in the family house. See the 1929 Model A Phaeton in the family room.

GAYS MILLS APPLE FESTIVAL

Gays Mills - *Downtown. The largest apple-orchard area in the Midwest hosts events all related to apples. The small town of Gays Mills attracts more than 20,000 Visitors enjoy all kinds of apple products, arts and crafts displays, flea market, a parade and a variety of live entertainment.* **www.gaysmills.org**. *(last weekend in September)*

GENOA NATIONAL FISH HATCHERY

S5631 State Road 35 (3 miles south Genoa on the west side of Highway 35)
Genoa 54632

- ☐ Phone: (608) 689-2605 **www.fws.gov/midwest/Genoa/**
- ☐ Hours: Monday-Friday 8:00am-3:30pm.
- ☐ Note: Nearby on SR 35, Lock and Dam #8 has several viewing areas to watch barges and boats navigate up or down the mighty Mississippi. FREEBIES: go to this link: ***www.fws.gov/midwest/fisheries/kidspage.htm*** for the US Fish & Wildlife Service Great Lakes Kids Page.

Each year, Genoa provides millions of eggs, fry and fingerlings of many different species to state fishery stations, federal hatcheries, National Wildlife Refuges, Department of Army installations and seven Native American Tribes to support ongoing fish management and restoration programs. Genoa's location and its ability to create different rearing environments and water temperatures, makes it one of the most diverse hatcheries in the nation. Nineteen ponds ranging in size from one-tenth of one acre to 33 acres, six raceways, and seven intensive rearing buildings make it capable of collecting, culturing, and rearing cold, cool and warm water fish species. Genoa raises, holds and rears more species of fish (15) and freshwater mussels (15) than almost any other federal fish hatchery! If you just pop in, the place seems pretty dull but if you plan to come for a tour, the fish scientists really give you a show. Depending on the season, you get a different tour as some fish move out and others are just growing and racing with delight. What are those colored jars along the workbench? Could it be fish eggs?

CHILDREN'S MUSEUM OF LA CROSSE

207 5th Avenue South **La Crosse** 54601

- ☐ Phone: (608) 784-2652 **www.funmuseum.org**
- ☐ Hours: Tuesday-Sunday 9:00am-5:00pm.
- ☐ Admission: $9.00/person (age 1+).

The museum is a colorful and clean refreshing atmosphere with three floors of hands on exhibits to engage kids 12 and under. Highlights are the dress up areas, the fire truck, a climbing wall, a giant mouth, and a water log table. Recently, they installed a crane to operate near the rivers and bridge exhibit and a two-story command center near the fire truck area. There is also a special area just for pre-schoolers. Look for dinos and a kid-sized bank too.

LA CROSSE QUEEN

405 East Veterans Memorial Drive (Riverside Park dock - next to the statue of Hiawatha) **La Crosse** 54601

- □ Phone: (608) 784-2893 **www.lacrossequeen.com**
- □ Hours: Daily - various departure times depending on cruise - (May-October).
- □ Admission: Sightseeing Cruise - $18.95 adult (12-59), $17.95 senior (62+), $9.45 child (1-11). Dinner cruises add ~$20.00+ adult, ~$10.00 child.
- □ Tours: Sightseeing Cruise 90-minutes. Other tours available with meals.

This paddle wheeler boat offers sightseeing trips up and down the Mississippi. Take one of the daily sightseeing cruises or a pizza cruise on the La Crosse Queen; an authentic replica of a 19th century stern-wheeler.

RIVERSIDE PARK

100 State Street (intersection of Mississippi River and State Street) **La Crosse** 54601

- □ Phone: (608) 789-7557 **www.cityoflacrosse.org/index.aspx?NID=1715**

Downtown, Riverside Park provides a perfect vantage point for watching river traffic and for boarding one of the two paddle wheelers that offer sightseeing cruises. Bald eagles are also often spotted swooping up and around the Mississippi River.

RIVERFEST

La Crosse - *Riverside Park. Top entertainers, Venetian parade. www.riverfestlacrosse.com.*

OCTOBERFEST

La Crosse - *Riverside Park. One of Wisconsin's largest autumn festivals, attracting 150,000 people annually. Held along the shores of the Mississippi River, this festival transports visitors' to Bavaria with music, entertainment, arts and crafts, ethnic food, carnival rides, parades. 608/784-FEST;* **www.oktoberfestusa.com**. *(last wkend in September through first weekend in October)*

La Crosse - *Riverside Park. Almost a million lights in the park. (day after Thanksgiving thru New Years Eve)*

UPPER MIDWEST ENVIRONMENTAL SCIENCE CENTER

2630 Fanta Reed Road **La Crosse** 54603

- ☐ Phone: (608) 781-9570 **www.umesc.usgs.gov/**
- ☐ Hours: Monday-Friday 8:00am-4:00pm.
- ☐ Educators: online links to quizzes, questions and fact sheets are under Teachers and Students, then Resources for Teachers.

Enjoy an interactive look at the wildlife and fish of the Upper Mississippi River. The center's hands-on displays include fur and feathers of creatures that make their homes in the river valley along with the shells of native mussels. Live fish common to the river, such as walleye, crappie, bluegill and perch, along with not-so-common shovelnose and lake sturgeon are also on display. Songbirds nesting in the Mississippi River Valley are also can be seen along with an inter-active CD-ROM program to help visitors identify songbirds and hear their calls. A quick walk outside reveals a boardwalk path to the Black River.

UPPER MISSISSIPPI RIVER NATIONAL WILDLIFE & FISH REFUGE

555 Lester Ave, Visitors Center **La Crosse (Onalaska)** 54650

- ☐ Phone: (608) 783-8405 **www.fws.gov/midwest/UpperMississippiRiver/**
- ☐ Hours: Monday-Friday 7:30am-4:00pm.

With more than three million people annually who come to fish, boat, hike, birdwatch, hunt, sightsee or just relax, the Upper Mississippi River National Wildlife and Fish Refuge is one of the country's largest and most visited refuges! Established in 1924, the 200,000-acre, 260-mile-long Upper Mississippi refuge features more than 265 bird species, 57 species of mammals, 35 species of reptiles and amphibians, and over 100 species of fish. No wonder this refuge is a nature-lovers wonderland! Special attractions along the La Crosse county shore of the river include boat and canoe rentals, the Long Lake and Goose Island canoe trails, with observation points at major pull-offs denoted by interpretive refuge signs. Displays of refuge wildlife are found at the US Fish and Wildlife Service visitors center.

PENDARVIS STATE HISTORIC SITE

114 Shake Rag Street **Mineral Point** 53565

- Phone: (608) 987-2122 **http://pendarvis.wisconsinhistory.org/**
- Hours: Thursday-Sunday 10:00am-4:00pm (mid-May - October). Last tour begins at 3:00pm.
- Admission: $12.00 adult, $8.00 child (5-12).
- Note: Store.
- Educators: full-bodied printable activity packets are found on the Field Trips/ Group Tours icons.

Costumed interpreters offer guided tours through the Pendarvis complex, recalling the days when Mineral Point was a rough and tumble lead mining camp. They explain what brought the Cornish, with their expert knowledge of mining and stone masonry, their Celtic superstitions, and their frugal foodways, to settle in this Shake Rag neighborhood. Learn how Wisconsin lead mining surpassed the appeal of the fur trading and farming for 19th-century settlers. The Merry Christmas Mine was one of the few large zinc mines in the United States where the original discovery of lead ore was made about 1825 and where much of the early mining was done. Today, you can hike the Pendarvis mine hill trail using a map guide that explains the restoration of 43-acres of native prairie, and the original "badger hole" mines and historic mining equipment.

Founded by Cornish miners, this town loves to tell tales of old. Each summer the town hosts Drolls of Old Cornwall, where storytellers share "drolls", or Cornish folktales. What's a "tommyknocker" or a "cousin Jack?"

CORNISH FESTIVAL

Mineral Point - *Pendarvis State Historic Site. The annual Cornish Festival celebrates the proud heritage of the immigrants who originally settled in the southwestern Wisconsin town of Mineral Point. Festivities kick off on Friday night with a traditional pub night at Pendarvis State Historic Site. The rest of the weekend includes authentic Cornish and Celtic music, traditional Cornish food, narrated bus tours featuring the town's historic stone cottages, live music and storytelling for all ages.* **www. cornishfest.org**. *(last full weekend in September)*

MEISTER CHEESE COMPANY
1160 Industrial Drive **Muscoda** 53573

☐ Phone: (608) 739-3134 **www.meistercheese.com**

Meister has been a Wisconsin family- owned and operated cheese factory since 1923. What can 3,000 local cows do for you? Meister Cheese Company uses that milk to produce Great Midwest Jack and Timber Lake Cheddar, a line of four uniquely flavored cheddar cheeses. You won't want to miss the observation window at the retail store. The company is innovative in flavors but also using renewable energy. The lumber plant next door has discarded wood chips. Meister uses a wood-burner to create heat and energy for their plant - eliminating use of gas resources.

WILDCAT MOUNTAIN STATE PARK
E13660 State Highway 33 **Ontario** 54651

☐ Phone: (608) 337-4775
http://dnr.wi.gov/topic/parks/name/wildcat/
☐ Admission: A vehicle admission sticker is required. Daily $8.00-$11.00. Annual passes available.

Located on a ridge rising steeply above the Kickapoo River, the park offers canoeing, unique campsites for riders and their horses, and an observation point overlooking the Kickapoo Valley. Features 38 campsites, showers, a dumping station, handicap- accessible picnic area and campsites, seasonal naturalist programs, vistas, shoreline, canoeing, fishing, 1.3 miles of nature trails, 2.5 miles of hiking trails, 15 miles of horseback trails (State Trail Pass required), horse-riders' camp, 7 miles of cross- country ski trails. Open daily 6:00am-11:00pm with overnight camping.

LAURA INGALLS WILDER MUSEUM
306 3rd Street (Hwy 35) **Pepin** 54759

☐ Phone: (715) 442-2142 **www.lauraingallspepin.com**
☐ Hours: Daily 10:00am-5:00pm (May thru late October)

Little House on the Prairie fan? This museum highlights local author, Laura Ingalls Wilder. The museum offers displays, memorabilia, antiques and souvenirs about Laura and the pioneer era. Volunteer staff answer questions and provide fascinating insights on Laura and her life. Souvenirs are on sale as well. A few miles northwest of town (take CR CC), the Little House Wayside sits on a small prairie site that includes a replica of the cabin she wrote about in Little House in the Big Woods. The cabin features informative displays about Laura and her family. The wayside is a modern and well-maintained, with picnic tables and restrooms. Fresh water is available as well -- but you have to pump it yourself, just as Laura did! Open year ' round.

LAURA INGALLS WILDER DAYS

Pepin - *Laura Ingalls Wilder Museum. Laura Contest: Contestants demonstrate their talents and knowledge of the life and times and literature of Laura Ingalls Wilder as articulated in her stories. The festival will include demonstrations of traditional crafts such as blacksmithing, woodworking, hand-spinning and quilting, an art & craft market, plus food sales. Other activities include: pioneer games & activities for children, guided bus tours to Laura's birth site. On Saturday night the candlelight traditional crafts demonstrations followed by traditional music evening performances and a bonfire. The festival's activities culminate on Sunday with the Grand Parade.*

THE MINING MUSEUM / ROLLO JAMISON MUSEUM

405 East Main Street **Platteville** 53818

- ☐ Phone: (608) 348-3301 **http://mining.jamison.museum/**
- ☐ Hours: Wednesday-Sunday 10:00am-5:00pm (May-October).
- ☐ Admission: Both museums - $12.00 adult, $10.00 senior (65+), $6.00 child (5-12). $3.00 child (under 5).
- ☐ Note: Accessing the mine requires walking down 90 steps and the mine is realistic – slippery, cold and dark – so dress appropriately.

MINING MUSEUM - The museum traces the development of lead and zinc mining in the Upper Mississippi Valley through models, dioramas, artifacts and photographs. A guided tour includes a walk down into the Bevans Lead, an 1845 lead mine which produced over two million pounds of lead ore in one year. Realistic dioramas depict men actually working. This real mine also includes a visit to a head - frame where you can see how zinc ore was hoisted from a mine and hand - sorted, and a train ride around the museum grounds in ore cars pulled by a 1931 locomotive.

ROLLO JAMISON MUSEUM - Rollo Jamison was born in Beetown, Wisconsin in 1899. He started collecting arrowheads on the family farm. This was just the beginning of his life - long interest in history and the objects used by people in their everyday lives which grew to a collection of 20,000 items. Exhibits of carriages, farm implements, tools, a tavern/general store, a kitchen and parlor, musical instruments and mechanical music boxes.

DID YOU KNOW? When the miners first arrived, they used to burrow into the hills when their work was interupted by rain or cold. Their burrows reminded on lookers of badger holes, hence the nickname of Wisconsin, the Badger State.

FORT CRAWFORD MUSEUM

717 South Beaumont Road **Prairie du Chien** 53821

- □ Phone: (608) 326-6960 **www.fortcrawfordmuseum.com/**
- □ Hours: Wednesday-Monday 10:00am-4:00pm. (May-October).
- □ Admission: $8.00 adult, $7.00 senior (55+), $3.00 child (6-17) $20.00 family.
- □ Tours: Self-guided. A brochure explaining the exhibits is available in the office.

An Urgent Care of pioneer days, this Medical Museum was set in a fort built in 1816 and saw the most activity during the Black Hawk War. Prairie du Chien is the oldest European settlement on the Upper Mississippi River. Located just above the confluence of the Wisconsin River, this fertile prairie was a major gathering place for regional Indian tribes and for the fur traders who followed. Many epic frontier stories were played out here. Visit the reconstructed military hospital of Fort Crawford, site of Dr Beaumont's famous experiments in human digestion. Extensive exhibits feature the growth and development of medicine in Wisconsin from Native American herbal remedies to modern practices. Some of the descriptions and displays of early medicine may be gross but the kids seem to be intrigued.

PRAIRIE VILLA RENDEZVOUS

Prairie du Chien - *St. Feriole Island along the Mississippi River. Rendezvous with history and learn about life during the fur trading days. Re-enactment participants from all over the country come to display furs, demonstrate period tools and guns, and prepare foods common in that era. Try a buffalo burger. Ongoing demonstrations on basketweaving, beadworking, and plants and medicines offer visitors insight into the lifestyle of the time period. With more than 400 lodges and tepees, this is one of the Midwest's largest trading rendezvous.* **www.prairieduchien.org.** *(third weekend in June)*

DROPPIN OF THE CARP NEW YEARS EVE CARP FEST

Prairie du Chien - *Parks and Rec locations around town. A fun filled event intent on bringing friends, family, and community together for the New Year! At the stroke of midnight on New Year's Eve, watch in awe a large, frozen carp, takes center stage during a 100-foot drop to usher in the New Year. Prior to the drop, the honored carp is put on a throne where participants are encouraged to kiss the fish for good luck. If that's not enough, folks can take a whack at the Carp Piñata and celebrate the crowning of the Carp King and Queen. Sound fishy? Not in Wisconsin! And the "carp-tastic" fun doesn't end there. The event has spawned 'Carp Fest' which engages the entire community into a series of unique, fun-filled events throughout the city's parks and facilities: arts & crafts, gym & swim, youth karaoke, ice skate parties, light show, torch light ski, hike and sled. Admission fees go to charity.* **http://droppingofthecarp. blogspot.com/.** *(New Years Eve)*

WYALUSING STATE PARK

13081 State Park Lane (5 miles W of US 18/ SR 35, 4 miles S of town. off Highway X - follow signs) **Prairie du Chien (Bagley)** 53801

☐ Phone: (608) 996-2261
http://dnr.wi.gov/topic/parks/name/wyalusing/
☐ Admission: A vehicle admission sticker is required. Daily $8.00-$11.00. Annual passes available.

Just south of the city, magnificent views of the Mississippi and Wisconsin Rivers can be enjoyed from the 500-foot bluffs of Wyalusing State Park. One of Wisconsin's oldest parks, Wyalusing features Indian burial mounds, canoe trail, bird watching. It's a place to go for fishing, boating, bicycling, picnicking, and enjoying nature. There is an interpretive center and four historical markers within the park. The state park doesn't have a beach, but Wyalusing Recreation Area, two miles south of the park entrance, has a beach as well as boat landing an picnic area. Young families will appreciate the shorter .8 mile accessible trail or the 2.4 miles of interpretive nature trails (signage along the way). Open daily 6:00am-11:00pm with overnight camping.

LITTLE FALLS RAILROAD & DOLL MUSEUM

9208 County Hwy II (near Cataract, midway between Sparta and Black River Falls) **Sparta** 54656

- Phone: (608) 272-3266 **www.raildolls.org**
- Hours: Saturday-Sunday 1:00-5:00pm. (May - October).
- Admission: $6.00/person. Train ride is $3.00 (no adult riders)

Located in three large buildings, the museum favorites for families are the 1,600 dolls, operating model trains, a garden railroad, caboose, and rides for kids aboard a park-model railroad. The kids can play on and around the 40 foot train and play with a twelve inch scale train. And, for those families with little ones, there's a Toddler's Trike Trail for those youngsters too young to ride a trail elsewhere. Bring your own trike, or ride theirs. There's a picnic area here, too.

LITTLE RED SCHOOL HOUSE MUSEUM

1318 Superior Avenue (located in Gillett Park on Superior Avenue, also known as Gasoline Alley) **Tomah** 54660

- Phone: (608) 372-2166 **https://www.tomahmuseum.com/content/ exhibits/little-red-school-house**
- Hours: Wednesday 1:00-4:00pm, Saturday 9:00am-Noon (Memorial Day - Labor Day).

Step into the 19th Century at the Little Red House located in Tomah's Gillett Park on Superior Avenue. Watermill School was built in 1864. The name Watermill was given because of the locality of the school. It was built near Mill Creek, and a mill had been erected for the lumber industry. School was called to order twice a year, spring and fall sessions. The first teacher, Marie Nelson, was hired to teach for 3 months for $3.00 a week. Twenty-two days constituted a month in 1871. No scholar living outside the school district could attend without paying $1.50 tuition. The Watermill School was one of the first in the area to supply free textbooks, beginning in 1912. When you tour you'll see the old wood stove, desks, volumes of old books and other memories of the past.

PERROT STATE PARK

W26247 Sullivan Road (2 miles S of SR 35/54 off US 53)
Trempealeau 54661

- Phone: (608) 534-6409
  http://dnr.wi.gov/topic/parks/name/perrot/
- Admission: A vehicle admission sticker is required. Daily $8.00-$11.00. Annual passes available.

Perrot is nestled among 500-foot bluffs where the Trempealeau and Mississippi Rivers meet, with breathtaking river views. Features 96 campsites, 36 electric sites, showers, a dumping station, handicap- accessible picnic area and campsites, nature center, seasonal naturalist programs, vistas, shoreline, canoeing, boating, fishing, 0.6 miles of nature trails, 11.5 miles of hiking trails, 8.5 miles of off- road bicycle trails (State Trail Pass required), 8.5 miles of cross-country ski trails-groomed and tracked after every significant snowfall. Snowshoes are available for rent for $3 per day at the park office. They are provided by the Friends of Perrot. Hiking, snowshoeing and pets are not allowed on any groomed ski trail.

WISCONSIN CRANBERRY DISCOVERY CENTER

204 Main Street (located in the historic Union Cranberry Warehouse in downtown) **Warrens** 54666

- Phone: (608) 378-4878 **www.discovercranberries.com**
- Hours: Daily 9:00am-5:00pm (Memorial Day - October) Hours vary the rest of the year, but are posted on website or call.
- Admission: $5.00 adult, $4.00 senior (65+), $3.00 student (K-12). $12.00 family.
- Note: The harvesting season typically begins the first week of October and continues through most of the month. FREEBIES: ready to try cranberries in some new recipes to make at home? Click on the website icon: RECIPES and you'll have about 100 to choose from.

Museum & gift shop dedicated to Wisconsin's cranberry industry. The self-guided tour starts with a seven minute video. Next, look at tools used in growing and harvesting cranberries. In the early days, cranberries were hand-picked. Later they developed the hand-rake method. The teeth of the rake did the work of 10 workers picking berries by hand. Through storyboards, video, sound recordings, static and interactive displays, the Exhibit Hall details the historic and contemporary aspects of Wisconsin's No. 1 fruit crop.

*Flooded cranberry marshes filled with a sea of bright crimson cranberries herald in the harvest as the "Cranberry Capital of Wisconsin" celebrates the tart fruit. Tour the marshes and enjoy Cranberry foods. Admission for marsh tours. **www.cranfest.com**. (last full weekend in September)*

KICKAPOO INDIAN CAVERNS

54850 Rhein Hollow Road (Scenic Highway 60 - 15 miles southeast of Prairie du Chien) **Wauzeka** 53826

- ☐ Phone: (608) 875-7723 **https://www.mississippivalleyconservancy.org/ land-protection/kickapoo-caverns**
- ☐ Admission: Please call or visit website for latest admission prices.
- ☐ Tours: Sunday, Monday, Thursday-Saturday tours begin at 11:00am, 2:00pm, 4:00pm. One-hour. Reservations recommended. (Memorial Day Weekend - October)

Welcome to the largest show cave in the Midwest. Guides walk you through marvelous stalactite chambers and genuinely natural formations formed eons ago by an ancient sea and later by the ancient river. This cavern was once used by Indians for shelter. Highlights include the ancient waters, the cathedral room, swirling waters and the frozen waterfall.

SNOWFLAKE SKI JUMP TOURNAMENT

Westby - *Westby Ski Club Nordic Center, Timber Coulee. Wisconsin is also home to the 118-meter Olympic-sized Snowflake Ski Jump Complex in Westby. The Snowflake Ski Jump Tournament features U.S. and international competitors from 13 countries. The competition is a must-see as jumpers shoot down the ramp in excess of 50 mph only to launch through the air for hundreds of feet. Ski jumping truly is the original extreme sport. Snow Money Pile for kids. Excellent food and drink available on site: pork sandwiches, brats, hot dogs and hot drinks. Admission. www.snowflakeskiclub. com. (first weekend in February)*

Travel Journal & Notes:

Activity Index

For updates & travel games visit: **www.KidsLoveTravel.com**

HISTORY

HISTORY

HISTORY (cont.)

MUSEUMS

OUTDOOR EXPLORING

SCIENCE

For updates & travel games visit: **www.KidsLoveTravel.com**

www.ingramcontent.com/pod-product-compliance
Lightning Source LLC
Chambersburg PA
CBHW060917120626
46553CB00001B/359